The Balanced Budget
A Republican Plan

The Balanced Budget
A Republican Plan

Congressman Gerald B.H. Solomon

Berkshire House Publishers
Stockbridge, Massachusetts

Library of Congress Cataloging-in-Publication Data
Solomon, Gerald B.H., 1930-
    The balanced budget : a Republican plan / Gerald B.H. Solomon.
         p.   cm.
         ISBN 0-936399-72-4
  1. Budget—United States. 2. Government spending policy—United States.
3. United States—Appropriations and expenditures. 4. Budget deficits—United
States. I. United States. Congress. House. Committee on the Budget. Balanced
Budget Task Force. II. Title
HJ2051.S645 1995
336.73—dc20   95-13202

                                 CIP

ISBN 0-936399-72-4

Printed in the United States of America
10 9 8 7 6 5 4 3 2 1

I know of no one better whose vision exemplified the principles and policies advocated in this book than Ronald Reagan. His keen interest in fostering a society dependent on limited government, dedicated to Judeo-Christian values, and devoted to the provision of real economic opportunity for all is truly an American endeavor.

Consistent with this vision is the necessity to rein in a growing government's unfettered appetite for consuming the right of our children and grandchildren to pursue the American dream. In honor of the groundwork laid by this great president, the legacy of fiscal responsibility left us by our forefathers, and the future generations of America, I dedicate this book and all of my efforts to balance our nation's budget.

But thou, O God, thou king from of old, thou mighty conqueror all the world over, by thy power thou didst cleave the sea-monster in two and break the sea-serpent's heads above the waters; thou didst crush Leviathan's many heads and throw him to the sharks for food.

Psalm 75:12-14 *(The New English Bible)*

Contents

Publisher's Foreword

February and March 1994 dumped ice, sleet, snow, hail, and rain in record numbers of inches on Washington, DC. Weather forecasters called it one of the worst winters in years. In the Rayburn House Office Building, just across from the nation's Capitol building, members of the House of Representatives were calling it one of the worst economic seasons. The weather forecasters looked at their computerized forecasting equipment and shook their heads. Even if they could forecast the weather accurately, they could do nothing to change its course. Unlike the weather forecasters, House members had the power both to forecast the country's economy and to do something about its dismal outlook.

By early February, President Bill Clinton's 1994 budget process was already well underway and was staying the course of his 1993 budget bill that had increased the individual income tax, the gasoline tax, the Social Security tax, and the corporate tax rate but was offering no new budget deficit reduction. The Republican budget took a different approach that reduced the deficit and taxes on families.

But Gerald Solomon (R-New York) wanted more than either side was offering. He wanted to know what it would take to accumulate enough spending cuts to balance the budget in five years. The Congressional Budget Office (CBO) offered an illustrative spending "path" to a balanced budget but no details on how to use it. Jerry Solomon wanted to find those details and compile them to see if they could lead to a balanced budget for those who wished to explore that potential destination.

On February 3, 1994, he set out on that path, circulating his ideas among other concerned House members, and began to gather a following that was willing to trek with him, to face the reality of a journey on an unknown path.

On February 10, a "Balanced Budget Working Group" drew up a preliminary roster of twenty-one members who were interested in exploring the path to an alternate solution. Some joined cautiously, others with great enthusiasm. Trekking along with Mr. Solomon were Republican members Wayne Allard (Colorado), Dan Burton (Indiana), Robert Dornan

(California), John Duncan (Tennessee), Harris Fawell (Illinois), Wayne Gilchrest (Maryland), Porter Goss (Florida), Steve Gunderson (Wisconsin), Mel Hancock (Missouri), Amo Houghton (New York), Peter Hockstra (Michigan), Nancy Johnson (Connecticut), Jim McCrery (Louisiana), Scott McInnis (Colorado), Toby Roth (Wisconsin), Olympia Snowe (Maine,) Fred Upton (Michigan), Bob Walker (Pennsylvania), Bill Zeliff (New Hampshire), and Dick Zimmer (New Jersey). Of those twenty-one daring to walk down the unexplored path, only fourteen would stay the course.

The trek evolved into a flurry of activity. During the day, Task Force staffers, under the leadership of Eric Pelletier, scrambled to gather information about programs and budgets, wasted money, and congressional budget gimmickry to compile, line by line, a list of items to be restructured, reduced, or eliminated. Many evenings Mr. Pelletier and his staff colleagues worked into the early morning hours as the wintry weather turned the city streets into a thin sheet of havoc. There were times when the federal government closed down to protect employees from the dangers of travel, but the Task Force moved forward.

Task Force members shuttled back and forth on the underground rail from the Capitol to the Rayburn Building for evening meetings in Congressman Solomon's office, where debate sparked fires of controversy amidst Mr. Solomon's collection of fire hats. The number of controversies far outnumbered his fifteen hats, and covered a greater range of colors than the red, yellow, and black. Staffers presented their first options list — fifteen legal-size pages of approximately $840 billion in cuts. Letters and memos circulated among House colleagues. Special interest groups poured letters upon the members. Task Force members debated on paper when they weren't debating in Mr. Solomon's office. Everyone worked at increasing speed to cover the vast territory in their limited one-and-a-half-month time frame.

Then the Democrat majority rescheduled the budget resolution debate, cutting the Task Force's time dramatically. A letter went out to all Task Force members from Mr. Solomon's office: ". . . in light of the recent scheduling change regarding the consideration of the Budget Committee's budget resolution, each member . . . should examine the attached draft list of possible spending cuts for those specific line items that should not be under consideration. . . ." The Congressman called for a meeting the next Monday, February 28, to compile changes into a master list that would be examined by Task Force members on March 1. He urged members to move quickly to ". . . ensure that [the Congressional Budget Office] can score our proposal and that the package can be sold to and understood by other members."

Suddenly, they were running down the path.

On February 28, using the options list as the format, Task Force members examined each item on the list, voiced their "yeas" and "nays," and struck those items considered to be the most controversial. If a member opposed a provision, he or she was required to substitute a new one to enable spending to stay at the same level. In the evening meetings, Mr. Pelletier kept pace with the questions, the debate, the slashing of programs from the list, the searching for new programs to add to the list. And Mr. Solomon, with the Capitol building silhouetted in the window behind his desk, doused one fire after another, much as he had done in his years of service as a volunteer fireman.

Mr. Dornan recommended changes regarding defense programs, specifically items that should be dropped. Later, he and Mr. Upton, sitting on opposite sides of the red-carpeted room, debated funding for the National Endowment for the Arts. Mr. Zimmer agreed with the proposal to eliminate the space station. Mr. Walker wasn't there to defend his position to keep it, so funding for the space station was cut. Unable to support a decision that would affect a program he held so dear, Mr. Walker was unable to support the Task Force's budget. Olympia Snowe, weighing her position on Medicare and her upcoming Senate race, left the Task Force. Others who also ultimately left included Steve Gunderson, Amo Houghton, Nancy Johnson, and Jim McCrery. But others had joined the race: Richard Armey (Texas), Roscoe Bartlett (Maryland), Mac Collins (Georgia), Chris Cox (California), Duke Cunningham (California), Tom DeLay (Texas), John Doolittle (California), David Dreier (California), Bob Ingliss (South Carolina), Dan Schaeffer (Colorado), and Bob Stump (Arizona).

The March 4, 1994, *Congress Daily* reported that Mr. Solomon and several GOP colleagues would ask the House Rules Committee the following week to allow the House to debate a substitute fiscal year 1995 budget resolution.

On Tuesday, March 8, a memo went out to Republican colleagues under the signatures of ten House members, promoting their plan as the only budget alternative that would actually balance the federal budget. "We've made hundreds of *speeches* about the need to make the tough decisions to make specific cuts in spending and balance the federal budget. But we've never had the chance to *vote* for such a budget because one has not been offered . . . *until now.* This week, the Solomon/Fawell/Upton budget alternative will give you the chance to vote for what you've been saying you would do: balance the budget by cutting federal spending."

Later that afternoon Representatives Solomon, Fawell, and Upton, with twenty-two other House members, unveiled "The Balanced Budget Plan" at a press conference, where Congressman Solomon said, "The naysayers say it can't be done. Our proposal says it can."

On March 9, the Task Force trio sent out a Dear Colleague letter with a different appeal, representing a different set of constituents: "Over the next several days, you will likely receive calls and letters from special interest groups asking for you to protect their favored programs from cuts by voting down our amendment. As you weigh the merits of their arguments, we urge you to keep in mind a group we are not likely to hear from — our grandchildren. The children of America do not have high paid lobbyists in Washington to promote their interests, and as a result, are being saddled down with an ever-increasing national debt in order to fund our consumption."

That same day the Task Force used the clout of a report from the General Accounting Office (GAO) that stated, "the key question facing policymakers is not *whether* to undertake major deficit reduction, but *when* and *how*." The report further stated that "regardless of the approach that is chosen, prompt and meaningful action is essential. In the end, action is unavoidable. The longer it is delayed, the more painful it will be."

March 9 also brought Mr. Solomon the opportunity to present the upcoming vote to members on the floor of the House. During his off-the-cuff speech, he told House members that the Senate also was preparing a similar balanced budget.

With the press racing to catch up with the unfolding story of a balanced budget, Task Force members and staffers were in high gear. Representatives Solomon, Fawell, and Upton met with outside groups — the National Taxpayers' Union, the Concord Coalition, and the Committee for a Responsible Budget — to arrange for the scoring if the CBO could not complete its task. They garnered a big leg of support from the other side of the aisle when Timothy Penny (D-Minnesota) said he would vote for and speak strongly in favor of the package, even though it had deep agricultural cuts. They dispelled rumors — no, the budget alternative did not raise the Medicare eligibility age to 67.

At 11:00 p.m. the evening before the resolution was scheduled to go to the floor of the House for a vote, officials from the CBO called to say they did not know if they would be able to get enough savings from the submitted provisions, mainly because they hadn't had time to analyze all of them. But, at the last minute the CBO brought what they had finished to Mr. Solomon's office. Those items, together with some already-scored options from the Senate's similar plan, gave the Task Force the level of cuts needed.

At midnight, staffers traveled through the underground from the Rayburn Building to the Rules Committee on the third floor of the Capitol building to present the resolution for the next day's debate.

On March 10, 1994, the House began to debate the budget resolution. Mr. Solomon was scheduled to present his plan after the proposed budgets of the Congressional Black Caucus and Representative Barney Frank (D-Massachusetts). Earlier in the morning, double-checking numbers that they had gathered the night before, staffers from the Solomon and Fawell offices met with CBO analysts until debate on the bill actually started. Other staff members raced around to gather needed information and speakers for the floor debate. Mr. Solomon talked with other House members, especially Democrats, to gather further support for the plan. The Task Force held a staff briefing so other offices would know details of the budget package.

Finally, the floor debate arrived and, after one hour of debate, the budget was defeated.

But, this was not the end of a short-lived drama that led a few Congressmen and the nation onto a path to federal solvency. It was just the beginning of a long, but necessary, journey. And this book is just one step along the way. According to Mr. Solomon, government spending adds $433,000 to the debt every minute. If it takes you ten hours to read this book, by the time you reach the last chapter the government will have added another $259,800,000 to the debt, a rate that we Americans cannot afford.

Preface and Acknowledgments

And to preserve [people's] independence, we must not let our rulers load us with perpetual debt. We must make our election between economy and liberty, or profusion and servitude. If we run into such debts, as that we must be taxed in our meat and in our drink, in our necessaries and our comforts, in our labors and our amusements, . . . as the people of England are, our people . . . must live, as they do now, on oatmeal and potatoes; . . . This example leads us to the salutary lesson, that private fortunes are destroyed by public as well as private extravagance. And this is the tendency of all governments. A departure from principle in one instance becomes a precedent for a second; that second for a third; and so on, till the bulk of the society is reduced to be mere automations of misery, to have no sensibilities left but for sin and suffering . . . And the fore horse of this frightful team is public debt. Taxation follows that, and in its train wretchedness and oppression.

Thomas Jefferson in a letter to Samuel Kercheval, July 12, 1816

As my family sat around the breakfast table every morning while my children were growing up, I always hoped for the best life possible for my five children and their families. Growing up in the freest nation on earth, protected from the centralized, statist nations of Europe and Asia by an enduring Constitution and the most powerful military in the world, my children enjoyed an opportunity most children of the world can only dream of having. Little did I know that the greatest threat to my children's future would come not from abroad but from within our own nation in the form of unfulfilled government financial obligations.

In 1979, when I was first elected to the House of Representatives, I carried to Washington a message that taxes were too high, spending was out of control, morality was being eradicated, and that government was not responsive to the true needs of citizens. At that time the budget deficit for 1978 was only $59 billion and the federal debt had risen to a high of $709 billion. Inflation and unemployment were skyrocketing while economic growth had stagnated. The economy was in shambles, the opportunity to pursue the American dream was threatened, and the government was a large part of the problem. My constituents elected me to Congress on an agenda to change the tide.

In 1981, Ronald Reagan came into office on a similar platform of lower taxes, lower spending, a balanced budget, and a restoration of our national defense. His visionary leadership helped to channel my legislative energies into those areas in which I could best make a lasting impact. That ongoing struggle has led me to this proposal today; it has carried me through the maze of federal laws, regulations, and bureaucracies to a strong stand behind the restructuring of the federal government as outlined in the chapters that follow.

The conclusions reached by our Task Force find most of their foundations in the economic and political philosophies that each of us carried into office. The governing philosophy that I adhere to is similar to that espoused by Ronald Reagan and most social and economic conservatives — limited government economic policy based on the free market, competition, and limited outside intervention. This is truly the only way our nation can maximize our economic resources while also maximizing the benefits of our economy for everyone. Not only has the philosophy of smaller government been shown to maximize individual liberty, but it also has been proven to be a superior way to create economic prosperity.

The fiscal policy known as supply-side economics was vindicated during the 1980s when President Reagan told us that we could have strong economic growth, lower unemployment, and falling inflation. The government's expansive economic policies of the 1960s and '70s led to declining productivity, rising unemployment and inflation, and the creation of a dependent underclass. Ronald Reagan liberated our economy from this fiscal straitjacket by enacting incentive tax cuts and deregulating business and industry. Despite the doom and gloom presented by many, the facts are irrefutable: seven years of strong economic growth; a peacetime record; 18 million net new jobs; unemployment cut in half between 1982 and 1990; inflation falling from 13 percent to 4 percent; interest rates falling from 20 percent to 8 percent; real per capita income rising; and, according to the Census Bureau, real average family income rising among all five income groups. Furthermore, contrary to many assertions, the poor did not get poorer. As a matter of fact, poverty actually dropped from 15.2 percent to 12.8 percent between 1983 and 1989.[1] Limited government brought about stronger and longer economic prosperity.

I believe that economic policy should not be based on a belief that wealth creation is a zero-sum game — one in which if any player gains, another player must lose. It was the French physiocrats of the early eighteenth century, led by Francois Quesnay, who first laid out the idea that there are natural laws governing economic activity and that if those laws were followed with minimal outside interference, the result would be increased productivity and maximum benefits for society as a whole.[2]

The federal government has for too long dug its claws into the economy, propping up some industries through government subsidies, promoting others through preferential tax treatment of laws — all essentially picking winners and losers in the economic marketplace. Congress historically has played a despicable role in this market manipulation, responsible to a large degree for our limited economic growth and wealth expansion. Adam Smith noted it best when he wrote,

> *The statesman, who should attempt to direct people in what manner they ought to employ their capitals, would not only load himself with a most unnecessary attention, but assume an authority which could safely be trusted, not only to no single person, but to no council or senate whatever, and which would nowhere be so dangerous as in the hands of a man who had folly and presumption enough to fancy himself fit to exercise it.*[3]

I believe the federal government's approach to economic policy has become increasingly self-defeating. The promotion of private sector expansion has for too long been painted by some as an incompassionate or antipoor endeavor. My own experience, both as a small-business man and a local government official, has convinced me that policies designed to enhance the ability of the private sector to thrive and expand on its own are much more beneficial than any government program instituted under the banner of public compassion. Again, referring to the writings of Adam Smith in the *Wealth of Nations*:

> *It is not from the benevolence of the butcher, the brewer, or the baker, that we expect our dinner but from their regard to their own interest. We address ourselves, not to their humanity but to their self-love, and never talk to them of our own necessities but of their own advantages . . . led by an invisible hand to promote an end which was no part of his intention, . . . frequently promotes [the interest] of the society more effectually than when he really intends to promote it.*[4]

Compassion, civic duty, volunteerism, economic opportunity, and ultimately individual liberty depend on the ability of citizens, whether through business or government, to create an environment in which such important virtues and activities can thrive.

Of course, there were some problems, most important of which was the budget deficit. But this had less to do with President Reagan's economic philosophy and more to do with his inability to alter congressional spending behavior, which was wildly out of control. He promised to scale back government; however, because of congressional irresponsibility, he was not completely successful. Spending growth was curtailed, but no serious or long-lasting cuts were made. One of the greatest lies of the last decade is that the 1981 tax cuts caused our budget problems. The trouble with this claim is that the facts don't bear it out. Federal revenues increased by $3,885 billion during President Reagan's two terms.[5] If lost tax revenue caused the deficit, then the six large tax increases Congress has passed since that time should have theoretically recovered that lost revenue and reduced the deficit. However, that did not occur.

Regardless of the causes, we must take steps to deal with this fiscal burden, which is the fundamental reason why I embarked on this journey to draft a balanced budget. The facts show that President Reagan's incentive-based tax policies released 290 million people into the economy free to exercise their economic abilities. However, increasing government spending and rising federal deficits and debt stifled the truly remarkable growth rates and economic expansion that could have occurred. Another ideal of President Reagan—a balanced budget—would have allowed for this stronger economic growth. Balancing the budget through a thorough restructuring of the federal government would remove this large burden from our nation's back.

Once again, this brings us back to the adventure detailed in the following pages. Restructuring the federal government requires an examination of every program and bureaucracy of the government. A French aristocrat named Alexis de Toqueville said it best when in 1833 he wrote, "In its deal to do good works the federal government covers the surface of society with a network of small complicated rules, minute and uniform, through which the minds and the most energetic characters cannot penetrate."

This was the challenge laid before the Balanced Budget Task Force, whose members rose to it with courage. Not every program reform or spending cut was unanimously approved — I do not even agree with all of the proposed reforms — but tough choices have to be made to reach the goal of a balanced budget.

It was Sir William Blackstone, one of the founders of English common law, who wrote that a contract was "an agreement upon sufficient consideration, to do or not to do a particular thing" and it was both morally and legally binding.[6] When I first took the oath of office to become a member of the House of Representatives, I made a contract with my constituents and with my country that I would do everything in my power to uphold the constitutional foundations of our democracy. A wise and efficient use of the power of the purse is my legal and moral obligation to the American people. I sincerely believe that if our nation could combine a form of tax policy similar to that begun under President Reagan with a budget policy based on a dedication to balanced budgets, we could experience rates of economic growth and improvements in the standard of living unprecedented in history. The work of the Balanced Budget Task Force is one reflection of the sincere desire of many members of the House of Representatives to fulfill this responsibility.

Acknowledgments

A dedication to the concept of balancing the budget and a resolve to limit government made this book possible. Such dedication and resolve from many congressional colleagues, private organizations and think tanks, and the American people enabled many of us in Washington to debate honestly the reforms necessary to produce a plan that can bring about a balanced budget and limited federal government.

The commitment of many colleagues in Congress to balancing the budget through responsible reform and economic growth made possible a discourse of the necessary steps and priorities to continue. In-depth research and analysis from many private firms and citizens' groups provided our government with a plethora of options, ideas, and proposals. The willingness of many American citizens to share in the sacrifice gave us the courage to make unpopular decisions.

First, I must express my sincere appreciation for the support and trust exhibited by the people of the 22nd Congressional District of the State of New York. For sixteen years I have had the privilege of representing its citizens in the House of Representatives. For years, they have stood by me as I have often rowed against the tide of business-as-usual in Washington, all the while seeking to bring about a better society through a more efficient and responsible government. Their continuous support has enabled me to place my beliefs and principles behind such a "radical" restructuring of the federal government as presented in this book. I am forever grateful for the opportunity to stand with them in their demands for a balanced budget.

Furthermore, the thorough work of our Balanced Budget Task Force in organizing and composing this budget resolution provided me with the opportunity to elaborate on the details and decisions made to formulate a balanced budget. Specifically, Representatives Wayne Allard, Roscoe Bartlett, Dan Burton, Bob Dornan, David Dreier, John Duncan, Thomas Ewing, Harris Fawell, Wayne Gilchrest, Porter Goss, Mel Hancock, Peter Hoekstra, Duncan Hunter, Bob Inglis, Toby Roth, Dan Schaeffer, Bob Stump, Fred Upton, Bill Zeliff, and Dick Zimmer were all original members of our group and contributed instrumentally to putting together this budget proposal.

I would be remiss if I did not also express my appreciation for the dedicated work of my colleagues on the House Budget Committee, led by my friend John Kasich. The work of the committee provided the foundation for much that we were able to do in producing our budget. The assistance of the committee staff was invaluable in developing our budget proposal and in explaining the proposal in this work.

It is also important for me to acknowledge the work that many groups contributed to this debate. As I said all along, the vast majority of this plan had already been written; it needed someone in government to sort out the various proposals and transform them into one comprehensive resolution. For the work of the Heritage Foundation, the Concord Coalition, the Congressional Porkbusters Coalition, the Congressional Budget Office, the General Accounting Office, the Cato Institute, the Grace Commission, Citizens Against Government Waste, the National Taxpayers' Union, the Department of Health and Human Services Inspector General Report of the Bush Administration, and the Citizens for a Responsible Federal Budget, I am grateful. The trench warfare performed by such groups laid the groundwork for our work.

I also must recognize the long hours and hard work of the congressional staff who compiled information, answered questions, and formulated suggestions as we put together this budget proposal.

More specifically to the writing of this book, I am indebted for the long hours and dedication of the Balanced Budget Task Force's staff director, Eric Pelletier, who spent a vast majority of his own time, knowledge, and resources in helping me draft this volume. I also must commend the long hours contributed by developmental editor Linda Wolfe Keister. Without their commitment to the completion of this work, it would have been impossible for me to have met the deadlines necessary to our objectives.

1   Alan Reynolds. "Upstarts and Downstarts," *National Review*. August 31, 1992, pages 25-30.

2   Forrest McDonald. *Novus Ordo Seclorum: The Intellectual Origins of the Constitution*. Lawrence, Kansas: University Press of Kansas, 1985, page 107. The physiocrats, who believed land was the only source of wealth and advocated total freedom of trade, were the first to refer to themselves as "economists" in the modern sense of the term.

3   Adam Smith. *Inquiry into the Nature and Causes of the Wealth of Nations*. Edited by R.H. Campbell, A.S. Skinner, and W.B. Todd, 2 vols. Indianapolis, 1981: 1:456 (bk. 4, chap. 2).

4   Ibid., 1:26-27 (bk 1, chap 2), 1:456 (bk. 4, chap. 2).

5   Total Federal revenues in 1981 were $606.8 billion. Total Federal revenues in 1989 were $1,013.3 billion. Total 1989 Federal revenues as expressed in 1981 dollars were $827.7 billion.

6   Norman B. Ture, "To Cut and To Please," *National Review*. August 31, 1992, pages 35-39.

7   Sir William Blackstone. *Commentaries on the Laws of England,* 12th edition. 4 vols. London, 1793-1795, 2:442-443, 447.

Part I - The Crisis

CHAPTER ONE

Facing the Crisis

O ur country is in serious trouble. We shake our money pouch and not even a penny clinks to the floor. We make excuses to bill collectors who knock incessantly at the door. We cringe as unwise spending haunts us with the distorted face of moral decline. We rip future chapters from our children's book of life. We risk losing everything we own, and even some that we don't. We spend money carelessly. We owe $4.96 trillion ($4,960,000,000,000).[1] We are poor stewards of freedom, opportunity, resources, and life itself. *We* are in financial trouble. Not they. *We*. We are America's people. We are in debt. And America's debt is America's crisis.

You say you want to help get us out of this crisis? Well, step right up. Get out your checkbook, every one of you — yes, every man, woman, and child — and write a check for $19,100. Or, if you're a family of four, you can write just one check — for $76,400. If this seems a steep price to pay and a bit cavalier, you have another option: the American Way. Step up to the task, make some sacrifices, and forge ahead. You must make one choice or the other. Why? Because America's debt is *our* crisis.

The American Way

Crisis is not new to America. In January 1981 — facing a 13 percent inflation rate, 22 percent interest rates, the Iranian hostage crisis, and the Soviet invasion of Afghanistan — Ronald Reagan, our fortieth president, stood strong when he declared:

> *We have every right to dream heroic dreams . . . the crisis we are facing today . . . requires our best effort and our willingness to believe in ourselves and to believe in our capacity to perform great deeds, to believe that together, with God's help, we can and will resolve the problems which now confront us. After all, why shouldn't we believe that? We are Americans.[2]*

I am unapologetic for my devotion to my friend and former president. His eloquent words ring just as true for me in 1995 as they did on that winter day in 1981. Today we are faced with another serious crisis in the United States, one of which all Americans must be aware. It is the national debt. But it is more than dollar signs and figures. As our new Speaker of the House, Newt Gingrich, clearly said, America needs a new vision, a new plan that, when implemented, will build on those elements of our society that have been a success and replace those portions that have not.

Improvement is key to building. We want to build, but we don't want to toss out everything old. We want to build upon and improve what we have achieved over more than 200 years. Politics in America historically has been a discipline premised on a genuine desire to improve the quality of life in America.

Despite the periodic shortfalls of many government leaders at all levels, our system of democracy is founded on the right of all American citizens to expect genuine service of its elected officials. Because of this right, political action is not taken in a vacuum without direction. Every member of Congress takes an oath to uphold the Constitution of the United States. This blueprint of democracy is our handbook for governing. All actions taken by our Congress should represent a fulfillment of the constitutional role created for the legislative branch — the Senate and the House of Representatives — by our Founding Fathers.

First and foremost of those responsibilities is to adhere to the preamble to the Constitution. Listen to the words of our fourth president, the father of the Constitution, James Madison:

> *We the People of the United States, in Order to form a more perfect Union, establish Justice, insure domestic Tranquility, provide for the common defence, promote the general Welfare, and secure the Blessings of Liberty to ourselves and our Posterity, do ordain and establish this Constitution for the United States of America.*

These words convey both beauty and political power. They provide for the "life, liberty and pursuit of happiness" that Thomas Jefferson called for in the Declaration of Independence. Those tenets of democracy have proven to be timeless as America has applied them to meet every challenge, domestic and foreign, that has risen since our nation's birth more than 200 years ago.

Franklin Delano Roosevelt, our thirty-second president, accurately characterized our ability in 1933 when he stated that "We have nothing to fear but fear itself," while confronting a 25 percent unemployment rate in the Great Depression. With each passing decade, our system of self-government has prevailed, unshaken by divisive forces outside or within the country. Just as our republic marched through the divisiveness of the Civil War under the steady hand of Abraham Lincoln, our sixteenth president, who ensured the "establishment of justice," I believe America will continue to rise to and overcome every challenge it faces.

America faces challenges every day. Whether it be abroad with the spread of terrorism around the world or at home with unemployment and poverty in America's streets, our nation confronts difficult choices and dilemmas. But we need to confront them in the American way. As President Reagan said, we are Americans and we will continue to keep our heads high as we march to overcome these crises, because we believe in our ability, with God's help, to achieve great things.

Today is no different. We are called to face the crisis and to make our nation again financially sound and morally strong. We are called to renew American society.

Taking the Crisis by the Horns

I believe that the one fundamental step necessary to renew American society is to balance the federal budget. This step is steep and difficult to climb. It will take a leap of faith — and certainly one of courage — to surmount the obstacles. But, look at where we must start the climb.

What is the year?	1995
How much does the federal government already owe?	$4,960,000,000,000
How much will the federal government spend this year?	$1,500,000,000,000
How much of the money spent will be borrowed?	$165,000,000,000
How much of the money spent will pay interest on the money already owed?	$235,000,000,000

Source: President's FY 1996 Budget, Historical Tables, page 90.

It is astounding to think that our national debt has built up to such an incomprehensible number because our government failed to balance the budget. If divided by the current population of the United States (260 million), the federal debt per person amounts to $19,100, which is why you were asked at the beginning of this chapter to write a check for that amount or, for a family of four, a check as large as $76,400. That amount is almost three times the average salary of a family of four in my New York State Congressional district. That debt payment would be enough to pay off the national debt, but only on condition that every American continued to pay taxes at the same rate paid now. (That means no decrease in tax rates.) As it is, every month, each family in America pays $440 in taxes just to pay the interest on the federal debt. That $440 does not help pay down the debt or serve any other useful purpose.

Traveling along the current budget path, the Clinton Administration projected the budget deficit will continue growing into the future without resolution. In 1997, according to President Bill Clinton, we will pay more in interest on the debt than we will pay for national defense. Take a look at where this path is leading us.

What is the year?	1997
What will we pay for defense?	$257,000,000,000
What will we pay in interest on the national debt?	$270,000,000,000

Source: President's FY 1996 Budget, Historical Tables, page 90.

What is the year?	2005
What will the national debt be?	$6,968,932,000,000 (7 trillion dollars!)
How much will the government pay in annual interest on this debt?	$412,000,000,000
What will the amount of debt be for each citizen?	$25,000
What will the amount of debt be for each family of four?	$100,000
How many tax dollars will a family pay each month for interest on the debt?	$570

Source: President's FY 1996 Budget, Historical Tables, page 90.

The sad truth is that this financial picture will only continue to get worse. Between the years 1995 and 2006, the government will pay $3,922,000,000,000 in interest on our debt. Over the next 11 years, we will pay as much in taxes just to pay interest on the debt as today's entire debt. None of that money will be spent on national defense or the education of our children. Not one red cent will be paid to help the elderly receive quality health care or to provide assistance to those trapped in poverty. Every penny of this money will go straight from the taxpayer's pocket to some holder of a portion of your government's debt. Many of those debt holders are overseas, which means that as soon as your hard-earned tax dollars leave your hand, they will be placed in the hands of a foreign investor who will spend your money in another country, adding to that country's economic growth and not our own.

Leonard Sloane, author of *The New York Times Personal Finance Handbook*, wrote in his financial guide for families that a family should know it is overextended when its debts exceed 15 percent of its take-home pay.[3]

Where does the government stand in relationship to such a formula? Interest alone on the federal debt already exceeds 17 percent of federal tax revenues. Soon it may be well above 20 percent, with no end in sight.

The Joint Economic Committee (JEC) of Congress recently offered an analysis that demonstrates the impact of interest payments on the debt over a taxpayer's lifetime.[4]

Taxpayer	Year of Birth	Interest Payments Over a Lifetime of 75 Years
Robert	1959	$75,851
Mary	1974	$115,724
Sally	1995	$187,150

The spending habits we have today saddle our children with a larger debt tomorrow. According to the JEC, Sally will have to pay $187,150 in taxes herself for interest on the debt *and* will pay more taxes for her parents' and grandparents' Medicare and Social Security before she pays taxes for any government service for herself.

That pattern of tax spending is not a new trend, but it is becoming worse. Look at what is happening even as you read.

Every second, government spending adds to the national debt. How much each second?	$10,000
Every minute, government spending adds to the national debt. How much each minute?	$60,000
Between now and 2002, how much will this spending increase the national debt?	38%

By the year 2012, the current budget plans will have left our children with a government that can only afford to pay interest on the debt and the cost of entitlements. That means no school lunches, no student loans, no national defense, no other discretionary government spending. Spending for those important programs will be beyond our means. On the other hand, if we set spending priorities now, the government will be able to continue to fulfill its obligations to its citizens. If we wait, the task before us will become that much harder, or even impossible.

A Bad Habit Is Hard to Break

Deficits have been a characteristic of the federal budget for a long time. In fact, Congress has balanced the budget only 27 times since 1901. That means the federal government has carried a shortfall for 67 out of the last 94 years. In recent history, the federal government has not balanced its books since 1969. For more than 25 years the president and Congress have allowed continuous deficits, adding billions of dollars to the debt each year.

Deficits did not begin with President Reagan, nor did they begin with President Jimmy Carter. They are neither Republican nor Democratic. Frankly, fixing blame for our situation would take too much time, and we don't have time to waste. We all must assume responsibility for allowing our system to get out of control. Regardless of the need for spending or the cause to fight for, we just plain cannot afford to continue sliding down our present course.

I believe that we must downsize the federal government in order to balance the budget. Those who oppose downsizing often claim that such restructuring lacks compassion for the poor and the less fortunate in our society who, they say, would be devastated by cuts in federal programs. But I say that every minute politicians continue to argue about whether or not it is wise to balance the budget, the number of this country's economically poor citizens continues to grow. Clearly, doing nothing but more of the same cannot be termed compassionate. When I look at what compassion has bought for those people, here is what I see.

- I see a failed welfare system that delivers goods and services to help people, but in the process actually hurts the poor.
- I see that system's failure reflected in violence, brutality, child abuse, and drug addiction, and shown in every local TV news broadcast.
- I see poor Americans saddled with rules that are antiwork, antifamily, and antiproperty.
- I see a system that forces poor Americans to live in unsafe housing and neighborhoods, to attend public schools that are equally as

dangerous and accomplish little, and to bear the human cost of a failed welfare state.

- Despite the creation of President Lyndon B. Johnson's "Great Society" war on poverty in 1965, the number of children in poverty has risen 40 percent since 1970.[5]
- Since 1965, the juvenile arrest rate for violent crimes has tripled.
- Since 1960, the number of unmarried pregnant teenagers has nearly doubled and teen suicide has more than tripled.
- For each 10 percent increase in single-parent families, there has been a 17 percent increase in violent crime by teenagers.
- For both white and black families, the decrease in the marriage rate has directly corresponded to the increase in teen crime.
- As the government has spent more and more money on welfare, the percentage of illegitimate births has continued to rise.
- A culture of violence increasingly permeates our entertainment industry and denigrates our civilization.[6]

I see a society that accepts a perverse view of life and the right to it. I see the failure of the welfare state striking at the heart of the American belief that every citizen is endowed by our Creator with certain unalienable rights, including life, liberty, and the pursuit of happiness. I think House Speaker Newt Gingrich said it best when he asserted:

> No civilization can survive with 12-year-olds having babies, 15-year-olds killing each other, 17-year-olds dying of AIDS, and 18-year-olds receiving diplomas they can't read. Furthermore, no civilization can survive with parents and grandparents cheating their children by refusing to balance the budget and live within their means. The welfare state cheats the poor. The unbalanced budget cheats every child.[7]

I agree with the Speaker completely. We are leaving our children a legacy of fiscal and moral bankruptcy.

As a grandfather, I cannot stand by and sell my grandchildren's future short just to avoid shaking up the current system. For too long, Congress has put off hard choices in exchange for short-term gain. I am ready to shake up the system, rock the boat, take risks, sacrifice comforts, and do whatever else is necessary to help us change course, to help us take that monumental step to balance the budget.

Turning Crisis into Opportunity

Just as America was forced to renew itself after the Civil War and after World War II, it must renew itself in the post-Cold War era. In the 1990s, the United States has an opportunity to redefine itself in a way that will allow the greatest democracy in the world to advance with strength into the twenty-first century.

We now have the opportunity to revitalize America by transforming our approach to government so that we will have a safer, more prosperous, and freer country. We must create new opportunities by reshaping American government and balancing the budget. If we reach inside ourselves to find that entrepreneurial American spirit, we, the American people, can join in a partnership to create a safe retirement for the "babyboomers" and a safer future for their children.

Franklin D. Roosevelt's declaration during World War II that "our generation has a rendezvous with destiny" applies today as we try to renew America through a restructuring of the federal government, a restructuring based on a dedication to balanced budgets. Our challenge is to have a federal government that spends no more than it receives each year and does it well enough to provide goods and services effectively without increasing our national debt. This book summarizes one such effort in this great democratic and economic struggle.

---

1 Throughout this book, all figures referring to the federal budget are from the Congressional Budget Office, unless stated otherwise.

2 Ronald Reagan. First Inaugural Address. Washington, DC: January 1981.

3 Leonard Sloane. *The New York Times Personal Finance Handbook*. New York: Times Books, 1995, page 72.

4 Joint Economic Committee analysis.

5 William J. Bennett. *The Index of Leading Cultural Indicators*. 1993.

6 The testimony of Robert Rector from the Heritage Foundation before the Committee on Economic and Educational Opportunity, January 18, 1995.

7 Newt Gingrich. Unveiling of the Contract With America Speech, September 27, 1994.

CHAPTER TWO

Drawing Blueprints for the Plan

I t was early February 1994 when the Clinton Administration, as required by the Budget Act, submitted to Congress its budget proposal for fiscal year (FY) 1995. President Bill Clinton declared that his 1995 budget continued the progress the country had accomplished with the passage of his 1994 budget package, which claimed $500 billion in deficit reduction over a period of five years. President Clinton's Omnibus Budget Reconciliation Act (OBRA) of 1993 increased taxes by $241 billion through increases in the top individual tax rate and the corporate tax rate, an increase in the gas tax, increased taxes on Social Security benefits, and other tax increases. On the spending side his budget made several changes in entitlement programs, placed annual caps on discretionary spending, and increased several users' fees. Despite all of these tax increases and program changes, the federal deficit was projected consistently to exceed $150 billion every year through the next five years and to be well above $200 billion, and even $300 billion, annually over the next ten years.

President Clinton's budget proposed to continue this "progress." My constituents were tired of being told to sacrifice, either through higher taxes or cuts in government programs, when in turn they only saw the deficit continuing to grow. The president's budget for fiscal year 1995 was more of the same. Under his new budget proposal the projected federal deficit was as follows:

Fiscal Year	Projected Deficit (in billions of dollars)
1995	$176.1
1996	$173.1
1997	$180.8
1998	$187.4
1999	$201.2

Source: President's FY1996 Budget, Historical Tables, page 14.

While the administration may have tried to reduce the deficit substantially the previous year, the problem continued to exist and the public debt continued to compound. The position of many of my congressional Democratic colleagues was not much different from the president's. One senior Democratic leader in Congress even went so far as to say, "With the improving economy, we just don't have this push for additional cuts that we had last year." [1]

If the nation were to follow the path set by the Clinton Administration the year before, as desired by Democratic congressional leaders, the debt would increase, spending would be restrained by less than one-fifth of 1 percent of the entire budget, and the government would continue to take more money out of the private sector for its own consumption. We had to do more. We needed a new approach.

A Republican Approach

Although congressional Republicans recognized the need for a new approach, they faced inevitable difficulty in getting their party's support for a bill that might never pass. Balancing the federal budget by cutting spending is not an easy task, nor a politically popular one. We hear many Americans saying, "I want to see the budget balanced," and they also say, "but don't cut *that* program, I *need that* program." Every program has a constituency that relies on federal support, and that constituency will fight to protect its own turf. So when it comes to cutting spending, what do we say to our fellow Republicans: "Vote for this balanced budget bill. . . . It will make your constituents hoppin' mad!"? This is one reason it is so difficult to cut federal spending: No matter how worthy the principles and laudable the rhetoric in a specific alternative budget, it can be very difficult to garner political support for it. It is not easy for a congressman to put his name on the line if he knows not only that the bill will never pass, but also that it will probably bring nothing but

political headaches. Supporting such a proposal can be a political kami-
kaze mission if it is not explained effectively.

However, a number of Republicans in the House believed we needed
to go further to balance the budget. This response came not so much
from a dissatisfaction with the proposed Republican budget as it did from
criticism of the Democrats and constituents. Republicans and Democrats
alike have claimed to support a balanced budget. However, no one in
recent congressional history has actually proposed a specific budget that,
if followed, would get the national budget deficit to zero.

Past budget proposals usually have been premised on deficit reduction but never on deficit elimination. Those budget proposals that did
call for a balanced budget at a future date consisted of spending caps,
not actual spending cuts. Gramm-Rudman-Hollings established deficit
targets based on spending caps that, if adhered to, would have balanced
the budget. The Omnibus Budget Reconciliation Act of 1990 established
similar spending caps and deficit targets. Neither approach worked. Congress needed to see the guts of what it would take to balance the federal
budget. Caps on spending only postpone the debate on the tough choices.
When it comes time to stand up and make those hard decisions, Congress has always lacked the courage. Proposing a budget that called for
the elimination, consolidation, reduction, and privatization of a wide
variety of government programs might jolt Congress and the American
people enough to realize what must be done.

Consequently, about 20 Republican members of the House of Representatives — moderates and conservatives — gathered in mid-Febru-
ary 1994 to form the Balanced Budget Task Force that would develop a
balanced budget resolution. From the beginning, they agreed that this
effort should be separate from the Republican leadership and that it
should be sold not as a substitute for the Republican budget proposal,
but as another alternative plan. The reason for this approach was that
the Republican leadership was dedicated to using the budget as a political document to highlight the major differences between Republicans
and Democrats, namely, a commitment to lower spending, lower deficits, and lower taxes. Because we were not in the position of setting the
congressional agenda, we were forced to take advantage of every opportunity available to show the American people what we stood for. Every
member of our group supported and agreed with these efforts.

However, we agreed that our efforts must be entirely consistent with
the principles underlying the Republican budget substitute. As a matter
of fact, the first action our group took in compiling our budget was to
adopt unanimously the Republican budget as the basis of our work. It
was determined that we would accept the specific spending cut and reform proposals presented by the Budget Committee and add more
spending reforms until we reached a balanced budget at the end of the

five years. This blueprint to a balanced budget is referred to as a budget resolution.

Before discussing the political process and dynamics that went into the development of the Balanced Budget Task Force's budget proposal, it is important to understand the budget process.

How the Budget Process Works

The process for determining the distribution of resources in the budget is set forth in the Budget and Impoundment Control Act of 1974, as amended. The congressional budget process is intended to pull together the multiple committees of Congress by developing an overall spending plan to guide Congress.

Step 1. The process starts in the spring when Congress adopts a budget resolution. Fundamentally, this resolution sorts out federal spending according to the following twenty budget functions that combine programs in similar subject areas.

1. National Defense
2. International Affairs
3. Science, Space, and Technology
4. Energy
5. Environment
6. Agriculture
7. Commerce and Housing Credit
8. Transportation
9. Community and Regional Development
10. Education and Training
11. Health
12. Medicare
13. Income Security
14. Social Security
15. Veterans' Benefits and Services
16. Administration of Justice
17. General Government
18. Net Interest
19. Allowances
20. Undistributed Offsetting Receipts

Step 2. The Budget Committee, in consultation with the authorizing committees, translates the amounts in this resolution into allocations to the Appropriations Committee for discretionary programs. Entitlement programs receive their funding allocations from various other authorizing committees based on targets of the resolution. All of these allocations, which tell the committee how much in total new budget authority or entitlement authority they may spend, serve as spending limits for each committee's jurisdiction. The Budget Committee reaches those amounts based on various assumptions regarding the particular programs. Our Task Force developed such a budget resolution, which established new allocations for each committee.

Types of Spending. The budget resolution deals with two types of spending in the federal budget, defined in the following table.

Types of Spending	
Discretionary Spending	**Entitlement Spending**
Represents about one-third of the government's $1.5 trillion in annual spending.	Represents about two-thirds of the government's $1.5 trillion in annual spending (excluding interest on the debt).
Involves programs for which Congress annually adopts specific levels of spending to occur each year.	Involves programs such as Medicare, Social Security, and Medicaid, which are referred to as mandatory spending.
Thirteen different appropriation bills, drafted by the thirteen subcommittees of the House and Senate Appropriations Committees, determine the spending levels.	These programs are based on benefits or cash provided to qualifying individuals. Once the eligibility standards and benefit levels of a program are determined and set in law, the government is required to provide the benefits or cash to every individual entitled to them — even if the total outlays exceed the amount the government had intended to spend on the program. That is why this kind of spending is called "mandatory" and why it is difficult to control.
Appropriation bills, which must be signed every year by the president, determine the maximum amounts that can be spent on programs in them.	Unlike discretionary spending, entitlements generally do not require annual appropriations; the authorization is all that is needed for spending to occur.
If added together, the amounts of the appropriation bills equal the corresponding spending amount established in the budget resolution.	For these programs, the authorization is what establishes the level of benefits to be provided to each recipient. For that reason, the kind of spending provided under such authorizing legislation often is called direct spending.

Spending Distribution. The budget resolution's spending distribution is implemented through two separate processes:

Spending Distribution Process	
Appropriations Process (Discretionary)	**Reconciliation (Entitlements)**
Involves passing and enacting the thirteen appropriation bills, which actually assign funds to individual programs.	Involves changes in entitlement programs and taxes and occurs only if the budget resolution calls for levels of entitlement spending or taxation that are different from what would occur if current law simply remained in place.
Example: The Labor, Health and Human Services, and Education Appropriations Bill provides funding for all programs in those respective departments.	Example: If the Food Stamp program is expected to spend $25 billion in the coming fiscal year, and the budget resolution calls for limiting the program to $20 billion, then the appropriate authorizing committee must rewrite parts of the Food Stamp program to reconcile the actual outcome in spending with what is indicated in the budget. If Congress does adopt a reconciliation bill, it must be signed by the president before its provisions become law.

A Painful Resolution to Give Americans What They Deserve

The Balanced Budget Task Force was committed to developing a balanced budget resolution that limited program funding and laid a specific pathway to a balanced budget through restructuring the federal government. With such a resolution, federal spending would be locked into balance. The specific and painful steps the government would need to take to reach that balance would be laid out for all the world to see. Not a pretty sight, but the resolution would be an honest and accountable presentation of the sacrifice needed to give the American people what they deserve. It would be an accurate dialogue for finding the best way to renew our view of America. It would return the government to its original role of enabling citizens to make decisions and create opportunities without an oversized bureaucracy stifling the choices.

From the beginning, the Balanced Budget Task Force recognized that our approach was not the only way, or not perhaps even the best way, to bring about a balanced budget. But we felt compelled to present a proposal that steered the debate in the proper direction. For years, both Republicans and Democrats proposed, debated, and passed deficit reduction packages. Those reduction packages inherently admit that the job is not complete. But the Task Force stood unified behind a proposal that continued this progression to the finish line. We were determined to show how to win the race by eliminating the deficit. We would not sit the race out while the rules were changed or the course extended. We believed our constituents deserved the specifics of a balanced budget, and we were committed to giving it to them.

Three Guiding Principles

In developing our budget proposal, the Balanced Budget Task Force adopted three guiding principles:
1.   No tax increases
2.   No cuts in Social Security or earned veterans' benefits
3.   No further cuts in defense spending

1. No Tax Increases. America's families and the capital that creates jobs and business opportunity already are taxed too heavily. The Task Force believes that increasing taxes is not the answer to balancing the budget. Keeping government spending in check, and allowing the nation to grow strong economically, *is* the answer — the answer for consistently balancing the budget. Taxes are a strong disincentive; they only serve to stifle growth. Taxes weigh business down; they place a fiscal burden on job creation. Moreover, overtaxing one sector of the population in an attempt to aid another sector only brings mixed results. Abraham Lincoln has been credited with saying, more than a hundred years ago, "You cannot help the poor by destroying the rich. You cannot lift the wage earner by pulling down the wage payer." By achieving a balanced budget through a restructured government and a renewed America, every American citizen, rich or poor, will reap the benefits.

Since 1977, Congress has raised taxes fifteen times. Yet research shows that tax increases have resulted more often in lower tax revenues than in deficit reduction.[2] Taxes were raised throughout the 1980s and twice in the early 1990s in efforts to balance the budget or reduce the deficit. Not once did these tax increases achieve that result! Congress would pass a tax increase with one hand and increase spending with the other hand, most often resulting in a net loss for the taxpayers.

This quick-handed method is exactly what Ronald Reagan came face to face with in 1982. In an effort to curb the increasing deficit, Democratic leaders in the House and Senate went to President Reagan and cut a deal. For every dollar in tax increases enacted in 1981, the Democrats promised two dollars of spending cuts. Being the new kid on the block, President Reagan agreed and supported an increase in taxes. However, when he tried to pass the promised spending cuts in 1982, he was stonewalled. Furthermore, passage of the tax increases led to the loss of the working conservative coalition Reagan had established after the 1980 election when many "boll weevil southern conservative Democrats," as well as Republicans, lost their re-election campaigns in 1982, and President Reagan was less effective in enacting his conservative agenda throughout the remainder of his term. Tax increases did not decrease the deficit then. They do not decrease the deficit now.

Raising taxes seems only to feed a growing government's insatiable appetite. If a businessman realizes that his spending has exceeded his income, he does not raise his prices to match his consumption. Neither should the government. Uncontrolled behavior will remain unchecked until there are no longer any expendable resources. The leviathan of government has swelled into a bureaucracy that is oversized, consumes too much of the economy, and forces competitive business out of the growth market. With this in mind, it makes no sense to provide this bureaucracy with more spending money. Instead, we need to pare back this beast's appetite to a level equal to the amount brought in by taxes.

2. No Cuts in Social Security or Earned Veterans' Benefits. From the start of the Task Force meetings, we took both Social Security and contractually earned veterans' benefits off the discussion table. We determined those to be important priorities that needed to be funded at their current levels. Why? Social Security is exempt from budget reductions because, as President Franklin D. Roosevelt said in 1935, at the time of its conception, Social Security is a trust between the government and an individual as a way to assist older Americans in retirement. Cuts in Social Security benefits would be a violation of this trust. Likewise, veterans and their families have a sacred contract with their country that must never be broken.

3. No Further Cuts in Defense Spending. The third guiding principle of the Task Force deals with our national defense. The fourth tenet of the preamble to the Constitution grants the federal government the responsibility to "provide for the common defense." Consequently, we believe that ensuring a level of defense spending sufficient to meet our defense challenges domestically and abroad must be a priority in the federal budget. The conclusion reached by the Task Force was that the scheduled reductions in defense spending by the Clinton Administration over the next five years placed our nation's military men and women in a dangerously compromised position. As a result, the Balanced Budget Task Force proposal asserts the need to maintain a sound national security policy that can meet predictable and unexpected events. We also agreed that the defense budget would not continue to be raided for other "priorities" in the federal budget. At the same time, we committed to make recommendations to ensure that the government spends defense funds in an efficient and wise manner, proposing that spending for low-priority or wasteful defense programs be rerouted to those more widely held defense programs.

A Credible Balanced Budget Proposal

After extensive discussion, research, and debate over a limited period of time, the Task Force, which had now grown to more than thirty-five members, compiled and approved a comprehensive list of program reforms and spending reductions. The budget scorekeepers at the Congressional Budget Office (CBO) thoroughly reviewed our proposals and gave us our official credibility as a balanced budget proposal. According to CBO, our program reforms would deliver a balanced budget by 1999, or the fifth year in which this budget plan would be in effect. Even more important is the fact that the plan would keep the budget balanced for as long as they could reasonably project. Compare the numbers of the Balanced Budget Task Force proposal with the present deficit numbers of President Clinton's budget:

Projected Deficits (in billions of dollars)

Fiscal Year	Balanced Budget Task Force	Clinton Budget
1994	- $230	- $230
1995	- $132	- $171
1996	- $ 69	- $166
1997	- $ 47	- $182
1998	- $ 12	- $180
1999	+ $ 8 (surplus)	- $204
2000	+ $ 5 (surplus)	- $226
2001	+ $ .030 (surplus)	- $258

Source: Congressional Budget Office

Look at the difference! Instead of showing deficits rising as they do under current law, our budget shows steady progress toward a balanced budget at the end of five years. If the nation does finally adopt a balanced budget amendment to the Constitution, it will be required to adopt a similar proposal that will gradually, but truly, bring our nation's accounts into balance over a seven-year period. The Task Force balanced budget proposal is real, honest, and verified. If you're wondering how we came up with those numbers, it was not magic. It came about through real tough thinking, honest discussions, and verification of facts and figures as we designed and detailed a blueprint for rebuilding the fiscal soundness of America.

Our budget blueprint provides a step-by-step approach through a maze of irresponsible government spending to fiscally responsible governing. Many of these proposals are not new, but they are real and they are far reaching.

According to the Congressional Budget Office, our budget resolution calls for reducing projected government spending by $698,000,000,000 over five years. Our proposal, which contains more than 500 specific cuts, redefines the role of government in American society. Through the outright elimination of 150 government programs, the consolidation of 35 more, and the privatization of 25 government agencies, this budget paves the way for producing a smaller government that is better equipped to deliver needed services to its citizens.

Here's the good news: The American people can have a balanced budget, the continuation of necessary government services, a more efficient government, and a stronger economy. However, despite the enormous amount of spending reduction mapped out in this budget, despite the restructuring, and despite the presence of a balanced budget, we must all understand that government spending will still increase by 3 percent, or $327,000,000,000, over the next five years — but we will be spending within reason.

Program Reform

The Balanced Budget Task Force proposal's important programmatic themes include a complete overhaul of federal job training by consolidating more than ninety duplicative programs into one comprehensive employment and job training block grant, giving states and businesses more flexibility in targeting and coordinating those resources. We believe the private sector is more effective in training individuals for real employment opportunity than the federal government.

Our budget also proposes comprehensive welfare reform based on the principles of time-limited benefits, paternity establishment, individual responsibility, cost control, discouragement of illegitimacy, and promotion of the family. Families with children who currently live in poverty and benefit from welfare programs should know that their welfare dependency will end and that their self-sufficiency will begin.

In devising this long, detailed list of program reforms, we pulled ideas from a wide variety of sources, including such congressional service organizations as the Republican Study Committee, the Congressional Budget Office, and the General Accounting Office. The Executive Branch provided us with suggestions in Vice-President Al Gore's *National Performance Review, Office of the Inspector General of the Department of Health and Human Services Cost-Saver Handbook: The Red Book* under the Bush Administration, and the report from the Grace Commission under the Reagan Administration. The Task Force also selected ideas from many active outside taxpayer support groups including the Heritage Foundation, Citizens Against Government Waste, the Cato Institute, the National Taxpayers' Union, the Committee for a Responsible Budget, and the Concord Coalition. Within Congress, many members came forth with individual spending reduction proposals. One of the co-chairmen of our Task Force, Harris Fawell (R-Illinois), was also chairman of the Bipartisan Congressional Porkbusters Coalition and, as such, was able to provide suggestions for further detailed cuts on programs gone awry.

Because those sources represent millions of Americans, the people had their voice heard in a truly bipartisan and inclusive discussion of budget priorities. Each one of those organizations proved invaluable to our Task Force's efforts to draft a real, credible, and realistic budget proposal that will place the United States back on a fiscally solvent track. All cuts presented in this budget represent hours of hard work, the spirit of bipartisan compromise, and an honest attempt to deal with a very complex problem. Not one of the members of the Task Force, including me, agrees with every cut in this proposal. However, we all do agree that every nook and cranny of the federal government should be called upon to contribute in this campaign to save our children's future.

Reading through the details of this budget in the following pages may cause alarm for some individuals and groups across America and, perhaps in many cases, rightly so. Nevertheless, I urge all who venture through these details to keep the proposal in perspective. *Every minute, government spending adds $10,000 to the national debt. Likewise, every newborn child enters this world with a personal debt burden of $18,000.* This situation must change, and change often involves pain, especially when it is as comprehensive as what we propose here. May you read these details and gain a new insight into what is really involved in the universal goal of balancing the budget. You may think it is a high price to pay. But the cost of inaction is a much higher price. For the sake of America's future and for my grandchildren, I commend the specifics to your concerted attention.

Until Congress passed the Budget and Accounting Act of 1921, an annual national budget was not required in the United States. With the passage of this statute, the president became responsible for presenting a budget to the Congress early every year. The president prepares the budget by reviewing agency estimates and coordinating them with overall government planning. As part of the budget preparation process, examiners from the Office of Management and Budget, which assists the president in preparing the budget, hold hearings and meetings with agency staff.

After Congress receives the budget and separates it into parts that are examined by the authorization and appropriation committees, budget committees prepare at least two annual resolutions: One in the spring provides "targets" for the committees, and the other in the fall sets binding totals. Resolutions specify totals for revenue, outlays, budget authority, expected surplus or deficit, and any change in public debt. Outlays and budget authority are further divided into functional categories for such broad areas as agriculture, defense, health, and transportation. The Congressional Budget Office gives Congress an independent, nonpartisan source of technical assistance.

The goal of the Congress is to complete action on authorization and appropriation bills by the start of the fiscal year, which begins October 1. If Congress fails to enact an appropriation bill for an agency, it may pass a "continuing resolution" to provide temporary stopgap funding authority.

The budget is not a static instrument, however. After the president submits the budget, he may send budget amendments to Congress. He also may submit supplemental requests for emergency or high-priority funding needs that cannot be postponed until the next fiscal year. At the same time, agencies are authorized to transfer funds from one appropriation account to another or from one program to another within the same account. Throughout the year the president may request deferrals to delay the expenditure of funds, or rescissions to terminate budget authority. The budget remains in a constant state of change throughout the fiscal year as the government responds to developing circumstances.

1 George Hager. "Clinton's Bid to Shift Priorities Constrained by Fiscal Limits," *Congressional Quarterly*. February 12, 1994, page 293.

2 Center for Policy Analysis. *Tax Briefing Book*. Dallas: Center for Policy Analysis, page 35.

Part II
Restructuring Programs

Balancing the budget is a lofty, abstract goal that most Americans claim they want Washington to accomplish. Nevertheless, many in Washington have shied away from such an adventure. Whether it may seem politically impossible, personally overwhelming, or logistically unfeasible, balancing the budget is a project into which most never venture alone. The federal budget is an intricate, complex, and detailed blueprint of numbers, projections, priorities, and vision that must not be examined loosely. To revolutionize the budget, it is necessary to dig into the specifics with a fine-toothed comb, setting priorities and making decisions that affect millions, if not billions, of people worldwide.

The Balanced Budget Task Force pulled out their combs and went to work examining the budget — line by line, program by program — to determine how best to rewrite this blueprint. Early on we recognized that balancing the budget necessitated a restructuring of the federal government from the top down. Only by a complete restructuring of the actual infrastructure of government could we maintain a government limited enough in scope to match our nation's limited revenues.

Part II of this adventure portrays what we found in the depths of these numbers and what changes and restructuring we recommended for adoption by the House of Representatives. These reforms have been organized so that you, the reader, can best understand how the changes will affect you through services now provided to you by the federal government. Every provision recommended by the Task Force is laid out in the following pages.

Since the entire federal budget is well over 1,200 pages long, space does not allow a complete analysis of each recommended provision of our budget. However, in addition to programs discussed in each chapter, we have listed the remaining provisions in tables at the end of each chapter. Furthermore, so that you can count the savings along with us as we proceed through the budget, each end-of-chapter table contains a running total of budget savings.

The program reforms outlined in the following pages will require a level of government restructuring unprecedented in recent history. As I mentioned earlier, many of these changes are not new ideas, but each of them is real and substantive. Many of these reforms have been considered and developed by individuals and organizations with a wealth of knowledge in the area in question. The hard work performed by these individuals and groups laid the foundation for much of our work. The ideas were submitted and the Balanced Budget Task Force pulled them together into a complete package.

The results of our concerted efforts are now before you — the taxpayer. See for yourself how the federal government could resolve our crisis and run our nation's books, just as individuals and companies throughout the country manage their own.

CHAPTER THREE

The Health and Livelihood of Citizens

<hr />

The preamble to the Constitution of the United States reminds us that an important function of government is to promote the general welfare. One way the government carries out this important duty is by fostering a society in which hard work is rewarded, the sick and elderly are cared for, and the basic needs of individuals and families are provided for by *both* private and public assistance. I believe that the federal government has intruded on the ability of many private citizens to aid their fellow man and that the principle of individual responsibility has been run roughshod over by the welfare state.

The Balanced Budget Task Force recognized the necessity of a partnership between the private and public sectors in any free society founded on limited government, and our budget proposal reflects an attempt to foster the growth of such a partnership. Because of the federal government's expansion of services in the areas of health, housing, and general welfare — and many of them are needed — welfare and entitlement programs have become the largest and fastest-growing programs in the federal budget. This Task Force budget proposal seeks to strike an equitable and fair balance between spending restraint and the provision of needed services for our citizens.

Reform Medicaid

Medicaid is a federal-state program designed to provide health care services to needy individuals. It functions under the direction of the U.S. Department of Health and Human Services (HHS) and usually is operated by state welfare or health departments, within guidelines issued by the Health Care Financing Administration (HCFA). Medicaid furnishes five basic services to needy individuals:

1. Inpatient hospital care
2. Outpatient hospital care
3. Physicians' services
4. Skilled nursing home services for adults
5. Laboratory and X-ray services

Those eligible for Medicaid include families and certain children who qualify for public assistance and may include aged, blind, and disabled adults who are eligible for the Supplemental Security Income (SSI) Program of the Social Security Administration (SSA). In addition, states may include individuals and families classified as "medically needy" who meet eligibility requirements except those for financial assistance. Each state decides who is eligible for Medicaid benefits and what services will be included. Some of the benefits frequently provided are dental care; ambulance services; and the cost of drugs, eyeglasses, and hearing aids. In determining eligibility for the program, a state may not hold adult children responsible for the medical expenses of their parents.

Medicaid spending is projected to grow at a rate of 9 percent every year from now until the year 2000. Its annual growth has exceeded 20 percent in recent years. Federal Medicaid spending has grown from $41.1 billion in 1990 to $85.9 billion in 1994.[1] Federal mandates expanding benefits and coverage, as well as additional state mandates, have contributed significantly to Medicaid cost increases.

Managed Care Systems for Medicaid Beneficiaries. Medicaid is inefficient and expensive; it costs $4,380 per enrollee, of which the federal share is $2,500. The Task Force proposal requires states to phase in managed care for Medicaid. States would receive waivers from federal Medicaid mandates to establish programs modeled after Arizona's access plan, and Medicaid reimbursement levels could be reduced to 94 percent of current levels. The savings come from more cost-efficient Medicaid health-care delivery, which would allow slower growth in reimbursement spending for Medicaid services. Medicaid cost increases for Arizona's managed-care system are 6 percent lower than average.[2]

Wisconsin's plan stands as another good example. The state moved its Medicaid program into a direct managed-care system and state Medicaid costs fell dramatically. For several years now, Wisconsin's Medicaid growth has been one-third to one-half lower than the national rate, and its cost savings occurred without any reduction in coverage or provider reimbursements.[3] Tennessee, Massachusetts, and Michigan have implemented similar managed-care initiatives, showing that, with flexibility, spending growth can be slowed while better services are provided.

Federal Share of Medicaid-Disproportionate Share Payments to Hospitals. In an attempt to control escalating health-care costs, Congress passed a law beginning with fiscal year 1993 that placed a national aggregate cap on the amount the federal government would pay to disproportionate share hospitals. Such hospitals are eligible for additional federal payments because they serve a disproportionate share of low-income patients. Unlike comparable Medicare payments, Medicaid payments must follow an established formula that considers a hospital's charity patients as well as its Medicaid caseload. The Task Force proposal reduces the federal share of disproportionate Medicaid payments to hospitals under the following phase-in schedule:

Year	Federal share reduced by (%)
1996	20
1997	30
1998	45
1999	60
2000	60

Medicaid-State Limits on Long-Term Care Beds. In 1993, nursing-facility care absorbed about 60 percent of Medicaid long-term care spending.[4] The supply of nursing home beds varies widely across the country, however, and these variations can be explained only partly by differences in the numbers of elderly people among states. The rate at which available beds are used — on average, about 90 percent — also varies, but the occupancy rate seems not to be related to the number of beds per 1,000 people. The Task Force proposal requires states to limit the growth rate in nursing home beds and thus reduce Medicaid spending on nursing homes.

States regulate growth in the number of nursing home beds eligible for federal funding through Medicaid, Medicare, or other federal programs by requiring that providers obtain a certificate of need (CON) to operate additional beds. For any specified area, states issue a CON only if the ratio of the number of nursing home beds to the population that is likely to need them falls below certain guidelines. The guidelines are set by the state, subject to federal approval.

If adding nursing home beds increases the number used, the number of beds could be limited to help curb further growth in Medicaid outlays. In the process, regulating the number of beds could make nursing home outlays more predictable for state budget planners. Guidelines also could be used to help change the balance between long-term care in nursing homes and other forms of care.

Federal Medicaid-Matching Administrative Expenses Rate. The Medicaid program provides medical assistance to low-income people who are recipients of Supplemental Security Income or who are current or recent recipients of aid to families with dependent children (AFDC) payments, as well as to certain other low-income individuals. The federal government pays half of most administrative costs, while state and local governments pay the remaining share. For some types of expenses, higher matching rates have been established as an incentive for local administrators to undertake more of a particular administrative activity than if such expenses were matched at 50 percent, which means the federal government is paying more than half of the expenses. The Task Force proposal reduces the federal Medicaid-matching administrative expenses rate to 50 percent.

All state Medicaid programs already have established computer systems and are currently operating units to control fraud and abuse, which should help alleviate the increased administrative burdens that may be imposed by implementing this provision.

Medicaid Coverage for Noncitizens. The Task Force proposal would eliminate all welfare benefits, except Medicaid, for noncitizens; exceptions would be refugees and permanent resident aliens over age 70 who have been legal residents for at least five years. This provision would restrict Medicaid coverage for noncitizens to emergency-only services.

The Cost of Welfare

The total cost of the "War on Poverty" has been enormous and has done little to reduce poverty in America. From its inception in 1965 to the present, welfare spending has cost the taxpayers $4.9 trillion in constant 1992 dollars, a figure greater than the entire national debt. Total welfare spending now absorbs 5 percent of the gross national product (GNP), compared to 1.5 percent in 1965. Welfare programs cost $305 billion in 1992 and are projected to increase by $510 billion by 1998.[5]

Our nation's current welfare system is laden with waste, fraud, and abuse, and welfare has become a way of life for many people. For more than forty years the welfare system has been paying for nonwork and single parenthood at alarmingly increasing rates. Examine these revealing statistics:

- More than 27 million American families currently collect Food Stamps.
- A record high of 5 million families (with 9.6 million children) currently are enrolled in the aid to families with dependent children program — up from 3.7 million families in 1988.
- 92 percent of children on AFDC do not have a father in the home.
- Fewer than 1 percent of AFDC parents are required to work.
- Out-of-wedlock births among teenagers between the ages of 15 and 17 have more than doubled since 1965.
- Funding for the twenty-five major social welfare programs doubled from $132 billion in 1975 to $277 billion in 1992.[6]

Those statistics represent the fruits of a welfare system that subsidizes out-of-wedlock births, penalizes marriage, creates dependents out of able-bodied citizens, and discourages recipients from breaking out of a detrimental cycle. Rather than alleviating social pathologies such as crime, drug abuse, and academic failure, the current welfare system has contributed to them. A fundamental approach to welfare reform must address three major areas:

1. Ending the subsidy of illegitimacy by requiring paternity establishment, implementing stricter child-enforcement measures, and eliminating AFDC payments to unwed minors.
2. Enhancing work requirements by limiting eligibility for AFDC benefits to two years.
3. Imposing concrete spending-control measures by converting savings into block grants to states to care for children and by imposing a spending cap of 3.5 percent on total welfare spending. (Individual programs would be permitted to grow at a higher or lower rate as long as the aggregate spending fell within the 3.5 percent cap, thus keeping the whole approximately within the level of inflation.)

This proposal will reverse the dismal results of the antiwork, antimarriage welfare policies currently in law. Taxpayers as well as welfare recipients would benefit from the lower costs of managing the welfare entitlement program.

Before placing these programs into block grants, the Task Force decided to firm up some of the rules for welfare spending under the current system. Those rule reforms included changes to eligibility criteria, federal-state cost sharing, administrative reimbursements, and certain program delivery costs. This effort enabled the Task Force to realize additional budgetary savings while also tightening up on the incidence of abuse and fraud in the system by both individuals and state bureaucracies. Such changes allowed us to maximize state flexibility in these programs while minimizing the number of strings attached to the funding once placed in block grants.

Reforms to the AFDC Program

Reforms to the aid to families with dependent children program creates a transition program in which welfare recipients are expected to work or prepare for work. The program's goal is to prepare recipients for employment in the private sector. Recipients must agree that, if after two years they have not secured paid employment, they will work in exchange for their AFDC benefits. Benefits are reduced or eliminated for recipients who fail to meet established criteria for participation in the program.

Also, as a condition for receiving benefits, paternity must be established for any dependent named on an AFDC application. The mother is exempt from this requirement if pregnancy was caused by rape or incest or if the state concludes that pursuing paternity will result in physical harm to the parent or child. Currently, states are required to establish paternity in 75 percent of cases before benefits are granted. This provision increases the requirement to 90 percent.

States also have the option of taking the amount of federal reimbursement they received for AFDC in 1992, plus a one-time inflation adjustment of 3 percent as a fixed annual cash payment, rather than continuing in the current AFDC program. Additionally, at their option, states may tighten the welfare roles in the following ways:

- Refuse AFDC benefits to single parents under the age of 18
- Provide new state residents with the same level of AFDC benefits as provided by the state from which the resident moved
- Decrease the total monthly AFDC benefit by up to $50 per month for up to six months for failing to comply with immunization or other health requirements
- Reduce monthly benefits up to $50 per month for families with school-age children who attend school less than a state-established minimum without good cause
- Deny additional benefits for children born 10 months or more after the date of application for AFDC
- Replace the current federal rules for disregarding income in setting AFDC levels
- Allow recipients who marry an individual other than the parent of their child and who become eligible for AFDC, to keep one-half of their current benefits for up to one year, as long as their combined family income is below 150 percent of the poverty level

• Require AFDC parents to participate in parenting classes and classes on money management during the transition program

Federal Share of Foster Care and Adoption. The Foster Care and Adoption Assistance programs, authorized under title IV-E of the Social Security Act, are open-ended entitlement programs that provide benefits and services to children in need. The federal government and the states jointly pay for the foster care assistance programs. The federal share of the costs of these programs varies with a state's per capita income. High-income states pay a larger share of benefits than low-income states. By law,[7] the federal share can be no less than 50 percent and no more than 83 percent. The 50 percent federal floor currently applies to fourteen jurisdictions: Alaska, California, Connecticut, Delaware, the District of Columbia, Hawaii, Illinois, Maryland, Massachusetts, Nevada, New Hampshire, New Jersey, New York, and Virginia.

The Task Force proposal lowers the floor for federal share of foster care and adoption to 45 percent. High-income states that choose to be generous should bear a larger share of the cost. If the floor is reduced to 45 percent, federal contribution levels are more directly related to the state's income, and nine of the fourteen jurisdictions would still be paying less than the formula alone requires.

Foster Care Administration. The federal Foster Care and Adoption Assistance programs also provide federal matching funds to assist states in providing foster care to children who meet certain eligibility requirements. In 1995, the program will serve about 255,000 children on average each month at a federal cost of $2.9 billion. Administration will account for about 42 percent of that total.

Each state administers its own program within the federal mandates established in title IV. The federal government reimburses states for one-half of certain administrative costs, including those for determining eligibility, certain preplacement services, and child placement services, as well as for administrative overhead.

During the 1980s, costs increased much more rapidly than caseloads. At some point in the past decade, many states' administrative costs increased sharply. In about one-half of the states, the annual increase in such costs per child exceeded 1,000 percent in at least one year,[8] supporting the theory that much of the growth resulted from changes in states' methods for claiming funds rather than from expanded services to children. Such costs increased from less than $50 million (in 1992 dollars) in 1981 to about $950 million in 1992.[9] The Task Force resolution limits annual increases in payments to each state for administrative costs to 10 percent a year.

Reforms to the Federal Feeding and Nutrition Support Programs

The Task Force proposes to consolidate all federal feeding and nutrition support programs into a single block grant to states and to reduce funding by 5 percent from the projected level of spending. The reduction would account for savings resulting from the elimination of benefit overlap, middle-income subsidies, and administrative duplication. The block grant is targeted to individuals at 185 percent of the poverty level and below. This level of spending allows for population growth and annual adjustments for food price inflation.

To assure that this block grant continues to service those who truly need aid, the program retains certain percentage requirements. For example, states must use 12 percent of their grants to fully fund Women, Infants, and Children (WIC) benefits for pregnant and postpartum mothers and their preschool children. Similarly, 20 percent of the block grants is earmarked for the school lunch and school breakfast programs.

Child- and Adult-Care Food Programs. Federal law provides a guaranteed federal subsidy for each U.S. Department of Agriculture (USDA)-approved meal and "supplement" (snack) served in participating child- and adult-care facilities. The Task Force proposes to reform child support programs by terminating the child- and adult-care food programs that are not carefully targeted to those who are in need. Three-quarters of the participating children in family day-care homes have household incomes above 185 percent of the poverty line.[10]

Food Stamp Program. The Thrifty Food Plan, the first food stamp program, was established in 1971 to reflect the average recipient household. Today's household can be represented by a single person living alone or a group of individuals living together. The Task Force agrees with the Grace Commission[11] recommendations to update the Food Stamp Program annually to reflect changes in average participant household size and composition. Savings achieved from this proposal are significant due to this demographic change. Some recipients may see a reduction in received benefits, but the newly adjusted levels more accurately reflect the needs of the recipients.

Food Stamp Monthly Payments Below $10. Food Stamp eligibility is based on income, with many households eligible for Food Stamp amounts of less than $10. In those situations, a minimum benefit of $10 is established. The Task Force proposal cancels Food Stamp monthly payments of less than $10 for all households.

Federal Matching Requirements of Food Stamp Benefits. The Task Force proposes to alter the federal matching requirements of Food Stamp benefits by requiring a 5 percent nonfederal match beginning in FY 1996 and escalating to a 25 percent match requirement by the year 2000.

Nutrition Assistance for Puerto Rico. Puerto Rico, a freely associated commonwealth of the United States whose residents pay no federal income tax, receives nutrition assistance from the U.S. government, including funding for Food Stamps, school lunch, school breakfast, summer service, nutrition education and training, state administrative expenses, and special milk programs. The Task Force proposal freezes all current nutrition assistance program fundings at their FY 1995 level for five years. The freeze does not affect current services but prevents any new expansion of services without subsequent reductions in other areas.

State Administrative Errors in the AFDC and Food Stamp Programs. State administrators often make substantial errors in administering benefits under the AFDC and Food Stamp programs, which results in misapplied federal funds. The Task Force proposal imposes a charge for state administrative errors in the AFDC and Food Stamp programs, requiring states to reimburse the federal government for all administrative errors made through overpayment in the programs.

Reforms to Assistance Programs

The federal government provides assistance to middle- to low-income individuals and families in the areas of emergency, heating, and energy aid. Reforms to these programs will ensure effectiveness in delivery and accurate targeting of this funding to those truly in need.

Emergency Assistance Benefits. The Social Security Act and federal regulations authorize emergency assistance to needy families with a child under the age of 21. The Task Force proposal will limit emergency assistance (EA) benefits to a single period of thirty consecutive days or less in a twelve-month period. Congress created the EA program so states could act quickly to meet a needy family's emergency needs in the event of a family crisis, intending that benefits be provided for a short time. However, some states are exceeding the congressionally mandated thirty-day limit because of vagueness in the federal regulation.

The Omnibus Budget Reconciliation Act (OBRA) of 1990 clarified this policy through the effective date of September 30, 1991. At that time the Department of Health and Human Services submitted a legislative proposal to Congress, instead of issuing regulations, to make the clarification permanent. But Congress never acted. This proposal clarifies that policy so that it complies with the original intent of the program. This recommendation is from the Inspector General of the Department of Health and Human Services under the Bush Administration.

Low Income Home Energy Assistance. The Low Income Home Energy Assistance Program (LIHEAP) helps pay the home energy costs of some low-income households. States may use the grants to help eligible households pay their home heating or cooling bills, meet energy-related emergencies, or fund low-cost weatherization projects.

Energy prices have declined by about one-third since LIHEAP was created. In fact, thirty states transferred up to 10 percent of their LIHEAP funds during fiscal year 1991 to supplement spending on five other social and community service block grant programs, which indicates that spending for energy assistance does not have as high a priority as other spending. This fact, plus the reduced prices of energy, warrants scaling back future LIHEAP appropriations by 50 percent. The Clinton Administration recommended a similar proposal in its FY 1995 budget.

Supplemental Security Income Reforms

The Supplemental Security Income Program is a means-tested, federally administered income assistance program established by the 1972 amendments to the Social Security Act. The SSI Program provides monthly cash benefits, in accordance with uniform, nationwide eligibility requirements, to the needy, aged, blind, and disabled. The number of SSI recipients increased from four million in 1974 to six million in December 1993. Total annual benefits paid under this program increased at an average rate of 7.9 percent, from about $5.3 billion in 1974 to $23.6 billion in 1993. Likewise, the monthly federal benefit rates for individuals and couples increased from $140 and $210 in 1974 to $446 and $669 in 1994, respectively. Large growth and cost increases over the last twenty years require a re-examination of this program for reform.[12]

Admission of SSI Recipients to Nursing Homes. The Task Force proposal calls for more timely reporting of the admission of SSI recipients to nursing homes to eliminate overpayment of benefits. Nursing homes will be required to report to the Social Security Administration admissions of SSI recipients within one day after admission. When SSI recipients are in nursing homes and the cost of care is funded at least 50 percent by the Medicaid program, monthly SSI payments are to be limited to $30.

SSI recipients or their representatives often do not report such admissions, resulting in millions of dollars in overpayments. Since nursing homes know whether Medicaid will be paying for the care of SSI recipients before they are admitted and SSI recipients may be impaired, the nursing homes should be required to report the admittance to SSA.

SSI Overpayments. At the outset of the Social Security program, Congress guaranteed the rights of eligible individuals to benefits that would be exempt from ". . . execution, levy, attachment, garnishment, or other legal process. . . ." As a result of this provision, SSA must obtain a beneficiary's consent to recover an SSI overpayment from Retroactive Supplemental Disability Income (RSDI) benefits.

The Task Force proposal for recovering overpayments through

offsetting reductions in Social Security payments pursues cross-program adjustment as a means of collecting the outstanding debts owed by former SSI recipients who are current RSDI beneficiaries. The amount of debts recovered through cross-program adjustment has decreased by nearly 50 percent since FY 1983, even though the ending balance of outstanding debt has increased.[13] Nearly half of the outstanding debts owed by former SSI recipients pertain to individuals who currently are receiving RSDI payments. The SSA's 1983 "SSI Non-Pay Overpayment" study indicates that a recontact with those individuals to remind them of their debt and encourage repayment will produce substantial recoveries. This proposal is based on a recommendation from the Office of the Inspector General of the Department of Health and Human Services under the Bush Administration.

Eligibility of Children for Supplemental Security Disability Income (SSDI). In addition to providing benefits to the elderly, blind, and disabled people who cannot work, the SSI Program also pays benefits to children under 18 who are blind or suffer other disabilities. From its inception in 1972 until 1990, the SSI children's disability program determined eligibility based on the legislative standard that the child's impairment be comparable in severity to that of the adult. But as a result of the February 1990 Supreme Court ruling in *Sullivan v. Zebley*, the Social Security Administration is required to take into account the child's "functional limitations" in determining the severity of the impairment, although that is not a standard used in determining the disability of adults. Nevertheless, federal regulations incorporating the new standard were issued in 1991.

Implementing the *Zebley* decision appears to have had an immediate impact on the caseloads of the children's disability program. In December 1980, 5.5 percent of SSI payments were made to blind and disabled children. By June of 1992, 9.9 percent of SSI payments were made to this group of recipients. Blind and disabled children now represent the fastest-growing segment of the SSI population.

Analysts and caregivers working in this area suspect that the fundamental cause of the rise in the children's disability caseloads is that the new federal regulations, consistent with the *Zebley* decision, include behavior that is not "age appropriate" as a disability. A plethora of disability claims have since been filed on behalf of children whose only "functional limitation" may be simply behavioral or emotional problems, but not severe impairments such as mental retardation or physical impairments.

Because public funds should focus on the most needy, Congress should examine whether to reverse the expansion of the definition of "functional limitation" relating to children that resulted from the *Zebley* decision. The Task Force proposes to terminate the eligibility of children for supplemental security disability income.

Income Exclusion for SSI. As a means-tested program, SSI benefits are reduced by a recipient's outside income. For unearned income, mostly Social Security benefits, the first $20 a month is excluded and any additional amounts reduce benefits dollar for dollar. Earned income is excluded more liberally. The Task Force proposal reduces the income exclusion for SSI from $20 to $15.

Reform Housing Programs

The federal government's housing programs are another area loaded with waste and inefficiency. Originally, they were set up to provide temporary assistance to people who lacked the resources to obtain good-quality housing and to help low-income families, whether urban or rural, young or old, to find affordable housing. Today's housing situation is quite different. A higher percentage of the population lives in public housing today than when these programs were started. Clearly the programs have not worked.

Housing programs are administered through four different departments and are implemented through an even more complex web of bureaucracy. The Balanced Budget Task Force budget seeks to examine these programs for overlap, reduce them to face budget realities, and restructure them to meet true need.

The U.S. Department of Housing and Urban Development (HUD) is responsible for programs concerned with housing needs and with the improvement and development of urban areas. Created by Congress in 1965, HUD provides for antidiscrimination in housing activities and aid to neighborhood rehabilitation. It absorbed the programs of public housing, urban renewal, urban planning assistance, and public facilities of the old Housing and Home Finance Agency, as well as the mortgage insurance programs of the Federal Housing Administration. It assumed responsibility for the new programs launched under the Housing and Urban Development Act of 1965, which includes a rent-supplements program to encourage private enterprise to construct desirable housing for low-income families. It also undertook the so-called Model Cities program of the Demonstration Cities and Metropolitan Act of 1966. HUD channels loans, grants, mortgage insurance, and technical assistance through communities, urban areas, states, and private and non-profit sponsors.

Operating Subsidies for Vacant Public Housing. HUD provides operating subsidies to public housing agencies (PHAs) to make up the difference between rental income and operating costs. Even though HUD has tried to stop payments for vacant public housing, Congress has continued funding for these units.

Some PHAs argue that the current operating subsidy formula does not provide adequate subsidies to cover costs. Therefore, they say, eliminating subsidies for vacant units will take away necessary funds. But because of massive increases for public housing modernization, operating subsidies, and drug elimination grants, all PHAs are receiving record funding amounts. The Task Force provision eliminates operating subsidies for vacant public housing.

Disposition of Multifamily Housing Units. HUD currently owns approximately 69,000 units of multifamily housing. HUD was never meant to function as a landlord, but the agency has not been able to sell the units because of restrictions in Section 203 of the Housing and Community Development Amendments of 1978 requiring that each unit be sold with fifteen-year project-based Section 8 assistance. That means that the federal government cannot just sell unused HUD-owned property but is required to lease it to someone. While most favor placing needy families in low-income housing, few believe the government should be prevented from availing itself of unused housing. Not only does current law force the government to subsidize housing, once the government purchases a housing unit for use in the Section 8 housing program, it is prevented by law from ever selling it. For a system designed to get individuals off the dole and on the road to self-sufficiency, this rule is a direct contradiction. Over the past several years, funding for Section 8 has been significantly reduced. The Task Force proposal loosens the restrictions in Section 203, allowing HUD to dispose of the multifamily units more easily. The Clinton Administration has recommended a similar reform measure.

Housing Slots. Housing assistance, although it establishes fifteen-year mortgages, was intended to be a vehicle to self-sufficiency, not a final resting place. Too often families become trapped in public housing for generations, never required even to attempt to strike out on their own and pursue the American dream.

The Task Force proposal calls for freezing all housing "slots" at 4.6 million units for the next five years to take advantage of the natural turnover process. This action still will allow the program to assist newly eligible households. The Secretaries of Housing and Urban Development and Agriculture are called upon not to reserve any new funds for additional housing units. All obligated funding for specific programs needs to be expended before entering any new commitments. Under existing contracts, those housing accounts already spend $15 billion to $20 billion a year. The selected number of housing units should be reduced by the appropriate levels as other portions of this budget are implemented. Such a change will ensure increases in savings to the taxpayer and a reduction in the number of federally assisted housing units. This proposed policy results in the creation of new households only when an existing household becomes vacant. Under this proposal the McKinney housing units[14] dealing with the homeless are exempt from both the caps and the definition imposed by housing slots.

Economies-of-Scale Adjustment Factors. The federal government uses certain factors in determining eligibility criteria and level of benefits for a variety of welfare programs. Those figures include regular economic data such as increases in the cost of living, inflation, and employment. They also attempt to reconcile the impact of those factors on the purchasing power of average families with the cost of maintaining a certain level of family need. Consequently, it is widely believed that these factors should be updated regularly.

The Task Force supports the Grace Commission[15] recommendation, which calls for modifying the economies-of-scale adjustment factors to reflect actual differences in purchasing costs based on family size. By adjusting the economies-of-scale factors so they are in line with a 1972 study of differences in purchasing power for different family sizes, welfare benefit levels will more accurately cover the costs of providing adequate resources for fulfilling the true need of welfare families.

Rental Assistance Commitments. Each year since 1975, HUD has made new commitments under the Section 8 and public housing programs. Those new commitments, which cover periods ranging from five to twenty years, provide rental housing assistance for additional lower-income households, thereby increasing the total number receiving aid. At the end of fiscal year 1992, about 4.7 million commitments for rental assistance were outstanding for all housing programs. The Task Force provision stops the expansion of rental assistance commitments by halting all new commitments for assistance under the Section 515 housing program.

Tenant/State Contribution. Most lower-income renters who receive federal rental assistance are aided through the Section 8 programs or public housing programs, which are administered by HUD. These federal programs usually pay the difference between 30 percent of a household's adjusted income and either the actual cost of the dwelling or, under the Section 8 voucher program, a payment standard. In 1992, average federal expenditures per assisted household for all of HUD's rental housing programs combined were roughly $4,200. This amount includes both housing subsidies and fees paid to administering agencies.

According to the Congressional Budget Office, savings could be achieved by reducing federal payments on behalf of recipients. The Task Force proposal increases combined tenant and state rental contributions over a five-year period from 30 percent to 35 percent of a tenant's adjusted income. In addition, this proposal requires changing the authorizing legislation for these programs, as well as cutting the annual appropriations for vouchers and public housing operating subsidies.

One rationale for involving states in housing assistance is that these programs generate substantial local benefits, such as improved quality of the housing stock. If all states paid 5 percent of the adjusted incomes of those receiving assistance, housing costs for assisted families would not rise. Moreover, since eligibility for housing assistance is determined by each area's median income, tying states' contributions to renters' incomes ensures that lower-income states pay less per assisted family than higher-income states. Finally, if a state chose not to participate and, consequently, rental payments by its households increased to 35 percent of their adjusted incomes, those out-of-pocket costs would still be well below the nearly 50 percent of income that the typical unassisted renter who is eligible for assistance now pays.

Direct Loans to Rural Homeowners (FmHA's Section 502). The Section 502 housing program, administered by the Farmers Home Administration (FmHA), provides mortgages to rural, low-income borrowers, many of whom live in areas with shortages of private mortgage credit. The FmHA's costs for this program include those associated with any future defaults on the loans and with the subsidies derived from the difference between the interest rates paid to finance the program and the rates borrowers pay to obtain the FmHA mortgages. The latter rates can be as low as 1 percent. During 1993, in the continental United States, more than 22,000 rural households with incomes averaging about $17,000 purchased single-family homes with reduced interest rate loans from the FmHA. The total value of all new Section 502 direct loans in 1993 was nearly $1.3 billion.

Through this program, eligible borrowers can purchase homes by spending a portion of their income — generally 20 percent — on principal, interest, property taxes, and insurance (PITI) throughout the full mortgage term, usually thirty-three years. Eligible borrowers with relatively low incomes, however, have to pay more than 20 percent to amortize the loan at 1 percent. Incomes are recertified annually and payments are adjusted as necessary. In contrast, almost two-fifths of all low-income homeowners in both metropolitan and nonmetropolitan areas spent more than 30 percent of income on housing in 1989.

During 1989, more than 25,000 rural households with adjusted incomes of about $14,000 bought homes through this FmHA program.[16] In most rural areas, qualified low-income borrowers can already acquire affordable private mortgage insurance, though certainly not at rates as favorable as those from the FmHA. Thus mortgage financing is available to low-income Americans in rural areas. Most rural borrowers differ little in income and other economic characteristics from other homebuyers, yet benefit from special government assistance unavailable to nonrural borrowers.

The Task Force proposal eliminates new lending under the Section

502 program. Additional savings are realized over time as the cost of administering a shrinking portfolio decreases. This option reduces the present value of the mortgage interest subsidies and the cost of future defaults, which under credit reform are scored as outlays when the loans are originated.

The current program may not be the best use of scarce federal resources. It makes sizable payments to relatively few households that, although they have low incomes, are better off than many that receive no housing assistance of any kind.

Specific Housing Credit Reform. The Task Force provision replaces all FmHA direct loans with loan guarantees, phased in over five years. The Farmers Home Administration direct program would be eliminated and replaced with an equal amount of subsidized guaranteed loans, for which lower interest rates have created greater opportunities for use. The Clinton Administration proposed reducing direct loans by 25 percent in FY 1994. The Task Force proposal also charges a 1 percent fee on FmHA single-family loan guarantees to defray the costs of administering the program. A similar fee is charged on other FmHA guaranteed loans.

This provision also increases the portion of eligible borrowers' income from 20 percent to 30 percent for payment on the mortgage loans. Increasing the borrowers' payments to 30 percent would reduce the present value of the mortgage interest subsidies and the cost of future defaults. It also would eliminate disparities between the FmHA Section 502 programs and home ownership programs sponsored by HUD.

This proposal turns originating and servicing for FmHA loans over to either private industry or a Government-Sponsored Enterprise (GSE) such as Fannie Mae, while retaining the federal government's role as a credit enhancer. The government has done a poor job originating and servicing loans and serving as a secondary market intermediary. For example, the FmHA mortgage approval process is inefficient and frustrating to the originating institution and homebuyer. In addition, FmHA has a multibillion dollar inventory of properties in foreclosure.

Rural Rental Housing Developers' Interest Rates. The Section 515 housing program, administered by the Farmers Home Administration, provides low-interest, fifty-year mortgage loans to developers of multi-family rental projects in rural areas. Under current rules, assisted tenants contribute the greater of 30 percent of adjusted income or the minimum project rent.

Maintaining rural rental assistance is inappropriate at a time when many other federal programs are being reduced. Increasing the tenant input percentage to at least 35 percent or raising the interest rate they pay to 5 percent would be more equitable. Even at a higher input rate, tenants still would be better off than the typical unassisted but equally poor renter who pays nearly 50 percent. The Task Force provision increases the rural rental housing developers' interest rate to 5 percent.

Modify Fee Structure for Public Housing Agencies. HUD pays fees to local and state PHAs for administering the Section 8 existing-housing certificate and voucher programs. For each assisted household, PHAs receive an ongoing annual fee and a one-time fixed fee when the new assistance commitment from HUD is first issued. Under current policy, the annual fee for commitments funded from pre-1989 appropriations ranges from 6.5 percent (for vouchers) to 7.65 percent (for certificates) of the local two-bedroom fair market rental (FMR). The fee for commitments funded from appropriations since 1989 is 8.2 percent for both programs. The ceiling for the one-time fee is now typically $275 for each new commitment.

A 1988 study based on data from a sample of large urban PHAs estimated that annual administrative costs for both the existing-housing certificate and voucher programs averaged about 5 percent of the two-bedroom FMR. The average start-up costs, however, amounted to about $590 per household.[17] In general, realizing these savings requires changing the authorizing legislation, as well as cutting the appropriations for vouchers to reflect the lower fee payments. Even greater savings might be realized if other private or public entities were allowed to compete with the PHAs for the administration of the programs.

Such a fee structure more accurately reflects the best available information about the costs of providing those types of housing assistance. The Task Force proposal modifies the fee structure for public housing agencies by equalizing fees for programs that appear to have similar administrative costs and eliminating the disparity among fees, which now vary according to the year the first commitment was first funded. Such changes would make it easier to administer the fees. Allowing other organizations to compete to administer the programs might lead to increased efficiency.

Entitlement Reforms

As stated earlier, entitlements are both the largest and fastest-growing programs in the federal budget. As such, serious and comprehensive attempts to grapple with the deficit and to restrain federal spending must reform entitlements. In 1993, the federal government paid more than $762 billion for entitlements.[18]

Historically, entitlement reform has been a hot political potato and will continue to be so. As evidenced by the merely philosophical conclusions of the 1993-1994 Bipartisan Commission on Entitlement and Tax Reform, dealing with these issues will not be easy. Our budget proposal seeks to lay out some options for reform in this area. While we in no way believe these reforms will come even close to solving our long-term spending crisis, we do believe they will start the country along the road to realistic and actuarially sound program reform.

Means-Test Current Nonmeans Tested Entitlements. The Task Force provision means-tests all current nonmeans entitlements, excluding Social Security, Medicare, veterans' benefits, and civilian/military pension programs, for middle- and high-income families. The federal civilian and military pension programs are exempted because they are part of a labor contract between the government and its employees. Changes in this contract resulting in changes in those benefits would erode the trust between government and employees associated with those programs.

This proposal also reduces benefits to those with incomes over $40,000 in proportion to their earned annual income for Medicaid, aid to families with dependent children, Supplemental Security Income, child nutrition, family support programs, and Food Stamps.

This approach, termed "global means-testing" by the Congressional Budget Office, results in decreased benefits for beneficiaries with the highest incomes. As beneficiaries' incomes rise, benefits are reduced, and the sliding scale imposes the costs of this approach on those most able to bear them. Global means-testing also curtails total payments to people who are receiving benefits from more than one program. This approach helps solve the problem of burgeoning entitlements more directly than cuts in individual programs.

As both a Concord Coalition[19] and Congressional Budget Office recommendation, this proposal reduces up to 85 percent of benefits on a graduated scale for families with annual incomes above $40,000. Those families would lose benefits under a graduated scale beginning at 10 percent for those incomes between $40,000 and $50,000 and increasing by 10 percentage points for each $10,000 of income up to 85 percent of benefits above $120,000 of total income. Nontransfer income would be considered first in determining the rate of benefit reduction, and benefits would be reduced only to the extent that they caused total income to exceed $40,000. It would index the income brackets for inflation, but the brackets would be the same for families of all sizes. This option affects unemployment compensation and other social services.

Eligibility levels, payment rules, and cost-of-living adjustments do not change. The projected 58 percent of Americans with incomes of less than $40,000 in 1996, when the means-test takes effect, would continue to receive full benefits and cost-of-living increases. Entitlement payments to the other 42 percent of Americans with incomes of $40,000 or higher would be scaled back in proportion to their incomes.

According to the Concord Coalition, "administering the entitlement means test would not require setting up a huge new bureaucracy or trying to coordinate one agency's payments with those of other agencies to account for multiple benefits received by the same individual. Instead, each entitlement payment would be accompanied by a special receipt telling the beneficiary and the government the amount received by that person. Individuals who expect the means test to reduce their benefits could file a withholding form with the Department of Health and Human Services or other appropriate agency to have benefits reduced. If a recipient's economic circumstances changed, withholding could be adjusted. At the end of the year, all entitlement receipts would be tallied on a form accompanying the federal income tax return and any needed adjustments based on entitlements and other income actually received during the year would be made."[20]

The Concord Coalition recommended that this global means-test be phased in over five years. During that time, there would be a 2 percent benefit reduction for each $10,000 of benefits in 1996, a 4 percent benefit reduction in 1997, a 6 percent benefit reduction in 1998, an 8 percent benefit reduction in 1999, and the full 10 percent in 2000, when the entire means-test would be in place. Maximum benefit reductions would be 8.5 percent in 1996, 17 percent in 1997, plus an additional 17 percent annually thereafter until the 85 percent maximum reduction was achieved in 2000.

Health and Livelihood of Citizens	Savings Over 5 Years (in dollars)
Implement managed care systems for Medicaid beneficiaries	28,200,000,000
Cut the federal share of Medicaid disproportionate share payments to hospitals	27,500,000,000
Consolidate welfare programs into block grants	21,275,000,000
Alter federal matching requirements of Food Stamp benefits	18,760,000,000
Means-test current nonmeans entitlements through increased targeting of certain programs through additional means-testing	17,700,000,000
Terminate the eligibility of children for SSDI disability	16,500,000,000

Health and Livelihood of Citizens	Savings Over 5 Years (in dollars)
Restrict Medicaid coverage for noncitizens	10,800,000,000
Reform child support programs by terminating the child- and adult-care food programs	10,400,000,000
Restrict SSI to noncitizens	9,400,000,000
Update Food Stamp program annually	8,653,000,000
Halt new commitments under Section 515 housing program assistance	8,190,000,000
Reduce AFDC, SSI, Food Stamps	7,700,000,000
Reduce annual contribution for certain assisted housing programs	5,295,000,000
Increase tenant/state contribution from 30 to 35 percent	5,230,000,000
Freeze housing slots at 4.6 million units for 5 years	5,190,000,000
Lower floor for federal share of foster care and adoption to 45 percent	4,550,000,000
Impose fees for non-AFDC child support enforcement	3,690,000,000
Limit emergency assistance benefits	3,320,000,000
Increase targeting of child nutrition subsidies	3,070,000,000
Modify economies-of-scale adjustment factors	2,950,000,000
Reduce the federal Medicaid-matching administrative expenses rate to 50 percent	2,650,000,000

Health and Livelihood of Citizens	Savings Over 5 Years (in dollars)
Reform operation of low-income housing through administrative reform	2,511,000,000
Restrict Food Stamps for noncitizens	2,280,000,000
Reform rural housing insurance fund	2,122,000,000
Eliminate direct loans to rural homeowners (FmHA's Section 502)	1,829,000,000
Impose FDA fees	1,817,000,000
Make AFDC contingent on paternity establishment	1,500,000,000
Institute housing credit reform	1,440,000,000
Stop expansion of rural rental housing	1,430,000,000
Reduce children and family services program	1,430,000,000
Increase rural rental housing developers' interest rate to 5 percent	1,380,000,000
Modify fee structure for public housing agencies	1,230,000,000
Reduce from $20 to $15 the income exclusion for SSI	1,000,000,000
Reduce HOME investment partnerships	759,000,000
Reduce rural housing community development service	753,000,000
Impose CDC baseline change	637,000,000
Use Medicaid-state limits on long-term care beds	625,000,000

Health and Livelihood of Citizens	Savings Over 5 Years (in dollars)
Freeze nutrition assistance for Puerto Rico	616,000,000
Reform severely distressed housing	568,000,000
President's food safety/inspection user fees	515,000,000
Allow the disposition of multifamily housing units	425,000,000
Reduce HUD general and specific risk account	407,000,000
Reduce low-income energy assistance	400,000,000
Cancel Food Stamp monthly payments below $10	300,000,000
Eliminate operating subsidies for vacant public housing	259,000,000
Charge for state administrative errors in the AFDC and Food Stamp programs	245,000,000
President's food safety/inspector service	244,000,000
Recover SSI overpayments through offsetting reductions in Social Security payments	220,000,000
Reduce substance-abuse treatment demonstrations	190,000,000
Reduce foster care administration by 10 percent	150,000,000
President's Agency for Health Care Policy and Research	136,000,000
President's Mine Safety and Health Administration	88,000,000
Refinance Section 235 mortgages	54,000,000

Health and Livelihood of Citizens	Savings Over 5 Years (in dollars)
Report admissions of SSI recipients to nursing homes	50,000,000
Reduce Office of Adolescent and Family/Health	38,000,000
President's Consumer Product Safety Commission	36,000,000
Restrict AFDC to noncitizens	(400,000,000)
Restructuring Programs that Affect the Health and Livelihood of Citizens **TOTAL**	**248,307,000,000**
Running Total of Savings	**248,307,000,000**

1 Committee on Ways and Means, U.S. House of Representatives. "Overview of Entitlement Programs," *1994 Green Book, 103rd Congress, Second Session.* Washington, DC: U.S. Government Printing Office, 1994, pages 296-297.

2 House Budget Committee.

3 Senate Budget Committee.

4 *1994 Green Book,* pages 125-127.

5 Patrick F. Fagan. *The Real Root Causes of Violent Crime: The Breakdown of Marriage, Family, and Community.* The Heritage Foundation, No. 1026. March 17, 1995.

6 The Heritage Foundation, National Center for Health Statistics.

7 Title IV-E of the Social Security Act.

8 *1994 Green Book,* pages 606-609.

9 Ibid.

10 According to the Bureau of the Census, in 1992 the poverty line for a family of four was $14,228.

11 See Glossary.

12 *1994 Green Book,* page 207.

13 *Office of Inspector General Cost-Saver Handbook: The Red Book*. Washington, DC: U.S. Department of Health and Human Services, 1993, Page A-4.

14 Stewart B. McKinney Homeless Assistance Act of 1988.

15 See Glossary.

16 Congressional Budget Office. "Reducing the Deficit: Spending and Revenue Options," *Report to the Senate and House Committess on the Budget*. Washington, DC: U.S. Government Printing Office, 1990, pages 253-255.

17 House Budget Committee.

18 *1994 Green Book,* page 1,266.

19 See Glossary.

20 "The Zero-Deficit Plan." A report from the Concord Coalition, 1994, page 29.

CHAPTER FOUR

The Health and Livelihood of Senior Citizens

A s we approach the twenty-first century, we take with us a large portion of the population who has lived through most of the twentieth century. Medical developments, health care improvements, and lifestyle changes over the past 100 years extended the average life span and increased the size of our current senior citizen population. In considering the program cuts that would give us a balanced budget, the Balanced Budget Task Force debated carefully about programs that affect this respected and contributing part of our population. We talked about Medicare and how we could make it more efficient. We discussed health insurance, pensions, and senior employment. The changes we propose will help balance the budget and, we think, will improve the day-to-day encounters that senior citizens have with systems such as health care and pensions.

Reform Medicare

Since the beginning of this century, our nation has grappled with the question of federal health insurance. Our current system traces its origins back to 1912 when President Theodore Roosevelt unsuccessfully attempted to introduce universal health insurance. During the 1930s,

President Franklin D. Roosevelt sought to include health insurance in his social insurance legislation, but advisors convinced him that it would jeopardize the chances of passing the Social Security Act of 1935. FDR's efforts were followed by President Harry Truman's similar push during the election of 1948. At the time, a bipartisan group of Republicans and Democrats defeated his bill because they thought it was too extensive.

In light of the political opposition to those proposals, proponents of government health insurance took a different route. As a first step, they sought to provide insurance coverage for those considered to be the poorest risks by the private insurance industry. This group consisted of elderly citizens who already were qualified to receive Social Security benefits and who were widely considered a deserving social group. Furthermore, the elderly's medical problems regularly came to the attention of their children and families and often created a heavy financial burden on successor generations. The government responded by passing President Lyndon B. Johnson's legislation during the 89th Congress in 1965.

Medicare, the popular name for the federal health insurance program for persons age 65 and over, operates under the direction of the Department of Health and Human Services (HHS). When the program went into effect in 1966, it was administered by the Social Security Administration (SSA). In 1977, the program was transferred to the newly created Health Care Financing Administration (HCFA). Medicare benefits are divided into two parts:

1. Part A, Medicare Hospital Insurance, is a basic hospital insurance plan that covers hospital care, extended care, home health services, and hospice care for terminally ill patients. The federal Hospital Insurance (HI) Trust Fund balances are dependent on the revenue received from payroll taxes. The funds raised from those taxes are required to be paid out in Medicare obligations. The amount of funds raised above the amount required for the obligations is deposited into the HI Trust Fund.

   Part A spending was projected to increase 11.3 percent in 1994, and more than 9 percent a year for the next five years. According to the 1993 Medicare Trustees Report, the HI Trust Fund is severely out of financial balance in the long range. Using the current rate to forecast, the outlook is grim. At best, this trust fund will reach exhaustion in 2001; at its worst, it will be insolvent by 1998. Programs that administer the HI Trust Fund are in desperate need of reform.

2. Part B, Medicare Supplemental Medical Insurance (SMI), is a voluntary medical-insurance program that covers physicians' fees, outpatient services, and other medical services. It is financed in part

by uniform monthly contributions from aged and disabled persons enrolled in the program and in part by federal general revenues. Seventy-five percent of Part B currently is subsidized by general tax revenues. In 1982 and 1984 Congress passed legislation to freeze at 75 percent the share of SMI costs covered by federal revenues. In 1994 a participant in the program contributed a monthly premium of $41.10.

The government meets Medicare costs through three sources of revenue: Social Security contributions, monthly premiums from participants, and general revenues.

In the early 1970s Congress passed legislation to extend Medicare to individuals under the age of 65 with certain disabling conditions. In 1994, about 32 million people were enrolled in Medicare in the aged category and 4 million in the disabled category.

In 1995, the Congressional Budget Office (CBO) projected that total Medicare spending will increase by 10 percent each year for the next five years. As the fastest-growing program in the federal budget, Medicare spending drives the rapid growth in overall federal spending. Consequently, the imminent crisis in Medicare funding is real, unavoidable, and must be corrected within the next few years. Under current trends, the Medicare trust fund deficit of almost $2 billion in 1996 will balloon to $71 billion by the year 2005. Rapid spending growth, due to the fast expansion of the eligible population served, will cause Medicare to go bankrupt in 2001. The Cato Institute[1] has estimated that if we wait until 2002, everyone, young and old, will pay for our failure to solve the problem. If we don't change our course, the Medicare portion of Federal Insurance Contribution Act (FICA) taxes for everyone will be raised 125 percent from their current level, and senior citizens will pay 300 percent more in yearly premiums.

Most everyone agrees we must change our course. The ship is out of control, and we cannot continue to float adrift as if lost at sea. We must take hold of the helm. The question becomes "How?"

Our Task Force firmly believes that Medicare provides vital services for older Americans and that we must take constructive steps to protect their program. We must transform Medicare from a centralized, government monopoly that is inefficient, wasteful, and too slow to adapt to new ideas into a system that provides every older person more choices in health care and more control over his or her life. The Task Force arrived at several recommendations for reform, many of which are not new and had been recommended in previous years. Our recommendations include reforming the systems for copayment, Part A and Part B premiums, and payments to hospitals.

Reform Medicare Copayment

Spending for home health benefits is the fastest-growing part of Medicare. Costs increased an average of more than 40 percent for the past four years, for a total spending of $10.184 billion. Over the next five years, the program is projected to spend $95.5 billion. The home health benefit is one of two Medicare programs without a coinsurance requirement. Clinical lab services is the second.

It has been charged that the coinsurance is a new "sick" tax. Clearly, Medicare beneficiaries or their medical insurance will have to pay a fraction of the cost of a service they now receive at no cost. The 20 percent coinsurance is reasonable, however, and brings home health services and clinical lab services in line with the rest of Medicare coinsurance requirements.

Health care economists agree that the days of providing benefits with no coinsurance are over. The propensity to overspend when using other people's money is proven by the data. Spending on benefits provided with no cost consciousness is unsustainable.

Home Health. Every year, 2.2 million Medicare recipients (7 percent) use home health services.[2] They receive care through home visits by health-care professionals such as skilled nurses, physical therapists, speech therapists, occupational therapists, medical social workers, and home health aides. The Task Force proposal institutes a 20 percent coinsurance for home health care (Part A). The Clinton Administration's health plan included a 10 percent coinsurance on home health services; this proposal takes that plan one step further to curb overspending and includes the following two important provisions to ease the burden of the coinsurance:

1. The coinsurance will not apply to Medicare beneficiaries at or below 150 percent of the poverty rate, which is $10,455 for individuals and $14,145 for couples.[3] No funds are required from this population and no unfunded state mandate is involved.
2. A prospective payment system (PPS), established by the Social Security Amendments of 1983 as a means by which Medicare would reimburse hospitals for inpatient services provided to beneficiaries, is set at 93 percent of the average rate that is charged beneficiaries. According to the House Budget Committee, most home health agencies support the new system.

The PPS also includes regulatory relief from current cost-reporting requirements. For some home health agencies, such reporting accounts for 40 percent of operating costs. The regulatory relief lowers costs, thereby lowering the charge to Medicare for services. The provision establishes standard rates, removing the variance between charges for the same service while protecting Medicare beneficiaries from being overcharged for a coinsurance payment.

Clinical Lab Services. Coinsurance for clinical lab services requires Medicare beneficiaries to pay 20 percent of the cost of services that include typical tests, such as blood test, urinalysis, electrocardiogram, and Pap smear, given at a doctor's office and analyzed in an office lab or in a clinical lab. President Clinton included a 20 percent clinical lab coinsurance in the Health Security Act. The clinical lab services program is a voluntary benefit and covers physicians' services in addition to lab services. A 20 percent coinsurance was charged for Medicare clinical lab services in the past but was removed when the payment system was changed. The Task Force proposes to reinstate the 20 percent coinsurance for clinical lab services (Part B), requiring nominal payments by the beneficiary. The coinsurance promotes cost-consciousness without causing an onerous burden on beneficiaries, and it reduces the incentive to overuse clinical lab tests.

Reform Medicare Part A Premiums

Medicare Part A is funded by a payroll tax of 1.45 percent paid by both employees and employers. The tax applies to all earnings. Because Medicare beneficiaries pay the tax over a lifetime, some argue that they should not be required to pay more for Part A services. Current beneficiaries, however, have paid an average of $7,000 in Medicare taxes and received an average of $40,000 in benefits.[4]

The Medicare Hospital Insurance (Part A) deductible has not been increased in line with inflation or private sector health plan deductibles. Beneficiaries currently pay the first $720 of a hospitalization regardless of income. Medicare pays all subsequent hospital costs for the first 60 days of a hospital stay. The Task Force proposes to reform Medicare Part A premiums by relating the Medicare Part A deductible to the enrollees' income. This proposal requires enrollees with retirement adjusted gross incomes of $70,000 ($90,000 for couples) and above to pay the first $2,000 of a hospitalization.

Reform Medicare Part B

Medicare Part B, the supplementary medical insurance program, generally pays 80 percent of the costs associated with covered services in excess of an annual deductible of $100. Those services include doctors' services (surgery, consultation, home office and institutional visits, dentists, podiatrists, and chiropractors), specialty medical services (laboratory and diagnostic tests, X-ray and radiation therapy, outpatient services, rural health clinic services, home dialysis supplies and equipment, artificial devices, and ambulance services) and medically necessary home health services.

Medicare Part B spending has been increasing at three to four times the rate of inflation, and the Congressional Budget Office projects a 12.6 percent annual increase over the next five years. Total Part B spending is projected to exceed $110 billion annually in five years.

Medicare Part B Premiums. Seventy-five percent of the cost of providing Medicare Part B services is paid from the federal government's general tax revenues (only Medicare Part A is financed by the Medicare payroll tax). When Medicare Part B was established, beneficiaries paid premiums. Today the premiums account for only 25 percent of program costs, which amounts to a substantial taxpayer subsidy.

The Task Force proposes that the government relate Medicare Part B premiums to enrollees' incomes by gradually reducing the Medicare Part B premium subsidy for those people who have an adjusted gross income of $70,000 for individuals and $90,000 for couples. The full national average premium ($164 per month) is paid by individuals above $95,000 and couples above $115,000 in income. The Clinton Administration's health plan contained a similar proposal.

Premiums for Program Costs. Under current law, a Part B premium is paid by or on behalf of all Medicare beneficiaries and is set to cover 25 percent of program costs. The Task Force proposes that the government continue the Medicare Part B premium at 25 percent of program costs. Without this extension, this provision will revert to an old formula that allows a much larger growth increase in the monthly premium amount. Extending the premium would not result in any reductions in services. It would continue current law and, at the same time, save $4.7 billion.

Premiums for Physicians' Services. The Omnibus Budget Reconciliation Act (OBRA) of 1993 established a basic premium of 25 percent of the costs for all enrollees under the Supplemental Medical Insurance program. This premium contains a hold-harmless provision to ensure that no enrollee's Social Security check decreases because an increase in the SMI premium exceeded the cost-of-living adjustment. This provision is set to expire in 1998. The Task Force proposal calls for extending the 25 percent premium for physicians' services (OBRA 1993) through the year 2000.

Reform Medicare Payments to Hospitals

A portion of payments that Medicare makes to hospitals is spent unwisely because of inefficiency in the hospitals' debt-collecting systems. In addition, Medicare overcompensates teaching hospitals for overhead costs.

Bad Debts. Hospitals are responsible for collecting certain deductibles and copayments from Medicare beneficiaries for inpatient services. Medicare fully reimburses unpaid balances for hospitals that have collection efforts. Currently, there is little incentive for thorough collection activities, and bad debt claims have more than doubled since program inception. Hospitals that serve the financially needy are compensated explicitly through other programs. According to the HHS Office of the Inspector General, eliminating Medicare payments to hospitals for enrollees' bad debts gives hospitals a financial incentive to expand their collection efforts, which would probably increase their recovery of enrollees' deductible and coinsurance amounts.

Indirect Teaching Adjustment. Medicare pays higher rates to hospitals with teaching programs to cover their additional costs of caring for Medicare patients. For example, under current law, payments to these hospitals are raised by approximately 7.7 percent for each 0.1 percent increase in a hospital's ratio of full-time interns and residents to its number of beds. The adjustment originally was established to compensate hospitals for indirect teaching costs.

The Task Force proposal better aligns payments with the actual costs incurred by teaching institutions. Also, since the training that medical residents receive will result in a significant increase in their future income, it is reasonable for some or all of a hospital's indirect training costs to be passed on to residents. This proposal lowers indirect Medicare education from 7.7 percent to 3 percent for each 0.1 percent increase in the intern and resident-to-be ratio. Although teaching hospitals have higher instances of indigent care and use the teaching reimbursements to cover losses from uncompensated care, other reforms in this proposal will alleviate the need for this use of the adjustment.

Support Selected Reforms of the President

The Task Force concurs with selected Medicare reform measures proposed by the Clinton Administration's fiscal year (FY) 1995 budget.

OBRA 93 — Continued Hospital-Market-Based Index. This recommendation lowers the update in payment rates for inpatient hospital services by 2 percent in 1997, 1998, and 1999, continuing the reduction required in 1996 under OBRA 1993. The government would save more than $7 billion dollars over FY 1996-1999.

OBRA 1993 Extension (Secondary Payer). This proposal continues current policies that make Medicare secondary to employment-based insurance held by enrollees (or their spouses) who still work. It keeps secondary-payer provisions uniform for aged and disabled enrollees, while continuing to limit the exposure of employment-based health plans to health costs for end-stage renal disease (ESRD) enrollees.

President's Cumulative Physician Fees. This provision eliminates adjustments in out-year fee targets for prior-year excessive growth.

Additional Administration Proposals. The Task Force also supports the president's cost-cutting proposals regarding research and demonstrations, survey and certification, competitively bid lab services and other services, high-cost medical staff, OBRA 93-skilled nursing facility care cost of living adjustment (COLA) and home health COLA, and outpatient overpayment.

Reform the Pension Benefit Guaranty Corporation

The Pension Benefit Guaranty Corporation (PBGC) was established by the Employee Retirement Income Security Act of 1974 to protect private pension beneficiaries from losing their entire pension contributions if their established pension plan goes belly up. The PBGC is a government-run corporation with a three-member board of directors that includes the secretaries of Labor (the chair), Commerce, and the Treasury. The PBGC is financed by participants' premiums collected from insured plans and assets in terminated underfunded plans for which the PBGC has become trustee.

The Clinton Administration's FY 1995 budget proposed comprehensive reforms in the Retirement Protection Act of 1993 to improve pension funding and protect workers and retirees. The legislation includes both administrative and financial improvements.

Eliminate the Senior Community Service Employment Program

The Senior Community Service Employment Program (SCSEP) gives grants to nonprofit and government agencies to pay for part-time employment of people age 55 and older who are unemployed and who meet income eligibility requirements. The Task Force proposal eliminates the SCSEP because we believe the organizations benefiting from this program should bear its cost.

Require Federal Agencies to Prefund the Government's Share of Federal Retirees' Health Insurance

Current accounting recognizes the cost of retired federal employees' health insurance coverage only when employees retire. According to the Congressional Budget Office, such accounting methods distort the true costs of labor to the government.

The Task Force proposal shifts recognition of employer costs of providing health care to annuitants and dependents to the years of active employment. Federal retirees' health insurance costs would receive the same accounting treatment as federal employees' retirement benefits. More than 80 percent of federal workers continue their employer-provided health insurance coverage under the Federal Employees Health Benefits program. The federal government does not recognize the cost until the employee retires and then funds the costs on a pay-as-you-go basis. Setting aside funds to cover the future cost of health benefits would be consistent with private sector financial management practices.

The Health and Livelihood of Senior Citizens	Savings Over 5 Years (in dollars)
Institute a 20 percent coinsurance for home health care	20,450,000,000
Lower indirect teaching adjustment to 3 percent	13,550,000,000
Require federal agencies to prefund the government's share of federal retiree's health insurance	11,550,000,000
President's cumulative physician fees	9,372,000,000
President's OBRA 93 — continued hospital-market-based index	7,396,000,000
Relate Medicare Part B premium to enrollees' income	7,350,000,000
President's outpatient overpayment	7,216,000,000
Reinstate a 20 percent coinsurance for clinical lab services	6,178,000,000
Continue Medicare Part B premium at 25 percent of program costs	2,003,000,000
Eliminate Senior Community Service Employment Program	1,810,000,000
Eliminate Medicare payments to hospitals for enrollees' bad debts	1,753,000,000

The Health and Livelihood of Senior Citizens	Savings Over 5 Years (in dollars)
Reform the Pension Benefit Guaranty Corporation	1,739,000,000
Relate Medicare Part A deductible to enrollees' income	1,650,000,000
President's OBRA 1993 extension (secondary payer)	1,631,000,000
President's OBRA 93 — home health COLA	1,512,000,000
President's high-cost medical staff	1,328,000,000
Extend OBRA 93 — 25 percent premium for physicians' services	1,295,000,000
President's competitively bid lab services	1,180,000,000
President's competitively bid other services	753,000,000
President's OBRA 93 — skilled nursing facility care COLA	605,000,000
Freeze funding for aging services	309,000,000
Reserve workers' compensation offset for disability insurance benefits	265,000,000
President's research and demonstrations	124,000,000
President's survey and certification	72,000,000
Restructuring Programs that Affect the Health and Livelihood of Senior Citizens TOTAL	101,091,000,000
Running Total of Savings	349,398,000,000

1 See Glossary.

2 House Budget Committee.

3 Ibid.

4 1994 House Budget Committee, based on data from the Congressional Research Service of the Library of Congress.

CHAPTER FIVE

The Health and Livelihood
of Veterans

At the outset of the Korean conflict, I left college to enlist in the United States Marine Corps. I served on active duty until July 1952 and remained in the Marine Reserves until discharged in 1959. It was one of the most important periods of my life, and in the military I learned the importance of duty, discipline, courage, and devotion. Moreover, my experience as a soldier helped mold my character, work ethic, and perspective on life. These lessons have been invaluable throughout my life, both as a small-business man and public servant.

My respect for the impact the Marine Corps had on my own life is evident in my position on the national defense of this country. I find myself constantly reminded of the fact that the federal government was primarily established for two purposes: The first was to represent the thirteen original states in international diplomacy, and the second was to provide for the security of the states. Our men and women in uniform perform one of the most important duties of our federal government — the protection of our citizens. We must never forget the selfless service these men and women provide.

I believe we owe them the assurance that as veterans they will be properly cared for, both as soldiers and as private citizens. I have the honor of representing a large number of American veterans in the state of New York. Consequently, the protection of our nation's veterans has been one of my most important tasks since I arrived in Congress, especially when I served as the ranking Republican on the House Veterans Affairs Committee during the 1980s. Protecting our veterans will remain a task of utmost importance.

One of the proudest moments of my life occurred in 1988 when I stood behind President Ronald Reagan as he signed into law a bill that created the Department of Veterans Affairs. With my good friend and colleague, G.V. Sonny Montgomery (D-Mississippi), Chairman of the Veterans Affairs Committee, I helped shepherd this bill through Congress to the president's desk. Service and care for our veterans improved by leaps and bounds after passage of this legislation.

Personal experience. Enormous respect. Tireless effort. A commitment to and respect for the military, as well as the Constitution and the American flag. I feel strongly about preserving all of these, which is why I have long fought to prohibit the burning of the American flag. For me, that is an affront to our nation's military men and women. With that commitment and with the perspective of providing and caring for those who gave so much, I, along with members of the Balanced Budget Task Force, met to determine how government expenses for veterans' programs could be minimized while continuing to deliver efficient services.

The Department of Veterans Affairs

The Department of Veterans Affairs (VA) is a cabinet-level branch of the federal government, independent of the Department of Defense. The VA assumed the functions of the former Veterans Administration, which had been established in 1930 as an independent government agency that administered national benefits for veterans. Following each military conflict that took place after 1930, Congress adjusted the federal laws under which the agency operated.

The VA provides a wide variety of services to eligible veterans and their eligible dependents and to the dependent survivors of deceased veterans. These services fall into seven main categories: education, insurance, counseling, health care and rehabilitation, pensions, home loans, and burial benefits. The VA, which is organized into three areas — medicine, veterans' benefits, and memorial affairs — has regional offices throughout the United States, as well as suboffices, hospitals, and domiciliaries.

Currently, benefits are paid under laws passed to help Spanish-American War, Mexican border campaign, World War I, World War II, Korean conflict, and Vietnam era veterans, as well as their dependents and survivors. Benefits such as home loans, nonservice disability pensions, hospitalization, education, and insurance are available even if a veteran was not injured while in the service, while others accrue only as a result of service-connected death or disability. Because some benefits go to widowed survivors, parents, and even adult offspring who became unable to care for themselves before the age of legal adult status, benefits may be paid for decades beyond the time when all the veterans of a particular war have died. Although benefits such as those for education, unemployment, counseling, and dental care may expire for a particular group, medical care, home loans, burial, and other benefits have no time limit but are subject to certain other restrictions.

Extend Veteran Program Provisions

A number of veteran provisions in law are scheduled to expire in fiscal year (FY) 1999. Many of those laws originally were established on a temporary basis but have been extended by such budget packages as the 1990 Budget Act and the Omnibus Budget Reconciliation Act (OBRA) of 1993. By extending those provisions temporarily, Congress can use the extensions as budget gimmicks, claiming spending reductions (reductions that are, in fact, phony) simply by again extending those provisions when they are scheduled to expire. If they are good policy, the provisions should be permanent. Four have been recommended for permanent extension by the Congressional Budget Office (CBO) and the Clinton Administration's *Vision of Change for America:* prescription charge/copayment, third-party payment provision, pension/medical care income verification, and resale loan loss. Extending all four of the proposals would save more than $900 million over five years.

Prescription Charge/Copayment. The VA operates a nationwide health-care delivery system for our country's veterans. The 1990 Budget Act imposed a temporary $2 copayment for each thirty-day supply of outpatient prescription drugs not related to the treatment of a service-connected (military-related) disability. OBRA 1993 extended the fee through the end of FY 1998. This fee has been extended three times by Congress and it is time to extend it permanently. According to the Clinton Administration's *Vision of Change for America*, which also proposed the permanent extension of this fee, "Cost sharing encourages more appropriate utilization of prescription drugs." A veteran pays a minimal $2 charge for prescription drugs. Most nonveterans' health insurance also includes at least a copayment for drugs. The Task Force proposal retains the fee indefinitely by permanently extending the prescription charge/copayment.

Third-Party Payment Provision. I have long believed that when veterans are working in the private sector and hold private insurance plans, these companies should reimburse the federal government for overlapping coverage of health-care costs. Many veterans are able to qualify automatically for a company's insurance plan after they become employed.

However, many of their health-care costs already are covered by the Department of Veterans Affairs. Consequently, the veteran is required to pay insurance premiums to the private sector while the federal government picks up the bill. Insurance companies should be prohibited from receiving this windfall. As the ranking member of the Veterans Affairs Committee, I wrote a bill, which eventually became law, to begin this policy of reimbursement of payments by third parties.

Companies that insure health care for veterans are willing to meet their obligation regardless of whether the veteran receives medical care in a VA or a non-VA hospital. An OBRA 1993 provision authorizes Veterans Affairs to collect the reasonable cost of medical care that the VA provides from any health insurer that contracts to insure a veteran who has service-connected disabilities. The current authority will expire October 1,1998. The Task Force provision permanently extends the provision for third-party payment.

Pension/Medical Care Income Verification. This OBRA 1993 provision, scheduled to expire October 1, 1998, authorizes the Internal Revenue Service (IRS) to assist the VA in verifying the incomes reported by beneficiaries for establishing eligibility to pensions and benefits. It is perfectly reasonable for the VA to assure the eligibility status of veterans receiving benefits, and the best source of income data is the IRS. The Task Force provision permanently extends pension/medical care income verification.

Resale Loan Loss Provisions. When a lender forecloses on a property purchased with a VA-guaranteed loan, the VA employs a formula to determine whether to pay the guarantee to the lender or to buy the property and resell it. The formula includes a "no-bid" computation that allows the Secretary of Veterans Affairs to determine whether it is less expensive to the government to purchase and resell a property in default or simply to pay off the VA guarantee. OBRA 1993 extended authority to continue the no-bid computation through September 30, 1998. The no-bid computation allows the VA another means of getting the best possible return on properties purchased with a VA loan guarantee. The Task Force provision permanently extends the authority to continue the no-bid computation (resale loan loss).

Reform Medical Care

The Department of Veterans Affairs has undergone tremendous financial and bureaucratic strains in its efforts to deliver quality health care for our nation's veterans. The Task Force's program reforms centered on two precepts. First, funds needed to be directed to those programs in which dollars were most required. Second, any reforms designed to improve delivery while also saving the taxpayers money deserved our support. Many of the suggestions here were proposed by the General

Accounting Office (GAO), the Congressional Budget Office, and a wide variety of outside taxpayers' groups.

Hospital and Medical Care. In its budget for FY 1995, the Clinton Administration proposed to reduce spending on hospital and medical care from the levels projected by the Congressional Budget Office. For all government programs, CBO projects annually how much the program will spend if the current policy remains in effect. The president proposed to reduce the projected increase for this program account by $220 million over five years. Believing that the VA needs more funds to meet its projected health-care costs, the Task Force concurs with the recommendations of the Republican Budget Committee FY 1995 Budget, which accepted only half of what the president was proposing.

Efficient Hospital Management. Studies from the General Accounting Office show that one-quarter of the inpatient days spent in VA hospitals are inappropriate or unnecessary because of inefficient management, the lack of less-costly options such as nursing-home care, and the availability of empty beds. A prospective payment system (PPS) at VA hospitals, similar to that now employed in Medicare, would classify each patient in a diagnosis-related group (DRG) that would entitle the hospital to a fixed payment designed to reflect the average cost of efficient care for such a patient. The use of prospective payments would promote greater efficiency in VA hospitals by squeezing funding for those that are using resources inefficiently. The Task Force provision promotes efficient hospital management by employing such a system at VA hospitals. The Clinton Administration's *Vision of Change for America* also recommended this proposal.

Inefficient Hospitals. The VA maintains a national medical network of hospitals, nursing homes, and outpatient clinics. While most are needed, the shifting of veterans' populations has caused the underutilization of some facilities. The Task Force proposes that underused units in hospitals be closed or converted into facilities offering services that are in demand. Such a move would improve resource allocation and efficiency in providing health-care services to veterans.

Third-Party Reimbursements for Service-Connected Veterans. To minimize the paperwork associated with claims while maximizing care for veterans, the VA needs authority to collect from insurance companies for care provided to veterans, including veterans with service-connected disabilities. The Task Force proposal reforms the third-party reimbursements for service-connected veterans by providing such authority through September 30, 1999.

Reform VA Housing

The Servicemen's Readjustment Act of 1944, popularly known as the

GI Bill of Rights, provided unemployment and education allowances as well as home, farm, and business loans, for millions of World War II veterans. Today, the GI Bill program also covers men and women who served in the armed forces between 1955 and 1976, but a limit has been placed on the period in which the program's benefits can be used after discharge. Loans for houses, condominiums, and mobile homes, however, are available indefinitely to men and women who served in the armed forces starting in 1940 and to their unmarried surviving spouses. Because entitlement to such loans can be reestablished as well, veterans may take advantage of this benefit more than once.

Multiple VA Housing Loan Guarantee Benefit. The Task Force proposal restricts use of the multiple VA housing loan guarantee benefit by allowing veterans to obtain a mortgage guarantee under the program only once. This provision affects only future applicants who have not used their entitlement in the past.

President's Loan Guarantee Program Account. The VA home loan guarantee program is designed to facilitate the extension of mortgage credit on favorable terms by private lenders to eligible veterans. As of January 1, 1990, the guarantee on all new loan origination is provided by the VA's Guaranty and Indemnity Fund (GIF), except for loans on manufactured homes. In cases of foreclosure, guarantee amounts made prior to the establishment of the new fund will be paid from the Loan Guaranty Revolving Fund (LGRF). The Task Force supports this proposal, which was recommended in the Clinton Administration's FY 1995 Budget. According to that budget, the guarantee protects lenders against losses in several ways. The following loan guarantee schedule is designed to minimize actual loss to the account and ultimately to the taxpayers.

1. For loans of $45,000 or less, 50 percent of the loan is guaranteed.
2. For loans greater than $45,000, but not more than $56,250, $22,500 is guaranteed.
3. For loans greater than $56,250, but less than $144,000, the lesser of $36,000 or 40 percent of the loan is guaranteed.
4. For loans greater than $144,000, the lesser of $46,000 or 25 percent of the loan is guaranteed.

In 1994, the VA spent $70,716,000 to administer the loan programs.[1] Merging the administrative and operating functions will eliminate bureaucracy and save the taxpayers $191 million over five years. As a result of this program reform, the VA will spend $59,371,000 or $11,345,000 less to perform the same duties. This proposal downsizes government, saves taxpayer dollars, and preserves essential programs for our nation's veterans.

Peace-Time Commitment

Because we rely on an all-volunteer military, we need to provide fair and adequate benefits to our service people, especially in peace time. Efficient and effective service to our nation's veterans is an essential part of that commitment. In addition, incentives must remain to ensure that individuals are induced to join and encouraged to serve in the armed forces. Measures such as the recent reforms to the GI Bill, which I helped to write, are crucial to preserving the attractiveness of the military and are ultimately the reward for serving our nation in this capacity.

Board of Veterans Appeals. Appeals of eligibility rulings are taking as much as two years to resolve. The Task Force proposal adds fifty full-time employees (FTEs) to the Board of Veterans Appeals to help reduce the backlog.

The Health and Livelihood of Veterans	Savings Over 5 Years (in dollars)
End low-rated compensation (0.6% to 10%)	4,712,000,000
Promote efficient hospital management	3,230,000,000
Reduce the increase for hospital and medical care	1,758,000,000
Promote cost sharing for VA long-term care	1,274,000,000
Convert inefficient hospitals	1,170,000,000
Reduce major construction	577,000,000
Coordinate Social Security and compensation benefits	555,000,000
Eliminate all OBRA 1993 sunset dates	545,000,000
Reform third-party reimbursements for service-connected veterans	368,000,000
Reduce medical and prosthetic research	337,000,000
Permanently extend third-party payment provision	225,000,000

The Health and Livelihood of Veterans	Savings Over 5 Years (in dollars)
Support president's loan guaranty program account	191,000,000
Restrict use of the multiple VA housing-loan guarantee benefit	125,000,000
Permanently extend prescription charge/copayment	72,000,000
Permanently extend pension/medical care income verification	23,000,000
Permanently extend resale loan-loss provisions	7,000,000
Add FTEs to Board of Veterans Appeals	(20,000,000)
Increase funds for veterans' medical care	(110,000,000)
Restructuring Programs that Affect the Health and Livelihood of Veterans TOTAL	**15,039,000,000**
Running Total of Savings	**364,437,000,000**

1 President's FY 1995 Budget, Appendix.

CHAPTER SIX

The Individual at School, in the University, and in the Research Setting

T he U.S. Department of Education was created by Congress in 1979 to ensure equal educational opportunity for all and to improve the quality of that education through federal support, research programs, and information sharing. It wasn't the first time the country had an education department. In 1867 the Congress authorized a Department of Education to collect information about education in the country. As a department, it functioned for about a year before it was abolished. The Department of the Interior assumed the information gathering and dissemination functions in a new Office of Education. In 1953 that office became part of the new Department of Health, Education, and Welfare.

Reform Elementary and Secondary Education

The Department of Education provides financial support to states and local school districts. The funds are earmarked for special areas such as providing vocational education, promoting bilingual education, assisting disabled and underprivileged students, and seeing racial integration. The Balanced Budget Task Force examined many Department of Education programs in search of ways to make better use of funds.

Impact Aid. Impact Aid, which carries out financial assistance programs under America's Schools Act, is intended to compensate school districts that have children who are enrolled there because their parents live or work on federally owned or subsidized property. Since that property is tax-exempt, this is theoretically reimbursement for revenue foregone by the school districts. The economic benefits from playing host to federal installations far outweigh the demands placed on schools, making the program unnecessary. In fact, the benefits are so substantial that local schools lobby intensely to forestall closing existing installations. The Task Force provision phases out Impact Aid over a period of five years.

Untargeted Funding for Math and Science Programs. Typically, federal funding for elementary and secondary education is targeted toward students with specific needs. Math and science education is necessary for training the next generation of workers, researchers, and innovators. The Task Force agrees that science and math education is the responsibility of the states and proposes to eliminate untargeted funding for science and math grants in elementary and secondary schools. States could offset the funding reduction because it accounts for less than 1 percent of total federal, state, and local expenditures on education.

Special Education Funding. Funding for certain special education programs is administered under the Individuals with Disabilities Education Act (IDEA). The Task Force proposes to freeze the funding at fiscal year (FY) 1995 levels for five straight years. A freeze on the total amount of funding spent on those programs under this act allows increases and decreases to occur among individual programs as long as the total amount spent under IDEA does not exceed FY 1995 levels. This recommendation was proposed by the Clinton Administration's FY 1995 Budget.

School Improvement Programs. A large number of specific education programs has been placed in the federal budget under the Department of Education in a category entitled "School Improvement Programs." Many programs that cannot be placed in other accounts under the department wind up here.

The Task Force provision freezes selected School Improvement Programs at their FY 1995 levels. Many of these programs are new, have had their funding increased, or have been consolidated for efficiency in the past three fiscal years. They include programs such as safe schools, magnet schools assistance, education for homeless children and youth, and inexpensive book distribution. The proposal does not eliminate funding for these worthy programs but limits the rate of their spending growth for the next five years.

Twenty-three Grant Programs in the Department of Education. For years the Congressional Budget Office (CBO) and many nonprofit groups have identified educational grant programs that duplicate private functions, are poorly targeted, or have had limited success. Many of these programs also are so small and involve such small sums that they make a very small impact on the promotion of education. The Department of Education funds more than 230 programs that address a range of problems at all levels of education. Some analysts have argued that a number of those programs have either largely or completely achieved their original purposes or could be supported by other funding sources.

For example, funding for small library programs is no longer necessary because access to public libraries is now virtually universal. The Follow Through program, which aids low-income children in elementary school, can receive sufficient funding at the state and local levels. The law-related education program succeeded in institutionalizing law-related education and is no longer needed since most law schools now offer clinical education.

The Task Force provision eliminates twenty-three such grants in the Department of Education, some of which were recommended for elimination by the Clinton Administration and Vice-President Gore's *National Performance Review*.

Reform Post-Secondary Education

The Department of Education also provides financial assistance to colleges and universities. For example, it provides funding for programs such as adult education and international studies, grants for improving instruction, and assistance for building facilities, as well as financial aid to students. The Balanced Budget Task Force sought to examine the various post-secondary education programs to improve the overall spending for the department, while ensuring the integrity of the programs.

Campus-Based Aid. The federal government provides campus-based student aid through three programs: supplemental educational opportunity grants, Perkins loans,[1] and work-study. Financial aid administrators at post-secondary institutions determine which eligible students receive aid under general federal guidelines. In 1994, the federal government provided $1.4 billion in campus-based aid, which will go to approximately 1.7 million students.

The Task Force proposes eliminating campus-based aid. The primary justification for eliminating such programs reflects the view that the main goal of federal student aid is to provide access to post-secondary education for those with low incomes. In contrast, campus-based aid is less closely targeted toward low-income students than is other federal student aid. In addition, because campus-based aid is tied to specific institutions, students with greater need at poorly funded schools may receive less than those with less need at well-funded institutions.

Post-Secondary Institutions Sharing in the Risk on Stafford Loans. Four types of loans are available under the Federal Direct Student Loan System of the Department of Education: direct Stafford loans,[2] direct unsubsidized Stafford loans, direct PLUS loans for parents, and direct consolidation loans. Students most commonly use the Stafford loans. In 1995, the federal government was projected to award Stafford loans at a cost of more than $4 billion.

The Task Force provision requires post-secondary institutions to share in the risk of Stafford loan lending by lowering the default rate to a one-year rate of 20 percent. Since the institution is primarily involved in the application and granting process of these federal funds, the institution should be more involved in sharing the risk of its decisions. This requirement will enhance efficiency in the application of the funds while providing yet another incentive for productive and responsible lending by participating institutions.

Participation in the Federal Pell Grant Program for Institutions Ineligible for the Federal Family Education Loans Program. Pell grant funds are limited and should be targeted where the best results are gained from the federal investment and where the government can be satisfactorily assured of repayment of the student loan. The Task Force provision amends the Higher Education Act of 1965 to prohibit an educational institution from participating in the federal Pell grant program if it has already been declared ineligible for participation in the Federal Family Education Loans (FFEL) program due to high default rates. Likewise, if an institution is ineligible to participate in the Stafford loan program, it also will be ineligible for participation in the Pell grant program.

Funding for Vocational and Adult Education Programs. Because of the budget concept of baseline budgeting, the spending increases in vocational and adult education programs implemented by the Clinton Administration during the past two years will remain available to expenditure. Baseline budget projects what it will cost the government to continue the current level of services into the future. As such, freezing the programs at their FY 1995 levels assures that they will continue to receive the same amount of funding next year as they received this year.

This recommendation, proposed by the Clinton Administration's FY 1995 Budget, calls for restructuring the vocational and adult education programs resulting in changes in program funding levels. The Task Force proposal accepts the recommendation that funding for vocational and adult education programs be frozen at their FY 1995 levels for five years.

Higher Education Reform. This proposal is based on an initial recommendation proposed by the Clinton Administration's FY 1995 Budget. The president called for a funding freeze on most higher education programs at the FY 1994 level. The Task Force proposal agrees and maintains funding levels in these programs consistent with perceived need.

Loan Origination Fee. Current law provides that students must pay up-front fees to the government for the benefit of receiving a federally guaranteed loan. For guaranteed student loans, the fee is 3 percent of the loan to the federal government and 4 percent to the guarantee agency. Under direct loans, the fee is 4 percent to the government. Raising the fees to 5 percent for both types of loans would contribute to reducing the federal deficit. The Task Force provision raises the loan origination fee for students to 5 percent of the loan.

Yearly Student Loan Limits. The Task Force proposal calls for a decrease of student loan limits along the following schedule:

Year	Proposed Reduced Loan Limit	Current Loan Limit
First	$1,500	$2,625
Second	$3,000	$2,625
Third	$4,000	$3,500
Fourth	$4,000	$5,500
Remaining undergraduate years	$4,000	

$10 Fee Paid to Institutions for Directors in Administration. The federal government currently pays fees to institutions for administering direct student lending. The original concern with direct student loans was that schools may choose not to participate. If paid $10 per loan, an institution was more apt to be involved. Now many schools are involved in the program and the initial incentive is no longer necessary. The Task Force proposal eliminates the $10 fee for direct lending. Because Pell grants are the most important and most vital student loan programs administered by the Department of Education, the $5 fee given colleges for administering the Pell grant program would be retained.

Home Equity Value in Determining Financial Need. The Higher Education Act specifies formulas to calculate a family's need for Stafford loans. The amount the family is expected to contribute is determined by what is essentially a progressive tax formula. In effect, need analysis "taxes" family incomes and assets — excluding house and farm equity — above amounts assumed to be required for a basic standard of living. Under the Task Force proposal, house and farm equity are used in the calculation of a family's need for financial aid for post-secondary education. In addition, the threshold under which most families with less than $50,000 in income are not asked to report any assets would also be lowered to its previous level of $15,000.[3]

Student Loan Interest Accrual and In-School Interest Subsidies for Graduate and Undergraduate Students. Under the subsidized portion of the Stafford loan program, the federal government incurs interest costs on the students' loans while they are in school. The Task Force proposal reduces federal subsidies on guaranteed student loans by having students accrue interest on their loans while in school, with their payments deferred until they finish school. Because of the payment deferral, students would not incur cash flow problems during school years. This proposal does not affect eligibility for student borrowers. The provision applies prospectively, so that only future loans, and not current loans, are affected. This provision applies to both graduate and undergraduate students.

Reform University Research/National Institutes of Health

Our nation has one of the most sophisticated and highly developed medical research fields in the world. Research at facilities such as the National Institutes of Health (NIH) has proven invaluable in our nation's quest for cures to cancer, the AIDS virus, and a host of other serious diseases. However, at a time when all sectors of the government are being asked to tighten their belts, university research should not be exempt. Furthermore, university research recently has come under increasing scrutiny as federal funds have been used repeatedly for questionable research projects. Placing a loose cap on this funding will not jeopardize needed research programs but will enhance the quality and efficiency of research performed as applicants compete for a more limited amount of grant funds. Also, our nation needs to ensure that we have a continued supply of financial resources for health research. If our deficit crisis is not dealt with in the near term, all funding for this important research will be in jeopardy. Current budget projections show that by the year 2013, all federal tax revenues will be consumed by interest payments and entitlement obligations.

Payment Rate on Federally Sponsored University Research. Federal spending for research and development performed at universities covers both direct and overhead (indirect) costs. The major direct costs of research are wages for scientists, engineers, and technicians and payments for materials and specialized equipment. Overhead costs allocated to federal research include research-related, administrative overhead; library and student services; buildings and equipment used in common; and operations and maintenance. The Task Force proposes imposing a 50 percent cap on the payment rate for overhead, which would motivate those institutions that are above the overall cap to become more efficient and cost-conscious.

Funding for the National Institutes of Health. The federal government provides money for research funded through grants and contracts awarded by the National Institutes of Health. Funding of projects is based on a rating system, with the proposals that earn the highest ratings receiving the awards. Approximately 60 percent of the grants go to universities and other nonprofit institutions. The remainder is spent on research by the NIH, industrial firms, state and local governments, foreign research firms, and NIH administration.

A reduction in NIH spending for health research and development could be softened by increases in private-sector expenditures. Between 1982 and 1992, private-sector spending for health research and development more than doubled, even exceeding the large increase in NIH spending. The Task Force provision freezes funding for NIH for three years.

Health Profession Assistance. The Public Health Service (PHS) subsidizes health profession education for training primary-care physicians, advanced nursing students, and minority and economically disadvantaged students. In 1995 Congress provided $288 million to the PHS in subsidies. Those funds primarily furnish institutional support through grants and contracts to schools for designated training programs in the health professions. A limited amount of the assistance is provided through loans, loan guarantees, and scholarships for students.

The Task Force proposal terminates all PHS education subsidies except those targeted at increasing minority or economically disadvantaged student enrollment at medical schools. The principal justification for this option is that market forces provide strong incentives for individuals to seek training and jobs in the health professions. Over the past several decades, physicians — the principal health profession targeted by the subsidies — have rapidly increased in number, from 142 physicians in all fields for every 100,000 people in 1950 to 161 in 1970 and 244 in 1990. Projections by the American Medical Association indicate that the total number of physicians per capita will continue to rise through 2000. In the case of nurses, if a shortage indeed existed, higher wages and better working conditions would attract more people to the profession and more trained nurses to nursing jobs, and would encourage more of them to seek advanced training.

Uniformed Services University of Health Sciences. The Uniformed Services University of Health Sciences (USUHS) is a medical school in Maryland created by Congress in 1972 to train physicians committed to long-term military careers. Operated by the Department of Defense (DOD) at a total cost of about $90 million in 1994, the school provides a full education for its participants, including a stipend to cover room, board, and books. Figures from 1991 show that USUHS is the most expensive source of military physicians, at $562,000 per person. Even after adjusting for the lengthier service commitment required of physicians trained at USUHS, their training cost is still higher than for physicians from other sources. In addition, USUHS has met only a small fraction of DOD's need for new physicians — less than 12 percent in 1992, for example.

The Task Force proposes closing the Uniformed Services University of Health Sciences. This proposal assumes that the class of students admitted in August 1993 would be USUHS's last and that the institution would close at the end of fiscal year 1997, after those students have graduated. Other programs for obtaining physicians would be expanded to offset some of the loss of physicians. The Clinton Administration also supports this program reform. On the basis of the findings by Vice-President Gore's *National Performance Review*, the Clinton Administration recommended closing this facility in 1997.

The Individual at School, in the University, and in the Research Setting	Savings Over 5 Years (in dollars)
Prospectively allow student loan interest accrual and eliminate in-school interest subsidies for graduate and undergradute students	9,560,000,000
Freeze funding for the National Institutes of Health for 3 years	4,077,000,000
Eliminate campus-based aid	3,230,000,000
Phase out Impact Aid	2,950,000,000
Eliminate 23 grant programs in the Department of Education	1,537,000,000
Raise loan origination fee to 5 percent	1,530,000,000
Terminate health profession assistance	1,427,000,000
Decrease yearly student loan limits	1,400,000,000
Eliminate untargeted funding for math and science programs	1,170,000,000
Cap the payment rate on federally sponsored university research	890,000,000
Reduce library services construction	762,000,000

The Individual at School, in the University, and in the Research Setting	Savings Over 5 Years (in dollars)
Impose home equity/Pell fee	700,000,000
Freeze funding for vocational and adult education programs	532,000,000
Eliminate $10 fee paid to institutions for directors in administration	405,000,000
Use home equity value in determining financial need	400,000,000
Freeze School Improvement Programs	371,000,000
Reform higher education	321,000,000
Close the Uniformed Services University of Health Sciences	190,000,000
Freeze special education funding	153,000,000
Require post-secondary institutions to share in the risk on Stafford loans	140,000,000
Prohibit participation in the federal Pell grant program for institutions ineligible for the Federal Family Education Loans Program	70,000,000
Eliminate FAA airway science educational grants	15,000,000
Restructuring Programs that Affect the Individual at School, in the University, and in the Research Setting **TOTAL**	**31,830,000,000**
Running Total of Savings	**396,267,000,000**

1 Resulting from the Carl D. Perkins Vocational and Applied Technology Education Act; formerly the national direct student loan (NDSL).

2 Awarded on the basis of financial need.

3 The Higher Education Act of 1992 raised the level from $15,000 to $50,000.

CHAPTER SEVEN

The Individual at Work

O ur country's economic growth and standard of living are
influenced by the size and quality of the work force. If the
people are healthy, well fed, and well trained and educated, we
will produce more goods and services more efficiently. To help build a
healthy and capable work force, the government created programs for
training, unemployment assistance, and pension plans. As with other
federally funded programs, many of these need to be restructured to trim
waste and redundancy.

Job-Training Block Grant

Federal job-training programs cost taxpayers more than $120 billion
over five years. The General Accounting Office (GAO) has identified 163
federal training programs scattered over fifteen federal agencies. Their
goals, clients, and services overlap and the results have not been positive.
We have too many programs, too many rules, and too much controversy.

The Task Force proposal consolidates ninety-three of these duplicative programs into one comprehensive employment and job-training
block grant. This policy is based on the precept that states rather than
the federal government are better equipped and situated to train and
place workers. Streamlining the federal role in running job-training

programs will grant states more flexibility in targeting and coordinating such programs. This proposal also cuts the costs of labor by reducing payroll taxes while increasing the take-home pay for low-income workers. With the consolidated programs, the states are directed to continue to serve the populations that were previously served and those that will benefit most from the services. Those targeted populations include disadvantaged adults, dislocated workers, veterans, displaced homemakers, disadvantaged youths, persons with disabilities, and those requiring vocational education.

Unemployment Insurance Reforms

The federal government first took steps to alleviate unemployment in the mid-1930s during the Great Depression. Through federal agencies such as the Work Projects Administration, the government provided millions of jobs. At the same time, Congress enacted the Social Security Act of 1935, which provided the first comprehensive social-insurance system in the United States. Through unemployment insurance, it provided workers who lost their jobs with a weekly compensation payment. The rationale behind such a program was that by maintaining the workers' purchasing power, the insurance would help stabilize buying patterns, which helps trade and industry. Since that time, the government's role in the area of unemployment and unemployment insurance has grown. The Balanced Budget Task Force proposes several measures for reducing federal funding in this area, including reducing the Unemployment Insurance Administration.

Uniform Two-Week Waiting Period for Unemployment Insurance Benefits. States set the eligibility standards for unemployment benefits, while the federal government manages the funding through the unemployment trust fund. While some states have two-week waiting periods before recipients are eligible for benefits, more states have shorter periods, increasing the costs to the federal government. Using a two-week waiting period for benefits greatly increases the incentive to work and encourages more people to find employment more quickly. The Task Force provision imposes a standard two-week waiting period.

Unemployment Compensation for Voluntary Military Quits. Civilian workers who leave their jobs voluntarily cannot apply for and receive unemployment benefits. However, personnel who leave military service voluntarily can receive unemployment compensation. The Task Force provision denies unemployment compensation for military personnel who voluntarily quit.

Reform Civil Service

The Civil Service Act, passed by Congress in 1883, created the foundation of the American Civil Service system as we know it today. As with other areas of the federal government, the Civil Service needs restructuring. The Task Force agreed that several areas needed specific attention: health insurance, thrift savings plan (TSP), Foreign Service disability and retirement, civilian retirement age, and military pension cost of living adjustments (COLAs).

Federal Employee Health Benefit Phantom Big Six Formula. Currently, the averaging formula uses a fictitious phantom insurer to compute federal employee health benefit payments. The Task Force proposal reduces the maximum government contribution toward a federal worker's health insurance by eliminating the fictitious sixth phantom insurer from the averaging formula used to determine the maximum contribution.

Thrift Savings Plan. The Task Force's proposed reform of the thrift savings plan maintains the automatic 1 percent of salary contribution, a dollar-for-dollar match for the first 3 percent, and a 50-cents-per-dollar match for the fourth percent. It eliminates the 50-cents-per-dollar match for the fifth percent of salary available under the current TSP. Remaining portions of the TSP will remain unchanged. This provision prospectively adjusts the plan. The reform applies only to new federal employees hired on or after January 1, 1996, not to current federal employees.

Foreign Service Disability and Retirement. This Grace Commission[1] recommendation modifies the criteria of Foreign Service disability. The Foreign Service retirement age would be raised to match the Civil Service Retirement System (CSRS) age, and the benefit formula would be changed to match the CSRS.

Civilian Retirement Age. The Task Force proposal raises the retirement age prospectively for all new federal hires. Currently, civilian employees can retire with immediate unreduced benefits at age 55 with thirty years of service, at 62 with twenty years of service, and at 65 with five years of service. For those hired on or after January 1, 1996, the retirement age will be increased to 65. The retirement age for current federal employees will remain unchanged. The annuities of federal judges, firefighters, law enforcement officers, air traffic controllers, members of the CIA, the disabled, and survivors are unaffected by this proposal. The proposal does not change federal annuity computations.

Military Pension COLAs. Starting on January 1, 1996, for all new enlistees into the armed services, the military retirement benefit is changed so that no cost of living adjustment on retirement benefits is provided until the retiree reaches age 62. At that age, there is a catch-up provision to account for the lack of a COLA since retirement, and a full COLA is provided for each year thereafter. This provision prospectively adjusts, so it does not affect the COLAs of disabled or survivors' benefits.

The Individual at Work	Savings Over 5 Years (in dollars)
Job-Training Block Grant	9,600,000,000
Impose a uniform two-week waiting period for unemployment insurance benefits	6,400,000,000
Prospectively adjust civilian retirement age	5,660,000,000
Repeal the Davis-Bacon Act	3,085,000,000
Reduce Unemployment Insurance Administration	2,614,000,000
Repeal the federal employee health benefit Phantom Big Six	1,450,000,000
Deny unemployment compensation for voluntary military quits	1,400,000,000
Reform employment programs by eliminating trade adjustment assistance cash benefits	660,000,000
Reform unemployment trust fund	443,000,000
Modify foreign service disability and retirement	170,000,000
Freeze the Equal Employment Opportunity Commission	143,000,000
Prospectively adjust the Thrift Savings Plan	86,000,000
Reform senior executive service accrued vacation and overtime leave	68,000,000
Prospectively adjust military pension COLAs	0

The Individual at Work	Savings Over 5 Years (in dollars)
Restructuring Programs that Affect the Individual at Work TOTAL	31,379,000,000
Running Total of Savings	428,046,000,000

1 See Glossary.

CHAPTER EIGHT

Citizens Who Farm

S ince the birth of our nation, agriculture has played a pivotal role in our nation's economy. The first political parties in the United States were largely divided between those who believed our national economy should be based on an agrarian society and those who believed it should be founded on a manufacturing base. Those who supported an agrarian-based society functioning with a weak national government in which all people would take part democratically, founded the Democratic-Republican Party, led by Thomas Jefferson and James Madison. Those who supported a commercial and manufacturing society with a strong federal government controlled by the commercial class, founded the Federalist party, led by Alexander Hamilton. Over the next 200 years the nation learned that both concepts had merit: Our economy needed both sectors to thrive and expand.

Likewise, the government's agriculture policy of today must recognize that important relationship. Without the manufacturing sector, farmers would not benefit from such technological developments as grain harvesters, tractors, planters, silos, and a number of other vital farming tools. Without the agricultural sector, factory workers on the assembly lines would have limited access to healthy food at affordable prices. The government must adopt policies that allow both sectors to expand in a vibrant manner.

To start with, the government needs to get out of the farming business. At the beginning of the twentieth century there were 5 million farms in the United States owned by hard-working farm families who developed America's agriculture resources as "the breadbasket of the world." At the time, the Department of Agriculture (USDA) had 3,000 employees. By 1935, there were 6.3 million farmers and 20,000 USDA employees. The ratio of bureaucrat to farmer was steadily rising.

Although farming had begun to decline in the nineteenth century with the advent of the Industrial Revolution, the rate of decline increased in the 1930s with the implementation of the New Deal. That decline has continued for more than five decades. Now there are approximately 2.1 million U.S. farmers, many of whom farm only part time. In sharp contrast, there are now 60,000 USDA employees. Author Martin Gross wrote, "As farmers have dropped to one-third in number in the last half century, federal farm bureaucrats have taken up the slack, increasing threefold."[1] If this trend continues, by the year 2040 there will be 150,000 USDA employees, equal to the entire number of full-time farmers in America. The Department of Agriculture should be downsized and our reliance shifted to the hard work and innovation of our nation's farmers.

Furthermore, our antiquated farming system costs farmers, taxpayers, and consumers too much to maintain. As James Bovard of the Cato Institute[2] explains: "For sixty years, the U.S. government has devotedly repeated the same agricultural policy mistakes. Unfortunately, the federal safety net is slowly strangling American agriculture."[3]

As I travel my 200-mile long congressional district in upstate New York, I am repeatedly reminded of its agricultural strengths of yesterday. While farming remains one of the most important industries in my district, the number of family farms has steadily declined. Government programs designed to assist small farmers have largely insulated them from the real incentives of economic competition. The federal government should limit itself to regulating interstate agricultural commerce and return the tax dollars spent on those assistance programs to the family farm so that it can compete, with all of its economic resources, on its own.

Some existing government programs are crippling the agricultural sector. When they were adopted and implemented many years ago, they were intended to serve specific needs. The needs no longer exist, but the programs do. It is time to let go of the programs and let the agricultural sector thrive on its own.

Reform Crop Subsidy and Insurance Programs

Three ways to work toward strengthening agriculture and, at the same time, balancing the budget are by eliminating all crop commodity programs (excluding dairy), replacing crop insurance with standing authority for disaster insurance, and terminating the Honey Program.

Crop Commodity Program Subsidies (excluding dairy). Farming is a timeless occupation. Many of our forefathers came from agricultural families in Europe, and every colony in America relied heavily on the ability of early settlers to provide the food necessary to sustain that colony.

Since then, farming has been a trouble-ridden occupation. Emerging from the nineteenth century, the industry was "sick" with its own special problems. This sickness was most evident throughout the 1920s, as farmers regularly bailed out of the industry or went into tenantry. Farm income continued to lag behind the average growth in the standard of living, and rural America fell well behind its urban counterparts in family income growth.

By its very nature, the small farm was at a disadvantage in the era of technological innovation. No longer was land the most precious variable in the farming equation. With the dramatic increase of farmable land that followed the expansion of railroads, the growth of storage combines, land speculation, and a rapidly growing economy, generational farmers were rolled over by this new technology era. Nonfarm output per worker rose by nearly 20 percent between 1910 and 1920, while output per farm worker actually fell.[3] Despite laudable efforts by those farmers, they could not seem to grow or raise enough to make a decent living.

The economic laws of supply and demand played games with the family farm. As a whole, Americans did not tend to increase their consumption of food products as prices fell. In contrast, when the price of manufacturing a good falls, the consumer is more apt to purchase that good. Increases in overall farm output resulted in much lower prices but not in larger cash profits for the small farmer. Consequently, farmers could produce more commodities than the consumers could or would buy.

In October 1929, the Stock Market crashed and America began its slide into the Great Depression, which bottomed out in 1932. Cash-strapped banks called in outstanding loans and stopped making new ones. Small and mid-sized farms were unable to repay such large amounts and many went bankrupt. Agricultural production screeched to a halt, and the gears of our national economy came to a stop.

Fortunately, President Roosevelt, and later World War II, got the economy working again. Under Roosevelt's New Deal, the revitalization of America's agriculture was front and center. According to Roosevelt and many economists of the time, the "market mechanism" did not produce a satisfactory result for farmers for two fundamental reasons. First, the demand for food was inelastic, which means that the percentage of change in demand is smaller than the percentage of change in price or income. This means that farmers could not depend on the market to show them the crop-production figure they needed to meet in order to count on a certain return in profit. Second, the agriculture industry could not limit its own output and thus constantly "broke the market" every time a bumper crop was produced.

That inelasticity of demand could not be changed because it was a product of man's desire for food. However, President Roosevelt did find a way to limit output: The Agricultural Adjustment Act established a way for farmers as a group to accomplish what they could not do as competitive individuals. In exchange for agreements on cutting back their acreage, and hence their output, farmers received payments from the federal government. It has been reported that in the first year after it was enacted, every fourth row of growing cotton had to be plowed under and 6 million pigs had to be slaughtered. As a result, in 1934 and 1935, 30 million acres were taken out of production in exchange for $1.1 billion in federal payments.[5] This economic experiment initially worked and the net income of the American farmer doubled by 1936.

However, the Roosevelt Administration was not finished. The New Deal sought to raise farm incomes further by establishing support prices at which the government would, if necessary, buy farm output. To guarantee farmers long-term stability in planning future production, the New Deal set these target prices higher than the point at which demand and price met. As a result, surpluses developed.

The government tried again. This time, it limited the acreage that farmers could plant if they wanted to qualify for support payments. This limitation, however, was soon overrun by the extraordinary increase in agricultural productivity from new technologies. Between 1940 and the late 1960s, farm acreage declined by 15 percent, while the yield per acre increased by more than 70 percent. Because of the increase, large levels of surplus output had to be purchased and stored by the federal government. And it was only because of the mass distribution of these supplies around the country in the 1960s that the surpluses did not become a national embarrassment. Despite the effort, the problem of surpluses and expensive subsidy payments re-emerged in the 1980s.

Nevertheless, this program has given farmers a little more stability in making long-term production predictions. The price supports prevent wide fluctuations in prices, allowing farmers to project with some degree of certainty their expected levels of profit. Price stability, no matter what the cause, also provides the consumer with predictable market prices over the long run.

Despite the short-term gain that may be realized from these commodity subsidies, numerous studies and our historical experience show that the program perpetuates government dependency, strains the market for these commodities, and discourages efficient farming growth and expansion throughout the nation. The Cato Institute has gone so far as to say that Congress and the USDA remain devoted to perpetuating the agricultural patterns of the 1930s and the prices of 1910.[6] Such subsidies often grant preferences to certain crops that have federal subsidies over those crop programs that do not, which manipulates the market in ways not beneficial to the consumer. The organization Citizens Against Government Waste reported that agriculture subsidies redistribute wealth from the poor and middle class to the wealthy. About two-thirds of all subsidy payments are to farmers with annual sales revenues of more than $1 million, or the top 15 percent of farms. For example, I recently learned when watching a national television program that Sam Donaldson, an ABC news correspondent, has been the third-largest recipient in the country of the wool and mohair subsidy.

The economic irrationality of these farm policies is well illustrated by America's sugar policies: The federal government keeps the price of cane and beet sugar high through price guarantees while restricting sugar imports. According to the Cato Institute, many times during the last decade American sugar prices have been on average twice as high as, and as much as 700 percent higher than, world market prices.[7] Thus the sugar program costs consumers $1.4 billion a year. In 1991, some 42 percent of the benefits to sugar growers, who are concentrated in Florida and Louisiana, went to 1 percent of all sugar-farming families. One family in Florida, the Fanjuls of Palm Beach, received $64 million in "higher profits and government handouts."[8] Clearly, the benefits of the sugar subsidy are not going to those farmers for whom they were intended.

The Crop Commodity Corporation provides subsidies for a wide variety of products including feed grains, wheat, rice, upland cotton, tobacco, soybeans, peanuts, sugar, wool, dairy, and disaster assistance. Each one of these crops carries its own story, its own problems, and its own solutions. However, government subsidies often serve as obstacles to the implementation of these solutions.

Economists Robert L. Heilbroner and James K. Galbraith summarized the current problem accurately when they wrote:

> Small-scale farming . . . is in a precarious state, and the majority of the million-odd small farmers now depend as much or more on income from nonfarm jobs — perhaps tending a gas pump — as they do on selling their small crops. Middle-scale farming . . . is sorely pressed by rising costs and heavy debts. . . . The farm sector has been severely hurt in recent years by a high dollar, which cost the United States much of its traditional agricultural export market. . . . The average American farmer . . . will not achieve [financial] security until the United States has again established a competitive place in the world economy.[9]

Of all sectors of the economy, American agriculture is one of the hardest hit by consistent annual budget deficits. This constrictive debt burden closes markets, hides capital, prevents investment, and minimizes farming income. Likewise, farm supports in 1995, based on 1930 estimates and a confined production capacity — accompanied by mandates such as wetland regulations, property takings, and zoning laws — strangles expansion, limits competition, overregulates the market, and stunts income growth. If the elimination of crop commodity subsidies was included in a package designed to balance the federal budget, pay down the national debt, and grow the economy, market opportunities for farmers would explode, allowing for market-determined food prices and long-term stability in crop production. Consequently, the Task Force proposal calls for the elimination over five years of all crop commodity subsidies, excluding the dairy subsidy and those subsidies for disaster assistance.

Decisions on excluding the dairy subsidy and disaster assistance were made because of the short time period in which we composed this proposal. First, the Hudson River Valley in New York, which I represent, produces more than 1 billion pounds of milk every year. The dairy industry is one of the largest industries in my congressional district. Advocating the outright elimination of this subsidy would have been politically difficult for me to do at the time. I recognize the duplicity that may be seen in such a position. However, I do believe there is substantial room for budget savings and reform in this program. We currently are trying to develop a reform program that maximizes the subsidy for small farms in the short term and curbs subsidies for the larger agribusinesses, all the while moving us down the road toward a complete removal of the subsidy. I intend to work with the farming community in my district toward this goal.

Second, removal of the federal subsidy for disaster assistance without moving its functions somewhere else may lead only to increased hardships for those it served. With more time we believed we could combine these reform efforts with those plans to reform disaster insurance and achieve acceptable and comparable results.

Replace Crop Insurance with Standing Authority for Disaster Insurance. For many years, the federal government has offered crop insurance to farmers through the Federal Crop Insurance Corporation (FCIC) to protect them against losses caused by natural disasters. The government pays all administrative costs, subsidizes farmers' premium payments, and covers losses in excess of premiums for this heavily subsidized insurance. Even with this program in place, the government has reacted in recent years to crop shortfalls from drought and other natural factors by providing cash or in-kind assistance. Phasing out the FCIC would save taxpayers billions of dollars.

The FCIC program covers more than fifty different agricultural crops with more than 85 percent of all U.S.-planted acreage eligible for FCIC protection. Nevertheless, less than half of the eligible acres currently are insured by the program. Even more disturbing is the fact that in some recent years the insurance rate has fallen to one-fourth of all eligible acreage. As with any insurance program, the smaller the number of farmers participating in the program, the smaller the number of premium-paying individuals. Consequently, the solvency of the FCIC is unstable. If this program works so well and possesses important safety benefits for the farming community, why do so few take advantage of it?

Congressional behavior has given farmers another answer. Despite the existence of disaster insurance, Congress has rushed to bail the agricultural sector out of their problems with large emergency appropriations. This happened in 1986, 1988, 1989, 1991, 1992, 1993, and 1994 and is occurring again in 1995. Why buy special insurance when you know that if a disaster strikes your farm, Congress will give you money to rebuild?

The Task Force proposal ends federally subsidized crop insurance offered through the FCIC and replaces it with federal disaster assistance, saving the federal government $1.6 billion over five years. It would expand the ability of the federal government to plan in advance for disaster assistance and would better protect the long-term interests of farmers and their crops. Some of the money saved by the elimination of this program could be rolled over into a special fund for unexpected disaster needs, whatever they may be. This fund would then be available to finance any future efforts to assist those affected by disasters.

Today, the private disaster insurance market is relatively small because the government's current policies have crowded out its business. By turning the FCIC over to the private insurance market, the government would strengthen and expand this market. Furthermore, this approach would relieve taxpayers of the burden of bailing out the farmers. In a private crop-insurance market, policyholders will take the necessary steps to mitigate potential loss and damage, much as they would with fire or other hazard insurance. In return, the government would treat farmers as the responsible business owners that they are rather than as potential victims of natural disasters.

Honey Program. According to Vice-President Al Gore's *National Performance Review*, "World War II also brought us federal subsidies for honey production. During the war, honey was declared essential because the military used bees' wax to wrap ammunition, and citizens replaced rationed sugar with honey. When honey prices dropped after the war, the federal government began subsidizing honey production. The program was intended to be temporary — at least until there were enough honeybees available for pollination. But more than forty years later, every beekeeper in the U.S. is eligible for federal loans."[10]

The General Accounting Office argues that price supports are no longer necessary to promote bee pollination. The GAO also points to the relatively few beneficiaries, since only about 2,000 commercial apiarists raise bees for honey production in the United States. Legislation to eliminate federal support for honey has passed the House and is pending in the Senate. This proposal for terminating the Honey Program assumes the termination of the program.

Reform Agricultural Research.

As part of the Department of Agriculture's function to gather and distribute information on farming and to administer laws to protect farmers and the public, the USDA conducts basic and applied research and provides technical assistance to farmers, as well as funding for rural education programs, through three programs: the Agricultural Research Service, the Cooperative State Research Service, and the Agricultural Extension Service.

The District of Columbia. The Task Force proposal to reform agricultural research eliminates payments to the District of Columbia. As our nation's capital, the District of Columbia is an important symbol of our nation. But the site chosen by George Washington himself has evolved over 200 years into a large metropolitan center, and within the borders of the District of Columbia, there is not one acre of farmland. Years ago, perhaps, there was an agricultural presence here, but that has disappeared. Nevertheless, the federal government continues to pay Washington, DC, money for agricultural programs. Those payments have almost doubled from 1993 to 1995, reaching a high of $2.9 million. The payments should stop.

Rural Technology Grants. The Task Force proposal to reform agricultural research also eliminates payments to rural technology grants. Early in this century the USDA established rural technology grants to assist farming communities by operating centers for the technological research and development thought necessary to compete with the urbanization of America. Technological development should be, and is, performed by the private sector at both corporate and university levels. Those research programs are entirely able to meet the technological needs of rural areas. The Clinton Administration agreed with this assessment and, in fiscal year 1995, asked Congress to terminate this program.

Agricultural Extension Work. The Smith-Lever Act established cooperative agricultural extension work. Since its inception, funding for these services has steadily increased as the number of farmers has steadily decreased. Since all of rural America now has electric service and nearly 98 percent has telephone service, these programs can be responsibly scaled back. The Task Force proposal calls for funding such programs at 85 percent of their fiscal year 1994 levels. According to the Congressional Budget Office (CBO), ". . . federal funding for some Extension Service activities could be reduced without undercutting the service's basic mission of educating and assisting farmers."[11]

Reform Foreign Agricultural Programs

We can decrease spending even more over the next five years by reforming the Foreign Agricultural Service (FAS), eliminating the Office of International Cooperation and Development, reducing loans made under the USDA Export Credit Program, and eliminating the Export Enhancement and Market Promotion Programs.

Foreign Agricultural Service. The Foreign Agricultural Service performs the market development agricultural activities outlined by the Agricultural Act of 1954. The FAS mission is to help American farmers and traders take maximum advantage of increased opportunities to sell U.S. agricultural commodities abroad and to help increase U.S. farm income.

The Task Force proposes to reform the Foreign Agricultural Service. The international diplomacy duties of the FAS duplicate similar functions already performed by the Department of State and the office of the United States Trade Representative. Consultations and negotiations with foreign governments should be performed by the State Department, while research and development studies should be performed by the private sector or the industry itself. In 1984, the Grace Commission[12] concluded that the FAS should be phased out gradually, but completely, in four years. It still exists.

Office of International Cooperation and Development (OICD). Under this office, the government promotes U.S. agriculture and the advancement of agriculture in developing countries through a number of complementary programs. According to the Office of Management and Budget, "Direct program activities include the administration of the Cochran Fellowship Program, which provides food industry training to senior and mid-level professionals from the public and private sectors of selected middle-income countries and emerging democracies, and the management of USDA's bilateral exchange and cooperative research programs with foreign governments and institutions."[13] Such programs are ongoing in more than eighty countries and are focused on such activities as land and water management, pest control, crop and livestock production, and conservation.

The OICD manages the Department of Agriculture's bilateral exchange research programs with foreign governments to strengthen the role of science and technology in the ongoing effort to stabilize world food supplies and to increase the efficiency with which the world's natural resources are used. I do not believe the government should be involved in determining what constitutes an environmental priority, at home or abroad, and I believe international relations should be coordinated by one central agent, the Department of State. The Department of Commerce could easily represent agricultural interests in their continuing overall trade negotiations with foreign governments.

The Task Force supports this nonimplemented Grace Commission recommendation to eliminate the Office of International Cooperation and Development and to turn over funding of these projects to the private sector.

Loan Guarantees Made Under the USDA Export Credit Program. The U.S. government guarantees short- and intermediate-term loans made by commercial banks to finance foreign purchases of U.S. agricultural commodities and products. Legislation requires that a minimum of $5.5 billion in loan guarantees be made annually, although actual levels of guarantees have been lower. There is no limit on the total amount of guarantees, but there is a requirement that borrowers be creditworthy.

When a foreign buyer misses a loan payment, the bank making the original loan submits a claim to the Department of Agriculture. The USDA reimburses the bank, takes over the loan, and attempts collection. The government guarantees 98 percent of the principal of the loan, except loans to the former Soviet Union. In these loans, the government has guaranteed 100 percent of the principal.

The Task Force proposal to reduce loan guarantees limits annual guarantees to $3.6 billion. The estimate of savings assumes the entire reduction would derive from lowering the value of loan guarantees for sales to the former Soviet Union, which is now considered the world's most risky borrower receiving guarantees.

Export Enhancement Program. The Department of Agriculture's Export Enhancement Program (EEP) gives subsidies to American exporters of agricultural products, primarily wheat. The program aims specifically at promoting exports to countries in which Americans face competition from subsidized products from other countries. Under EEP's complex subsidy scheme, the American exporter negotiates a tentative price with foreign buyers. The exporter then seeks EEP commodity certificates, which the exporter may redeem for U.S. government-owned commodities. Thus, an exporter can tempt foreign purchasers with lower prices since part of his exports are provided free by the federal government. The primary foreign beneficiaries of this program have been the former Soviet Union and the People's Republic of China.

According to an April 1990 report from the General Accounting Office (GAO),[14] the EEP, like other agricultural subsidy programs, has had unpredictable and mixed results. In fact, the EEP at times has harmed American consumers directly. A June 1991 Congressional Budget Office study[15] determined that greater export demand effectively reduced supplies available for domestic use, which raised the domestic price. It is also questionable whether American taxpayers' dollars, through the EEP, should be used to help the government of the People's Republic of China, a major human rights abuser. Furthermore, the breakup of the former Soviet Union requires a complete reexamination of America's trade and assistance to the resulting new republics. The Task Force proposes to eliminate the Export Enhancement Program.

Market Promotion Program. In 1990 the federal government eliminated the Targeted Export Assistance (TEA) Program and replaced it with the Market Promotion Program (MPP). The TEA was created in 1985 to "counter or offset the adverse effect of subsidies, import quotas, or other unfair trade practices of foreign competitors on U.S. agricultural exports."[16] After five years, this protection program was replaced by another that relied more on the participation of the private sector. The MPP channels federal funds to private companies and agricultural producers to assist them in advertising and marketing their products in other countries.

Despite its laudable goals, the Market Promotion Program has become nothing more than a handy source of free cash for wealthy businesses. Taxpayers would be astounded to learn where these funds have gone. The world's largest food chain, McDonald's Corporation, received MPP funds to advertise Chicken McNuggets overseas. Actor Paul Newman's food company, Newman's Own, Inc., received $100,000; Pillsbury Company (a subsidiary of the British conglomerate Grand Metropolitan PLC) received $1.14 million; and Ernest and Julio Gallo Winery, Inc., received $2.2 million. Liberals and conservatives, Democrats and Republicans, have long referred to such payments as prime examples of corporate welfare.

Furthermore, the GAO also learned that the Department of Agriculture has no record of who actually receives these subsidies or how much is actually given out. After a year of time-consuming research, the GAO was able to compile a complete list of recipients. The names on this list included such huge agribusinesses as Blue Diamond Growers (Cooperative) almonds, Sunkist oranges, and Moyle mink furs. Surely, the taxpayers should not be in the business of subsidizing the promotional campaigns of America's largest corporations. The Task Force proposes to eliminate the Market Promotion Program.

Restructure and Reform the Administration of Agricultural Programs

The Task Force also examined administrative areas in which the government could save additional funds over the next five years.

Non-Farm Service Agencies. In addition to the Farm Service functions, the Department of Agriculture performs a number of other duties that do not traditionally fall under the title "Agriculture." Consequently, the Task Force proposal calls for a restructuring of such agencies through downsizing and resetting priorities.

The Bush Administration in 1992 presented a proposal to consolidate and restructure non-farm service agencies and to improve the safety inspection process through automation. The consolidations recommended by this proposal have been 90 percent completed; however, only proportional reductions have been made in the Soil Conservation, Bureau of Extension, Agricultural Stabilization and Conservation Service, Federal Crop Insurance, and FmHA offices. The Task Force proposal would fulfill the initial Bush Administration recommendation by completing the consolidation. The Clinton Administration agreed with this position and also recommended such a completion in its budget for fiscal year 1995.

Reform Agricultural Loans

We can realize additional savings by reducing FmHA loans for farm ownership and duplication with the Small Business Administration (SBA), as well as terminating state mediation grants.

FmHA Loans for Farm Ownership and Duplication with the SBA. The Farmers Home Administration, as part of the Department of Agriculture, provides credit for agriculture and rural development, including housing. The FmHA makes direct loans at below-market interest rates, gives loan guarantees, and provides relief on interest payments to single-family home borrowers. The expertise of the FmHA is supposedly in the area of farming, yet a sizable portion of its current activities involves housing, business, and community-development loans, clearly duplicating existing SBA functions. These activities can and should be done through the SBA or the private sector.

State Mediation Grants. The federal government spends $3 million each year to help states administer agricultural loan mediation programs. Under the Agricultural Credit Act of 1987, the Department of Agriculture makes a grant to a state that has been certified by the Farm Service Agency as having such a loan program.

A loan mediation program is designed to promote settlement between conflicting parties through the intervention of an outside party. In other words, state officials are used to reconcile contract differences between individuals or businesses. I question why there is a federal need to intervene in such disagreements. State and local authorities, if needed, should be more than able to assist in this area. Furthermore, I believe one of the reasons for our justice system is to provide citizens the opportunity to reconcile disputes and receive recompense for wrongdoing. Moreover, under existing law the federal government only becomes involved in running the program after a state has established it. If the state can start it, why should federal tax dollars be used to keep it open? Local disputes, especially those involving local dollars, are best left to local officials using local money to resolve.

For these reasons, the Task Force has agreed with both the Bush and the Clinton administrations that state mediation grants should be terminated.

Citizens Who Farm	Savings Over 5 Years (in dollars)
Eliminate all crop commodity program subsidies (excluding dairy)	37,044,000,000
Reduce loan guarantees to high-risk borrowers	2,460,000,000
Reform agricultural research	1,245,000,000
Eliminate the Export Enhancement Program	1,044,000,000
Replace crop insurance with standing authority for disaster insurance	986,000,000
Reduce the number of farm agencies' field offices	905,000,000
Restructure the non-farm service agencies	535,000,000
Eliminate the Market Promotion Program	500,000,000
Reduce FmHA loans for farm ownership and duplication with the SBA	201,000,000
Reduce SBA loans to farmers	201,000,000
Reduce loan guarantees made under the USDA Export Credit Program	155,000,000
Reform FAS and eliminate the OICD	33,000,000
Terminate the Honey Program	31,000,000
Terminate state mediation grants	15,000,000

Citizens Who Farm	Savings Over 5 Years (in dollars)
Restructuring Agricultural Programs TOTAL	45,355,000,000
Running Total of Savings	473,401,000,000

1 Martin L. Gross. *The Government Racket: Washington Waste from A to Z*. New York: Bantam Books, 1992, page 9.

2 See Glossary.

3 *The Cato Handbook for Congress*. Washington, DC: The Cato Institute, 1995.

4 Robert L. Heilbroner and James K. Galbraith. *The Economic Problem,* 9th edition. Englewood Cliffs, NJ: Prentice Hall, 1990.

5 Ibid., page 495.

6 *The Cato Handbook,* page 222.

7 Ibid., pages 218-219.

8 General Accounting Office. *Addressing the Deficit: Budgetary Implications of Selected GAO Work for Fiscal Year 1994*. Washington, DC: U.S. Government Printing Office, September 1993, page 103.

9 Heilbroner and Galbraith, page 497.

10 Albert Gore. *National Performance Review*. Washington, DC: U.S. Government Printing Office, September 1993, page 103.

11 Congressional Budget Office. "Reducing the Deficit: Spending and Revenue Options," *Report to the Senate and House Committess on the Budget.* Washington, DC: U.S. Government Printing Office, February 1995, page 133.

12 See Glossary.

13 President's FY 1996 Budget, Appendix, U.S. Government Printing Office, April 1990.

14 General Accounting Office. *1990 Farm Bill: Opportunities for Change*. Washington, DC: U.S. Government Printing Office, 1995.

15 Congressional Budget Office. *The Outlook for Farm Commodity Program Spending, Fiscal Years 1991-1996*. Washington, DC: U.S. Government Printing Office, June 1991.

16 General Accounting Office. *Agricultural Trade: Review of Targeted Assistance Programs*. Washington, DC: U.S. Government Printing Office, May 1998.

CHAPTER NINE

Individuals in Business

I n a free market system the relationship between individuals in
business and individuals in government is, by design, supposed
to be limited. Over the years, as the federal government expanded,
this relationship has become blurred. Now, to promote a thriving business sector with limited government involvement, significant reforms
to a wide variety of government programs are necessary to break many
forms of government shackles off the arms of business and industry.

Reform How the Government Conducts Business with the Private Sector

The federal government and private businesses often interrelate in
providing and delivering certain public services. The government can
provide a public service by contracting out its delivery to a private business, which may provide any service ranging from printing to prison
operation. Government's cost is reduced because private providers will
offer the service at a lower cost as they compete with each other and
minimize expenses to produce profits. And private businesses often have
access to less-expensive resources for providing the service.

The government also can privatize, or allow the private sector to carry
out, certain functions. A decision about privatization may be reached

when government determines that the private sector can provide a service in a more cost-effective and efficient manner than it can itself. Privatization represents, in part, an undoing of decades of government takeover of functions that initially were private. It makes good sense because services are provided, private-sector jobs are created, increased corporate profits become taxable income, and financing incentives lead to more rapid and efficient building of projects. Also, because the private facility operates to make a profit, it is generally more consumer-friendly.

Federal Procurement. The Task Force proposal accepts the Clinton Administration's recommendations on "reinventing" federal procurement practices described in the vice-president's *National Performance Review (NPR)* and in the Fiscal Year (FY) 1995 Budget. According to the *NPR*: "The Federal Government does at least one thing well: It generates red tape."[1]

Service Contract Act. The McNamara-O'Hare Service Contract Act of 1965 sets basic labor standards for employees on government contracts whose principal purpose is to furnish labor, such as laundry, custodial, and guard services. Contractors covered by this act generally must provide employees with wages and fringe benefits that are at least equal to those prevailing in their locality or those contained in a collective bargaining agreement of the previous contractor.

The Task Force proposal modifies the Service Contract Act to repeal the successorship provision. By permitting successor contractors to pay lower wage rates or to provide less costly fringe benefits than those provided by their predecessors — yet still being subject to the rules on prevailing wages and fringe benefits — federal procurement costs would fall, because it would promote greater competition among contractors.

Advanced Technology Program. The Omnibus Trade and Competitiveness Act of 1988 established the Advanced Technology Program (ATP) within the Commerce Department's National Institute of Standards and Technology. The program awards research and development (R&D) grants on a merit basis to individual companies, independent research institutes, and joint ventures. The grants support research in generic technologies with applications to a broad range of products, as well as precompetitive research. Many question whether the federal government is capable of picking projects with the most potential for technological and commercial success. Furthermore, those projects that stand out as clear "winners" might have been funded by the private sector anyway. One privately funded study suggests that as many as half of ATP projects in 1990 would probably have been undertaken without ATP support. The Task Force proposal eliminates the Advanced Technology Program.

Government National Mortgage Association. The Government National Mortgage Association (Ginnie Mae) was created in 1968 to insure banks and savings and loan institutions that make loans guaranteed by the Department of Housing and Urban Development (HUD) or the

Department of Veterans Affairs (VA) against a loss to the lender when selling those loans to other investors.

Only the riskiest borrowers really need Ginnie Mae insurance, and HUD and the VA are not in a position to make loans to such risky borrowers. In practice, this program gives lenders a way to make loans and sell them quickly, getting a check from the government to make up the difference. Taxpayers' money should not be used to guarantee investment bankers against losses due to unquestionable loans.

The Task Force proposes to privatize the Government National Mortgage Association. The existing loans would be sold to the private sector with guarantees that the terms of the loan, as brokered by the federal government, would remain within reason. The government needs to get out of this business — plus it duplicates similar efforts at the Farmers Home Administration.

Helium Processing and Storage Facility. To conserve helium for essential government use and promote the development of a private helium industry, the federal government, in 1960, began purchasing and storing helium. This action was taken in anticipation of a predicted critical shortfall of helium supply for federal users. Defense activities, such as the intercontinental ballistic missile program and the space program, greatly expanded both the immediate and future demand for helium. The government now owns a large helium stockpile in Amarillo, Texas, that is capable of meeting projected needs for about the next 100 years. In addition, the Department of Interior has been successful in its efforts to spur the growth of a private helium industry.

The Task Force provision would sell all physical assets associated with the federal helium industry, excluding the government-owned inventory of crude helium, which would be retained. In addition, we assume that government agencies can purchase helium from the private sector.

National Oceanic and Atmospheric Administration Fleet of Sea Vessels. The National Oceanic and Atmospheric Administration (NOAA) owns and operates a fleet of sea vessels for scientific research and other duties. The vessels carry out scientific experiments and maintain buoys and navigational beacons.

The General Accounting Office (GAO) has criticized the government-operated fleet for being too expensive to maintain and operate and recommends that it be phased out and privatized over a five-year period. Says the GAO, ". . . NOAA vessels' daily costs range from $100 to $22,000, compared to $465 to $4,955 for private-sector ships. . . ." NOAA should purchase services from the private sector, which would be more cost effective and would increase private competitive forces.[2] The Task Force proposes that NOAA sell its fleet to the private sector and contract with the buyers for other services.

Private Power Cogeneration. The Task Force proposal to permit private power cogeneration also was part of Vice-President Al Gore's *National Performance Review*, was included in the so-called Penny-Kasich amendment, and was in the Government Reform and Savings Act of 1993. By permitting private power cogeneration, the government would realize savings because civilian facilities could avoid the cost of rebuilding existing facilities that provide steam for building heat and industrial processes. Also, agencies could lower their utility costs if the private providers sold steam and electricity at lower rates than the agencies now pay.

The Department of Defense (DOD) can enter into cogeneration arrangements with private power producers. Those producers build and operate facilities at defense installations to provide electricity and heat, selling off any excess electricity to private users.

Alaska Power Administration and Southeastern Power Administration. The Alaska Power Administration (APA) and the Southeastern Power Administration (SEPA) are two of the government-run power management facilities in the Department of Energy (DOE). The government has dominated these markets for years and, while these Power Management Administrations (PMAs) may generate revenue, they also poignantly symbolize big government. If the federal government does not have to do this — and it doesn't — it shouldn't.

Regarding the Alaska Power Administration, Vice-President Gore's *National Performance Review* advocated that the federal government should divest its interest in the Alaska Power Administration. SEPA is a logical PMA for divestiture, since it does not own or operate any transmission facilities. In a ten-state area of the Southeast, SEPA markets power that is generated at Corps of Engineers hydroelectric generating plants. Deliveries are made via transmission facilities owned by others. SEPA sells power at wholesale rates, primarily to publicly and cooperatively owned electric distribution utilities, using wheeling and pooling arrangements with the region's large private utilities to provide firm power to its customers. Since producing electricity should be a commercial, not governmental, activity, the Task Force proposes to sell the Alaska Power Administration and the Southeastern Power Administration and recommends developing an orderly process to divest the government of the remaining PMAs.

Hydropower Leasing. When the Federal Power Commission was established in 1920, hydroelectric plants were being built; but with the simultaneous development of larger and more cost-efficient steam-power plants, only very large and costly hydroelectric installations could compete effectively. At this point the federal government stepped in to assume a major share in their construction. Then, in 1933, motivated by the search for additional uses of water resources, such as navigation, flood control, and irrigation, the Tennessee Valley Authority (TVA) started the government's participation in large-scale waterpower development.

Essentially all Americans now have access to electricity and technological opportunities and, although the government's policy in this area can be said to have succeeded, the original need no longer exists. Now the program must stop. The Task Force proposal initiates hydropower leasing by allowing private entities to finance improvements in federal hydroelectric facilities in exchange for the right to sell some of the additional electricity resulting from the improvements. This "partnership" could cause an increase in the efficiency of hydroelectric power production, a decrease in the federal government's role in the area of hydroelectric power, and an expansion of services provided for consumers. The Clinton Administration recommended a similar proposal.

Naval Petroleum Reserves. The Naval Petroleum Reserves (NPRs) are two taxpayer-owned and operated commercial oil fields at Elk Hills, near Bakersfield, California, and Teapot Dome, near Casper, Wyoming. The NPRs were set aside by Presidents William Howard Taft in 1912 and Woodrow Wilson in 1915 to assure the U.S. Navy a reserve supply of oil as its fleet converted from coal to oil. Later, when U.S. oil reserves proved more plentiful than originally expected, the two NPR fields stood mostly idle. The 1973-1974 oil embargo by the Organization of Petroleum Exporting Countries (OPEC) caused Congress in 1975 to sell oil and gas on the commercial market as a way of reducing oil imports and earning money to pay for the start-up of the Strategic Petroleum Reserve.

Oil now produced from the NPRs accounts for only about 1 percent of U.S. domestic output and, thus, is hardly vital to national security. The Clinton Administration's FY 1995 Budget stated, "Producing and selling this oil is a commercial, not a government activity. There is good reason to believe that private industry can run Elk Hills quite well, since it accounts for most U.S. domestic oil production." Chevron already has expressed keen interest in managing the facility to bring the field up to commercial production standards so it can be sold. The Strategic Petroleum Reserve is a much better emergency stockpile than the NPRs, particularly since oil can be pumped out of the SPR more than 30 times faster than out of the NPRs. The Task Force supports the Clinton Administration's proposal to sell the Naval Petroleum Reserves.

Uranium Enrichment Corporation. The federal government enriches uranium at federally operated plants in order to provide U.S. utilities with nuclear fuel. The Uranium Enrichment Corporation was created by the 1992 Energy Policy Act with the vision that it would eventually be privatized. The Task Force provision fulfills this vision by proposing to privatize the corporation in fiscal year 1998.

Minimum- to Medium-Security Mainstream Federal Prisons. Many prisons throughout the United States are managed by private corporations. Where implemented, correctional privatization has not produced either the wave of litigation or the deficient delivery of correctional services many critics anticipated. Private correctional facilities at the state level have lower escape rates and fewer disturbances by inmates than do public facilities. In general, staff and inmates both feel more secure at the privately operated facilities. The experience of state governments is that privatizing prisons reduces operating costs by 3 percent to 5 percent.

The Task Force proposal recommends that the Federal Bureau of Prisons, an agency within the Department of Justice, privatize the minimum-to medium-security mainstream prisons called Federal Correctional Institutions (FCIs). This proposal would be implemented over five years, with an equal percentage of prisons being privatized each year. It is assumed that current government-employed prison workers (guards, for example) would be hired by the corporations taking over the prisons. In addition, the plan involves only takeovers of existing prisons, not new prisons.

Neither the U.S. Constitution nor federal law prevents a private company from being in the corrections business. In fact, the federal government has numerous contracts for the private incarceration of federal prisoners. Furthermore, exposure to liability would be minimized by the superior, efficient service provided by private firms.

Restructure How the Small Business Administration Conducts Business

The Small Business Administration (SBA) was created in 1953 as an independent agency of the federal government to promote business development and assist small businesses in several areas, including making loans to small and economically disadvantaged businesses and homeowners affected by natural disasters, aiding and supporting women and minority groups, developing managerial skills, marketing, and providing protection through licensing and regulation.

SBA Direct and Guaranteed Loan Programs. The SBA provides both direct loans and loan guarantees to qualified small businesses. Under the loan guarantee program, the federal government guarantees 90 percent of the principal for business loans up to $155,000 and between 70 percent and 85 percent for larger ones. The interest rate on guaranteed loans is about 2.5 percentage points above the prime rate; in addition, the SBA guarantee has a charge equal to 2 percent of the amount guaranteed.

SBA loans and loan guarantees go primarily to businesses that have been rejected by conventional providers of financing. Perhaps as a result, they have a high default rate. It also can be argued that financial markets are now more efficient and less susceptible to the types of market failure that justified the SBA program when it first began. Reduction or elimination of SBA loans would result in administrative savings. The Task Force, therefore, proposes to end all SBA direct and guaranteed loan programs.

Servicing Fee on SBA Assistance. The Task Force proposal would impose a $15-per-hour fee on individuals obtaining assistance from Small Business Development Centers (SBDCs). Rather than pay for consulting, business owners often will go to the SBDC where they can obtain specialized assistance at no charge. Charging a low fee would still give business owners the help they need at a substantially reduced rate from what private consultants would charge. Such a service fee is a user fee in the classic sense: It is a collection for a voluntary, business-like transaction.

Administrative Expenses of SBA Loans. The Task Force provision ends the administrative expenses of SBA loans by transferring to the applicants the costs associated with administering the loans.

Proposed SBA Fees. The Task Force provision establishes four users' fees to help the SBA service its customers: SBDC fee, publication fee, servicing fee, and SBA on-line fee.

Restructuring Outdated Programs

Many government programs were created to address specific needs at specific times. Today, many of the needs have been met, but the programs continue to gobble up taxpayers' money. In our attempt to balance the budget, the Task Force has identified such programs for restructuring.

Clean Coal Technology Program. The Clean Coal Technology Program (CCTP) was created in 1986 to help private industry develop commercial technologies that would use coal in environmentally sound ways. The technologies developed are intended primarily to reduce the emissions of sulfur dioxide and nitrogen oxides from normal coal combustion.

Federal support for new clean coal technologies may no longer be necessary. Since the passage of the Clean Air Act amendments of 1990, the private sector has faced a clear legislative mandate for lowering coal emissions. The private sector is fully capable of sponsoring commercial research on combustion and pollution abatement equipment and, if granted more flexibility under clean air regulations, would have strong incentives to do so. The Department of Energy's efforts also may be redundant in light of independent research efforts by utilities and by states that produce high-sulfur coal and want to maintain the product's sales. The Task Force proposal eliminates future funding for the Clean Coal Technology program.

Mining Royalty. Currently, the government receives no financial compensation for hard-rock minerals extracted from federal lands. The General Mining Law of 1872 governs access to hard-rock minerals — gold, silver, uranium, copper, molybdenum, and most other metals — within the boundaries of public lands. In 1990, hard-rock minerals worth at least $1.2 billion were extracted from federal lands, while known, economically recoverable reserves of hard-rock minerals remaining on federal lands were valued at $64.9 billion.

The Congressional Budget Office (CBO) estimates that an 8 percent royalty would yield additional receipts to the federal treasury of $70 million a year, beginning in FY 1996. The Task Force would impose mining royalties by charging a price for the use of federal lands and their resources.

Public Telecommunications Facilities Program. More than $500 million has been spent by the Department of Commerce on grants to bring public radio and television to remote areas. More than 95 percent of Americans now receive public broadcasting, fulfilling the goal of this program created in the early 1960s.[3] The program has strayed from its original mission and is now used as an operating subsidy to upgrade existing stations. The Task Force proposal calls for a reduction in the Public Telecommunications Facilities Program.

Energy Technology Development. The Department of Energy and its predecessors have funded technology development projects for several different energy sources since the first oil crisis, in 1973. DOE's track record for developing new technologies is poor. According to the Congressional Budget Office, few successful energy technologies have emerged from these research and development programs. The Task Force proposes that fossil energy R&D be reduced by 25 percent of its baseline levels over five years. Commercial companies already spend considerable funds to develop new technologies. The major new technologies for enhanced oil recovery, for example, have been developed in the private sector.

Energy conservation, magnetic fusion, and solar and renewable energy R&D programs would be reduced to 50 percent of baseline levels, phased in over five years. Concerning nuclear energy R&D, the Task Force proposal reduces funding for Energy Technology Development by terminating the Advanced Neutron Source Program and freezing the remaining funds for nuclear fission R&D in fiscal years 1996 through 1999.

Government Sponsored Enterprise Fees. Government Sponsored Enterprises (GSEs) were originally created to allocate credit to specific sectors of the economy. Most are now privately owned. As a result of their "quasi-governmental" status, these agencies enjoy certain privileges that give them a competitive edge against their purely private counterparts. Financial markets treat their securities more as if they were issued or backed by the Department of the Treasury rather than as issues of private corporations. Charging fees on new securities issued after September 30, 1994, would bring the GSEs' debt and security costs closer to the costs of similar credit to private borrowers. The GSEs affected by the proposal include the Student Loan Marketing Association (Sallie Mae), the Federal National Mortgage Association (Fannie Mae), the Federal Home Loan Mortgage Corporation (Freddie Mac), and the College Construction Loan Insurance Association (Connie Lee).

Individuals in Business	Savings Over 5 Years (in dollars)
Reinvent federal procurement	10,642,000,000
Privatize the Government National Mortgage Association	3,000,000,000
Reduce funding for energy technology development	2,530,000,000
Impose Government Sponsored Enterprise fees	2,354,000,000
End all SBA direct and guaranteed loan programs	1,440,000,000
Modify the Service Contract Act	1,050,000,000
Eliminate the Advanced Technology Program	830,000,000
Sell the Southeastern Power Administration	613,000,000
Sell the Naval Petroleum Reserves	498,000,000
Transfer administrative expenses of SBA earmarks	425,000,000
Privatize the Uranium Enrichment Corporation	357,000,000
Privatize minimum- to medium-security mainstream federal prisons	273,000,000
Impose railroad inspection fees	171,000,000
Impose SBA proposed fees	130,000,000
Cut the Public Telecommunications Facilities Program	85,000,000

Individuals in Business	Savings Over 5 Years (in dollars)
Permit private power cogeneration	61,000,000
Impose a $15/hour servicing fee on SBA assistance	60,000,000
Sell the Alaska Power Administration	57,000,000
Initiate hydropower leasing	54,000,000
Impose mining royalties	45,000,000
Sell the helium processing and storage facility	27,000,000
Establish BATF users' fee	25,000,000
Eliminate funding for the Clean Coal Technology program	19,000,000
Reduce minority business development	8,000,000
Restructuring Programs that Affect Individuals in Business **TOTAL**	**24,754,000,000**
Running Total of Savings	**498,155,000,000**

1 Albert Gore. *National Performance Review.* Washington, DC: U.S. Government Printing Office, September 1993, page 11.

2 Government Accounting Office. *Status of Open Recommendations: Improving Operations of Federal Departments and Agencies.* Washington, DC: U.S. Government Printing Office, January 1991, page 695.

3 House Budget Committee.

CHAPTER 10

Citizens in the Arts
and Culture

A merican history flourishes with remarkable examples of artists, authors, musicians, and entertainers who influenced our way of life and creatively preserved slices of our nation's personality. American painters such as Henrietta Johnston, John Singleton Copley, Thomas Cole, Winslow Homer, Grandma Moses, Thomas Eakins, and Norman Rockwell proved that American society could produce creative figures capable of absorbing the European experience without losing their "Americanism." Henrietta Johnston's execution of some of the earliest pastel portraits carved a niche for American women, while Thomas Cole's detailed landscapes captured the majesty of the wilderness. Their lives on canvas presented the United States to the Western cultural tradition in a totally unprecedented manner.

Likewise, the poetry of Anne Bradstreet, Ralph Waldo Emerson, and Walt Whitman brought the cherished American ideals of freedom, tolerance, patriotism, and spiritual unity to complete poetic expression — an expression that has been read and re-read by families around fireplaces and dinner tables, and by teachers and students in countless classrooms, for decades. Novelists James Fenimore Cooper, Nathaniel Hawthorne, and Herman Melville created detailed and spellbinding accounts that, even today, invite us into adventures in colonial America and on the high seas.

Early American composers wrote timeless hymns and patriotic songs, many of which we still hear in church sanctuaries, school auditoriums, and town parades across the country. American ballads spread the message of freedom and the importance of unity among our troops in both the Revolutionary and Civil wars. Francis Hopkinson, America's first poet-composer, who also designed the American flag and signed the Declaration of Independence, created ballads in the Revolutionary spirit. And Julia Ward Howe's "Battle Hymn of the Republic," which was first published in the February 1862 edition of the *Atlantic Monthly*, swept the country during the Civil War and has been sung in classrooms, churches, and meeting halls ever since.

The United States always found ways to support, promote, and develop the arts and humanities as the nation expressed its beliefs through painting, poetry, and music — long before the federal government began paying for this promotion. Early in our country's history we relied on many European cultural traditions, but over time we created our own. The common threads of democracy and freedom run through our history and culture, from the day the Pilgrims first walked ashore in Massachusetts to the day American astronauts first walked on the moon. The promotion of the arts and humanities is the promotion of our history, values, and principles, all of which have emerged from our experiences as "the American people." When the government subsidizes this promotion, Americans are relieved of their duty to remember, and uphold, what makes America so different from the rest of the world.

In light of recognizing our part as citizens in shaping America's history and facing our burgeoning federal debt, the Balanced Budget Task Force was forced to examine why the federal government subsidizes the arts and humanities. Some members of our Task Force, including me, proposed eliminating funding entirely for the National Endowment for the Arts (NEA), National Endowment for the Humanities (NEH), and Corporation for Public Broadcasting (CPB). Others, however, did not think all funding should be cut. The final proposal reflects, after careful study and healthy debate, a compromise of the Task Force — a deliberative conclusion.

The Task Force chose to hand some of the funding responsibility back to the private sector by reducing the federal government's funding by 50 percent for the NEA, the NEH, the Smithsonian Institution, the National Gallery of Art, and CPB. Many arts and humanities programs benefit higher-income people, so much of the loss in federal funds could be made up through admission fees or private contributions. The real effect of this reduction will depend on how much of the loss can be made up through private contributions and fees. Both the Bush and

Reagan administrations, as well as the Congressional Budget Office (CBO) and various government think tanks, recommended reducing funding for these programs throughout the 1980s and early 1990s.

National Endowment for the Arts. Created in 1965, the National Endowment for the Arts awards grants to individuals, state and regional art agencies, and nonprofit organizations to fund the arts and to increase public understanding and appreciation of them. The Task Force proposes to reduce funding for the NEA by 50 percent over five years. While it may be true that reduced funding may result in fewer NEA activities — that is, proposed exhibits, works, or demonstrations that qualify for a grant from the Director of the NEA — private funding can and should be able to fill the gap. In fact, federal subsidies account for a mere fraction of what is actually spent on the arts. In 1990, American individuals and corporations donated nearly $8 billion to the arts, culture, and the humanities. It is clear the commitment to the arts goes far beyond the NEA — it belongs to the American people.

Recently, the National Endowment for the Arts has come under criticism for some of its so-called "art." I personally have considered some exhibits to be an affront to religion and the moral backbone of our society and believe such displays should not be funded by the federal government. NEA funds should be targeted to only those projects that meet widely held standards and criteria.

National Endowment for the Humanities. The National Endowment for the Humanities, like the NEA, was created in 1965 as part of the Foundation for the Arts and Humanities, an independent agency in the executive department of the federal government. It is charged with funding activities that improve the quality of education and teaching in the humanities, strengthening the scholarly foundation for humanities study and research, and advancing the understanding of the humanities among general audiences.

The NEH receives support through outright federal grants, matching grants, or a combination of both. Eligible applicants for these funds include schools, higher education institutions, libraries, museums, historical organizations, professional associations, other cultural institutions and individuals. The rationale for this spending reform is similar to that detailed above for the National Endowment for the Arts. The Task Force chose to reduce funding for the NEH by 50 percent over five years.

Smithsonian Institution. When James Smithson, a British mineralogist and chemist, died in 1829, he willed his fortune of $500,000 to the United States for the creation of "an establishment for the increase and diffusion of knowledge." Little did he know that more than 150 years later the U.S. government would be spending $125,000,000 each year to carry out his bequest.[1]

The Smithsonian Institution, an independent agency of the U.S.

government, was founded in 1846 by an act of Congress under the terms of Smithson's bequest. To accomplish Smithson's objectives, the institution maintains collections of scientific and artistic interest, sponsors scientific research and exploration, publishes books and periodicals, and provides for the international exchange of publications.

The Smithsonian Institution, as a center for basic scientific research, is responsible for the management, exhibit selection, and program financing for many of our national museums. The Smithsonian, now the largest museum complex in the world, conducts research in the natural and physical sciences and in the history of cultures, technology, and the arts. By acquiring and preserving for reference and study more than 100 million items of scientific, cultural, and historical importance, it maintains public exhibits in a variety of fields. Currently, the Smithsonian operates and maintains fourteen major exhibition buildings, a zoological park and animal conservation and research center, and other research facilities. Associated with the Smithsonian, but operated by a separate board of governors, is the National Gallery of Art. In addition, the libraries of the Smithsonian Institution contain nearly a million volumes that invite researchers in science, natural history, and the humanities.

Over the past few years, critics of the Smithsonian have accused it of using some of its exhibits to placate certain special interests through political correctness. I personally support the veterans who recently criticized the Smithsonian's perspective of the exhibit featuring the "Enola Gay," the World War II bomber that was used in 1945 to drop an atomic bomb on the Japanese city of Hiroshima. I do not believe taxpayers' dollars should be used to fund programs that portray the United States as the "bad guy" in its efforts to bring an end to the war activities of an aggressor nation.

Corporation for Public Broadcasting. The Corporation for Public Broadcasting, established by the Communications Act of 1934, disburses federal aid to 300 radio stations and 170 television stations for program production and acquisition. At one time, the CPB was necessary to supplement limited radio and television with quality programming.

Today, however, with the spread of cable television and the proliferation of educational channels and viewing options, government funding is not appropriate. If there is indeed a market for such programs, above and beyond the cable channels, private money can provide support.

The Balanced Budget Task Force agreed to reduce funding for this program by about 50 percent over five years. Since this program is funded two years in advance of the time in which the funds are actually spent, public television and radio stations should be more than able to prepare and adjust their priorities to account for this reduction in federal funding.

Although, public television is one of the few channels that carries quality programs that people of all ages can enjoy, it will continue to thrive without federal support. Currently the Public Broadcasting Service (PBS) receives only 14 percent to 15 percent of its funding from the federal government and National Public Radio (NPR) receives only 3 percent of that. In other words, in addition to more than $100 million in assets, producers and contractors get nearly $1.5 billion from nonfederal sources and receive only $272 million of that from the government.[2]

Institute of Museum Services. The Institute of Museum Services, an independent, grant-making agency established by Congress in 1976, assists museums, including the Smithsonian, in maintaining, improving, and increasing their services to the public. In 1981, the Institute was established as an independent agency within the National Foundation for the Arts and Humanities. As with the other organizations in the foundation, the institute's director is appointed by the president, with the advice and consent of the Senate, and is authorized to make grants to museums subject to policy directives and priorities set by the Institute of Museum Services.

The Institute of Museum Services awards grants on a competitive basis to support the efforts of museums in conserving our historic, scientific, and cultural heritage; to maintain and expand their educational role; and to ease the financial burden borne by museums as a result of their increasing use by the public. Given the increase in charitable contributions over the last decade (nearly $8 billion in 1990), the private sector could easily handle the management, maintenance, and oversight of our nation's museums.

The Balanced Budget Task Force recommends the privatization of the Institute of Museum Services. Under this proposal, the advisory role could be retained without the need for federal financial support.

Citizens in the Arts and Culture	Savings Over 5 Years (in dollars)
Reduce funding for the Corporation for Public Broadcasting	700,000,000
Reduce funding for the Smithsonian Institution	625,000,000
Reduce funding for the National Endowment for the Humanities	493,000,000
Reduce funding for the National Endowment for the Arts	477,000,000

Citizens in the Arts and Culture	Savings Over 5 Years (in dollars)
Limit funding for the National Gallery of Art	185,000,000
Privatize the Institute of Museum Services	145,000,000
Terminate federal funding for the John F. Kennedy Center for the Performing Arts	102,000,000
Restructuring Programs that Affect Citizens in the Arts and Culture TOTAL	2,727,000,000
Running Total of Savings	500,882,000,000

1 House Appropriations Committee.

2 Ibid.

CHAPTER ELEVEN

Conservation, Recreation, and the Environment

The federal government passed its first important pollution control law in 1899, a law that made it a crime to dump any liquid wastes except those from sewers into navigable waters. The law could have been extremely effective in lessening water pollution, but it was almost never enforced. Until the 1960s few other significant federal pollution laws were passed.

Today, the federal government provides Americans with a variety of government programs designed to promote conservation, recreation, and the environment. As our nation attempts to ensure that the provision of these services will continue indefinitely, numerous program reforms are necessary. I believe the government has an important role in promoting conservation and protecting the environment, roles that need to be continued. However, at a time of daunting budget deficits, we need to take measures to slow spending in these areas.

Inland Waterways. According to the Congressional Budget Office (CBO), Congress annually appropriates $560 million for the operation, maintenance, and construction of our nation's system of inland waterways. Almost half of all such construction is funded by revenues from the inland waterway fuel tax. This users' fee is a levy on the fuel consumed by barges using most segments of the inland waterway system.

The Task Force proposes that such users' fees be increased gradually to cover more of the costs associated with the management of the waterway system. Reducing subsidies for water transportation would improve resource allocation by leading shippers to choose the most efficient route rather than the most heavily subsidized one. Furthermore, users' fees would encourage more efficient use of existing waterways, thus reducing the need for new construction to alleviate congestion. Also, CBO believes users' fees would help identify the additional projects likely to provide the greatest net benefits to society.

Conservation Reserve Program. The Conservation Reserve Program (CRP), created by the U.S. Department of Agriculture (USDA) and authorized by the Food Security Act of 1985, pays farmers to remove "highly erodible cropland and other environmentally sensitive land" from production for either ten or fifteen years. The act prevents farmers from overplanting their land and, at the same time, promotes wildlife habitat.

At an annual cost of more than $1.6 billion, the CRP encourages farmers to set aside 35 million acres of land, an area equivalent to the size of Illinois. By 1995, the program hopes to enroll an additional 4.5 million acres, three-quarters the size of New Jersey. Between 1985 and 1995, taxpayers will pay farmers $20 billion to let this land lie fallow.

The USDA already spends nearly $800 million per year to teach farmers erosion prevention methods. Even this seems unnecessary since farmers, as businessmen, have every incentive not to ruin their land through overplanting: If they ruin their land, they destroy a capital resource. Most of the land taken out of production by the CRP is low-quality farmland that, most likely, would not be planted were it not for the many federal government crop subsidy programs that make farming marginal land profitable. Lucrative federal subsidies make it worthwhile to seek short-term profits at the expense of long-term resource management. The CRP functions less as a program for preventing erosion than as yet another program to channel taxpayers' money to farmers. Moreover, the program's destructive effects extend beyond land values. In 1988, the USDA estimated that taking this much farmland out of production would cost 150,000 jobs.[1] In light of all these factors, the Task Force recommends eliminating the Conservation Reserve Program.

Commercial and Recreational Uses of Public Lands. The federal government owns and manages nearly 650 million acres of land in the United States. The land is used in a wide variety of ways, including recreation and water reclamation. For most commercial and some recreational uses, the government is compensated — often by fees. In some cases, those fees may not provide the government with a fair return, and underpricing may lead to overuse. Better pricing could increase federal receipts, alleviate overuse by rationing commercial and recreational activity, and relieve taxpayers of paying for services that benefit only users. The Task Force provision improves pricing for commercial and recreational use of public lands.

Park Service Entrance and Users' Fees. In 1993, the National Park Service of the U.S. Department of the Interior spent an estimated $230 million in services for visitors. Although entrance and users' fees are charged at some sites, the fees generally cover only a small portion of the costs for services provided to visitors. For example, in that same year, the Park Service recovered only an estimated $90 million in fees. In 1991, the Department of the Interior's Inspector General reported that the Park Service did not collect as much as anticipated because the fees collected were not returned to the individual parks. Such handling of fees led to a lack of incentive, which, together with staffing and funding shortfalls, resulted in the Park Service's failure to collect an anticipated $105 million during that fiscal year.[2]

The Balanced Budget Task Force proposes to implement Vice-President Al Gore's *National Performance Review (NPR)* recommendation and support the Interior Department's follow-on report to the *NPR* by reforming the pricing structure of entrance fees at recreational sites to help defray direct costs to the federal government and shift the cost burden from taxpayers to the beneficiaries of the services — those who enjoy the recreational activities.

The government will deposit half of the additional revenues raised, minus the costs associated with actually collecting them, into a new, mandatory National Park Renewal Fund. The other half of the revenue will be returned to the parks to offset the costs of running the parks.

Not only would the added revenue reduce the operating costs of the National Parks System, it would enable individual parks to, in effect, become self-sufficient (at existing funding levels) in their day-to-day operations, providing incentive for managing funds more efficiently. Additional funding for expansion, new facilities, or special projects could be obtained on a case-by-case basis through requests to the National Park Service General Fund.

Arctic National Wildlife Refuge. In 1980 Congress passed the Alaska Lands Bill, which excluded more than 42 million hectares (more than 104 million acres) in the state from commercial development. Many Alaskans opposed what they felt were unjustifiable federal attempts to limit use of the state's resources.

I believe the federal government already owns too much land, especially in the state of Alaska. Many private oil and gas companies have expressed an interest in leasing these lands from the federal government. We believe an equitable agreement could be worked out between interested parties in the private sector and the federal government that promotes industrial production while protecting the natural beauty and innocence of this Alaskan wildlife refuge.

The Task Force proposal authorizes the leasing by the Department of the Interior of 1.5 million acres of the 19-million-acre Arctic National Wildlife Refuge (ANWR) in Alaska. One hundred percent of the receipts would be deposited in the U.S. Treasury. ANWR offers an opportunity potentially to add billions of barrels of oil and trillions of cubic feet of natural gas to the U.S. reserve base. If oil is found in the ANWR, it could increase the gross national product (GNP), reduce the trade deficit and the federal budget deficit, and produce many jobs.

Below-Cost Timber Sales. The Forest Service manages federal timber sales from 119 national forests in the national system. In seven of the nine national forest system regions, annual cash receipts from federal timber sales consistently have failed to cover the Forest Service's annual cash expenditures.[3] Critics charge that these sales contribute to the national deficit, deplete timber resources through uneconomic harvests, destroy road-free forests valued by recreational visitors, and interfere with private timber markets. The Task Force provision eliminates below-cost timber sales, thereby requiring the sale of timber at market rates.

Fuel Tax Subsidy for Ethanol. The oil shortage of the 1970s revitalized an interest in alternative fuels, and the call from the Environmental Protection Agency (EPA) for a complete ban on leaded gasoline in the 1980s fueled another flurry of activity in developing alternatives such as ethanol fuel.

Today, producers of ethanol fuel receive a federal subsidy for developing ethanol. Some of its proponents consider ethanol an environmentally friendly alternative fuel, although some studies estimate that ethanol has nearly 40 percent greater "greenhouse" emissions than gasoline.[4] Although some other alternative fuels receive federal subsidies, none receives as large a subsidy as ethanol. We believe the ethanol sudsidy gives ethanol an unfair advantage over other alternative fuels. The Task Force proposal reduces the current federal fuel tax subsidy for ethanol by 50 percent, bringing it more in line with subsidies provided for other alternative fuels.

Strategic Petroleum Reserves. The Strategic Petroleum Reserves (SPRS) were authorized in 1975 by the Energy Policy and Conservation Act to help the United States survive interruptions in oil imports, such as the oil embargo of the Organization of Petroleum Exporting Countries (OPEC) in 1973-1974. Today, the Department of Energy continues to operate six underground salt-dome storage sites on the Gulf Coast of Louisiana and Texas containing a total of 568.5 million barrels of petroleum.[5]

During the Persian Gulf conflict, the target size of the SPRS increased from 750 million barrels to 1 billion barrels — an expensive overreaction to a short-term problem that the market could rapidly have corrected. The target number of days for oil security is 90. At 750 million barrels, our reserve is targeted to last 100 days; at 1 billion barrels, 135 days. The Task Force proposal halts purchases of oil for the Strategic Petroleum Reserves and eliminates the authority to spend unspent funds for acquisitions.

   Coast Guard Alteration of Bridges. The Clinton Administration urged the elimination of the Coast Guard's share of the costs for altering or removing bridges that obstruct navigation. Under the Task Force proposal, the federal share of Coast Guard projects for the alteration of bridges will be financed from bridge program funds of the Federal Highway Administration.

Conservation, Recreation, and the Environment	Savings Over 5 Years (in dollars)
Impose users' fees for inland waterways	3,130,000,000
Lease 1.5 million acres of the Arctic National Wildlife Refuge for development	2,600,000,000
Reduce the current federal fuel tax subsidy for ethanol by 50 percent	1,690,000,000
Eliminate below-cost timber sales	1,550,000,000
Reduce funding for the National Forest System	1,550,000,000
Improve pricing for commercial and recreational uses of public lands	720,000,000
Reduce funding for resources, conservation, and development	609,000,000
Reduce Agricultural Conservation Program	462,000,000
Capture savings implied in the baseline — National Oceanic and Atmospheric Administration (NOAA) procurement and modernization	445,000,000
Eliminate the Conservation Reserve Program	364,000,000
Collect Park Service entrance and users' fees	324,000,000

Conservation, Recreation, and the Environment	Savings Over 5 Years (in dollars)
Reduce funding for the operation of the National Park System	311,000,000
Halt purchases of oil for the Strategic Petroleum Reserves and eliminate the authority to spend unspent funds for acquisitions	308,000,000
Improve compliance on harbor maintenance	285,000,000
Reduce NOAA construction	244,000,000
Freeze National Park Service construction	225,000,000
NOAA aircraft procurement	181,000,000
Freeze Fish and Wildlife Service construction	154,000,000
Abandon mine reclamation fund	149,000,000
Eliminate Coast Guard alteration of bridges	51,000,000
Impose Environmental Protection Agency/pesticide registration fee	30,000,000
Reduce funding for NOAA sanctuary and aeronautical chart	30,000,000
Impose a National Marine Sanctuary fee	15,000,000
Charge fees to support the costs of maintaining and distributing aeronautical charts	15,000,000
Restructuring Programs that Affect Conservation, Recreation, and the Environment **TOTAL**	**15,442,000,000**
Running total of savings	**516,324,000,000**

1 James Bovard. *The Farm Fiasco*. San Francisco: The Institute for Contemporary Studies Press, 1989, pages 221-224.

2 Congressional Budget Office.

3 Congressional Budget Office, "Reducing the Deficit: Spending and Revenue Options." *A Report to the Senate and House Committees on the Budget.* Washington, DC: U.S. Government Printing Office, February 1995, page 124.

4 House Budget Committee.

5 Thomas W. Lippman. "Filling it to the Billion Barrel Rim," *The Washington Post*, August 5, 1991.

CHAPTER TWELVE

Science, Space, and Technology

For many years the federal government has been involved in the promotion of science, space, and technology, of which the best known enterprises are the space shuttle and the space station.

I strongly believe a priority of the federal government should be to encourage scientific research and technology. However, our limited resources must be directed at those programs that represent the most pressing needs of space and science technology. The federal government must actively participate in those areas where the private sector has been unable to fund adequate research activities. Likewise, the government should not compete with or duplicate research initiatives undertaken by the private sector. The Balanced Budget Task Force proposal sought to strike an equitable balance between these two important responsibilities of the federal government.

Assure Previous Planned Spending Reductions

Under the Congressional Budget process, Congress can actually vote to reduce spending for a program and then roll the future savings into other pots in the budget to spend the available money on other programs. In previous years, Congress voted to cancel the Advanced Solid Rocket Motor (ASRM) and the Superconducting Super Collider (SSC). Together those cancellations have resulted in billions of dollars in savings that should be used to reduce the deficit. The House Budget Committee, in consultation with the Congressional Budget Office (CBO), found that substantial budget savings could be achieved if honest budget procedures were applied to the provisions. The Balanced Budget Task Force concurred with this conclusion and recommended such proposals in our package.

Advanced Solid Rocket Motor. The National Aeronautics and Space Administration (NASA), an independent agency of the federal government, was established by the National Aeronautics and Space Act of 1958 to plan, direct, and conduct all U.S. aeronautical and space activities, except those that are primarily military. The scientific community plans for scientific measurements and observations to be made through use of aeronautical and space vehicles and disseminates information on results. NASA also develops programs of international cooperation in space activities. With the advent of the space shuttle program, NASA became more frequently involved in military activities, although its original intent was to function as a civilian agency. Also, after the 1986 Challenger disaster,[1] when NASA experienced long program delays, the military started expanding its own space-related programs.

After the Challenger disaster, NASA designed the Advanced Solid Rocket Motor as a safer motor that could carry heavier cargoes and attain higher orbits. Over the years, however, the program's projected cost increased significantly. In 1993, Congress voted to cancel that proposal. The Task Force proposal captures savings implied in the baseline as a result of canceling the Advanced Solid Rocket Motor.

Superconducting Super Collider. The Superconducting Super Collider was a fifty-four-mile proton accelerator under construction by the Department of Energy (DOE) to investigate the origin of mass and to test the current theories about the unity of electromagnetism and radioactive decay. As the world's largest physics experiment, the SCC was set to consume 6 percent of all federal basic research spending over the next five years. Many individuals contend this large a share of federal resources is well out of proportion to the likelihood that the SCC will produce usable science or technology.

America's Superconducting Super Collider is quickly becoming America's super boondoggle. Perhaps to avoid Congressional criticism, the Department of Energy consistently has underreported the total cost of the project. DOE's original estimates of construction, equipment, and development costs exceeded $5 billion, with an additional $1 billion in local infrastructure cost donated by the state of Texas. By early 1991, however, DOE revised the estimate to more than $8 billion. The General

Accounting Office (GAO) now projects the total cost to nearly $12 billion in 1990 dollars. Moreover, the SSC project was to have received $1.6 billion in foreign contributions, which DOE says is essential; no money has yet arrived, reports the GAO. Furthermore, a similar project is underway in Europe, and the scientific information could be shared by the world community.

As a result, in 1993 Congress appropriated $640 million to terminate the SSC. James Watkins, then Secretary of Energy, estimated it would cost $278.1 million to terminate the program, although other estimates have been considerably higher. The Task Force proposal, assuming that no additional funds are required for the SSC, captures savings implied in the baseline as a result of completely cutting the Superconducting Super Collider.

Administrative and Research Savings

Streamlining the bureaucracy and personnel costs associated with scientific research can result in significant budgetary savings, as well as a more efficient use of scientific resources and personnel.

General Science and Research Activities. The Department of Energy currently funds a number of programs designed to promote energy research in the areas of high energy physics, nuclear physics, and general science. In previous years this account has undergone both a reduction in funding and a reorganization of personnel.

The goal of the nuclear physics research program is to understand the interactions and structure of atomic nuclei by providing support and experimental equipment to qualified scientists and research groups conducting experiments in nuclear physics accelerator facilities around the world.

The Balanced Budget Task Force provision calls for a freeze on all funding for research in the General Science and Research Activities account on nuclear physics beginning in fiscal year (FY) 1995. The freeze follows a 1994 reduction in the account for nuclear physics proposed by the Clinton Administration.

National Science Foundation and NSF Grant Application Fee. The National Science Foundation (NSF), an independent agency of the federal government, was established by an act of Congress in 1950 ". . . to promote the progress of science; advance the national health, prosperity, and welfare; and secure the national defense." The NSF's divisions include physics, chemistry, materials research, mathematical and computer sciences, astronomical sciences, atmospheric sciences, earth sciences, ocean sciences, behavioral and neural sciences, social and economic sciences, and science education development research. The NSF develops a national science policy, supports basic research and education in the sciences, provides funds to educational institutions, supports supplemental training for science teachers, helps graduate students gain advanced education, encourages the modernization of science curricula, coordinates national research programs, facilitates methods of disseminating scientific information, and supports international science programs.

Over the past few years annual funding for the National Science Foundation has increased dramatically to approximately $3 billion for fiscal year 1995. The Task Force proposal limits the rate of growth of the National Science Foundation by permitting all NSF accounts to grow at a rate of only 1 percent less than inflation.

The NSF receives nearly 70,000 grant applications annually and currently does not charge any processing fee. Such a fee would help cut down on "frivolous" grant applications, but should not discourage the average grantee. (The average grant awarded in 1993 was approximately $164,000.) The Task Force provision imposes a $50 National Science Foundation grant application fee.

High Performance Computing Program. The High Performance Computing Act of 1991 established the multiagency High Performance Computing and Communications (HPCC) program to further the development of technology for supercomputers and high-speed computer networks. A supercomputer is a large, extremely fast and expensive computer used for complex or sophisticated calculations. It can perform the enormous number of calculations required to draw and animate a moving spaceship in a motion picture and can be used for weather forecasting, large-scale scientific modeling, and oil exploration.

The Congressional Budget Office has recommended reducing the program by 25 percent and concentrating the reductions on research and development for supercomputer technology. They suggest, "Focusing any reductions . . . on supercomputer R and D makes sense because the federal government's efforts to promote the commercial use of parallel supercomputer technology are running counter to the direction that the computer field is taking." The Task Force proposal reduces spending for the High Performance Computing Program.

Specific Program Reforms

In addition to examining budget cuts through assuring previous planned spending reductions and streamlining the administration of programs, the Balanced Budget Task Force debated ways to reduce spending in individual programs. With a focus on saving money while ensuring the integrity of those programs that benefit the American people as a whole, we selected several programs for restructuring.

Space Station. The National Aeronautics and Space Administration has been planning the space station "Freedom" for nearly two decades.

The station supposedly will facilitate scientific experiments requiring the zero gravity of space, make possible studies of the biological effects of space flight, and act as a way station for future flights to the moon and Mars. Projected costs for the station have quadrupled from $10 billion to nearly $40 billion.[2]

The station is unlikely to meet NASA's own self-proclaimed goals. A special Presidential Advisory Commission report said, "We do not believe that the space station Freedom . . . can be justified solely on the basis of the (non-biological) science it can perform, much of which can be conducted on Earth or by unmanned robots."[3]

Even where a space station is needed, private suppliers have been anxious to sell station services to other private concerns and to the government. And NASA officials admit that not manning the station for three or four years might work out well since a human presence would be too disruptive for many sensitive experiments.

It is questionable whether experiments in space biology alone can justify the station's $30 billion to $40 billion price tag. It is also questionable whether the station could be completed. Assembly of the station will take at least twenty-seven shuttle flights. Yet a 1990 study, *Access to Space*, by the congressional Office of Technology Assessment, finds that there is a 50 percent chance of losing another shuttle in an accident over the next thirty-four flights. Such a loss, with a replacement cost of $4 billion to $5 billion per shuttle, probably would bring both shuttle and station activities to a permanent halt.

The space station helps only select American businesses while harming the science community by wasting scarce resources and eliminating opportunities for the private sector. Perhaps when our deficits have been eliminated and the debt has been reduced, funding the space station could once again become a spending option. In the meantime, the Task Force proposes to cancel the space station.

National Aerospace Plane. During the 1980s, DOD embarked on a joint effort with NASA to design and build a hypersonic aircraft — the National Aerospace Plane (NASP) — to deliver payloads into orbit from conventional runways. Since then, however, NASP has experienced technical difficulties, management changes, and severe cost escalation. This program will cost three times its original estimate of $3.1 billion, and the launch date will be at least three years later than planned.

None of the government entities involved seems strongly committed to the program: DOD has not budgeted for NASP in its future year's defense program, and a NASA advisory committee concluded it did not merit high-schedule urgency. In addition, DOD could accomplish most of the missions intended for NASP with the space shuttle and Titan IV rockets. Consequently, the Task Force proposes to cancel the National Aerospace Plane.

President's NASA Proposal. The Clinton Administration proposed to restructure the budget accounts for those programs administered by the National Aeronautics and Space Administration. Such restructuring will allow the budget for NASA to reflect its programs more accurately while saving the federal government money through lower administrative costs. Because the Task Force also proposed to reduce funding for or to restructure other programs within NASA, we accepted only half of the president's NASA reforms, thereby preventing any overlapping of program reforms.

Science, Space, and Technology	Savings Over 5 Years (in dollars)
Cancel the space station	10,400,000,000
Capture savings implied in the baseline — complete cut of the Superconducting Super Collider (SSC)	3,762,000,000
Accept 50 percent of president's NASA cut	2,269,000,000
Reduce spending for the High-Performance Computing Program	1,226,000,000
Eliminate the Atomic Vapor Isotope Separation Program	500,000,000
Capture savings implied in the baseline — cancel the Advanced Solid Rocket Motor	496,000,000
Freeze the General Science and Research Activities account	324,000,000
Limit the rate of growth of the National Science Foundation	321,000,000
Cancel the National Aerospace Plane	200,000,000
Impose a $50 National Science Foundation grant application fee	19,000,000

Science, Space, and Technology

Science, Space, and Technology	Savings Over 5 Years (in dollars)
Restructuring ograms that Affect Science, Space, and Technology TOTAL	19,517,000,000
Running Total of Savings	535,841,000,000

1 The U.S. space shuttle Challenger exploded and was destroyed 73 seconds after lift-off from the Kennedy Space Center on January 28, 1986.

2 Congressional Budget Office.

3 *Report of the Advisory Committee on the Future of the Space Program.* Washington, DC: U.S. Government Printing Office, December 1990.

CHAPTER THIRTEEN

States and Communities

E very community, no matter how large or small, must invest in its
infrastructure, business, and environmental well-being. I believe
this investment should be locally funded from the public and private sectors. Infrastructure spending may include funding the construction and repair of bridges, roads, airports, utilities, water treatment plants,
service areas, and parks, as well as the provision of emergency services,
education, and, in some parts of the country, social services. Over the
past few decades, the federal government increasingly has become a larger
source of funding for infrastructure investments. As we continue to move
toward the renewal of federalism, the federal government can take substantive measures to save taxpayer dollars while transferring more power
and authority to the local level.

The principle of federalism established a well-designed governing
partnership between states, localities, and the federal government.
Through a wide variety of programs in the Department of Commerce,
the federal government attempts to help state and local governments
and businesses meet the demands in trade, development, and commerce
that confront them. Initially, the Department of Commerce was created
to help the federal government regulate interstate commerce. Today, the
Department of Commerce consists of more than 36,000 employees who
are engaged in a much broader array of activities. Many commerce

programs have become vehicles for special-interest porkbarrel spending, have hindered local economic growth, and have discouraged long-term investment in communities. Fundamental reform to delivering and funding these assistance programs will go a long way to stimulating local markets, reducing government regulations, and promoting business development.

The federal government also has responded to states and communities in the area of the environment. As the congressional representative of the Adirondack State Park and Hudson River Valley in upstate New York, I have a keen interest in government programs that affect the environment, yet I believe our nation must adopt an environmental policy that strikes an appropriate balance between technological development and environmental protection. No American wants to see industrial production run rough-shod over the environment. However, economic growth through manufacturing expansion and technological development should not be smothered by overregulation.

Over the past two decades especially, the business sector has been buried by state and federal environmental regulations, stifling the potential for strong, long-term economic growth in many areas of the country. Overly restrictive environmental regulations have forced many manufacturing businesses into the position of choosing between hiring more people or throwing dollar after dollar into projects to comply with environmental regulations. In my state of New York, entire families have lost their jobs as a greater share of industry profits has been consumed by higher taxes and more regulation, resulting in industry cutbacks and closings. While the initial justification for these regulations may have made sense, imposing a one-size-fits-all mandate on industry has resulted in killing the entrepreneurial spirit that built this country.

In recent years, even local municipalities have felt the over-reaching of these mandates. In many areas, local governments have been forced to raise taxes and cut local services so they can dedicate limited fiscal resources to compliance programs. Some areas with especially heavy regulations have pushed individuals and companies right out of the state or county. If the business "environment" is not balanced with a realistic environmental policy, we will see an increase in unemployment, government social-service spending, and poverty, together with a decrease in economic growth, job creation, and the standard of living. Those programs that duplicate or overregulate industry should be scaled back or eliminated.

The Balanced Budget Task Force examined closely the issues of infrastructure, business, and environment in the relationship between the federal government and state and local governments. Our proposals, summarized here, align us more closely with the federal government mapped out by our forefathers.

Highway Demonstration Grants. The 1992 Intermodal Surface

Transportation Efficiency Act (ISTEA) included more than $5 billion in demonstration projects. (Demonstration projects usually are narrow in scope, have only local impact, and often are earmarked by Congress in an appropriation bill.) Nearly 4 million miles of public roads and approximately 577,000 bridges make up the country's interstate system and key feeder and collector routes. According to the House Appropriations Committee, the federal government provides grants to states to help finance the construction and preservation of about 920,000 miles (24 percent) of these roads. The Federal-Aid Highways Program provides funds to states in a variety of ways, one of which is demonstration projects.

According to the Congressional Budget Office (CBO), a survey of demonstration projects authorized in the 1987 Surface Transportation Bill found that about half of those projects did not appear in state transportation plans. Furthermore, more than 10 percent of the projects would not have qualified for funding under the usual highway grant programs. Consequently, the survey concluded that funding for demonstration projects often encourages construction that neither state transportation officials nor the broader federal highway program would classify as priorities.

For example, the fiscal year (FY) 1995 Transportation Appropriations Bill contained $352 million in the account for highway demonstration projects. Of the $352 million, 47 percent of the funding was for West Virginia. And of the $165 million received by that state, $140 million was for one project. Taxpayers in 49 states should not be paying for one other state's local highway improvements. The Task Force provision eliminates highway demonstration grants.

Highway and Mass Transit Grants. Each year the federal government spends about $3 billion in grants to fund capital projects for mass transit, mostly in urban areas. However, only 6.5 percent of journeys to and from work are made by mass transit.[1] Reducing the federal share of capital costs for mass transit might improve local investment choices, as a similar reduction seems to have done with federal subsidies for construction of local wastewater treatment plants. Further, transit agencies serve mainly downtown areas, whereas most of the growth in urban travel has been in the suburbs. By consolidating highway and mass transit grants, federal aid could be reduced responsibly without jeopardizing existing services, yet resulting in significant deficit savings. The Task Force proposal consolidates highway and mass transit grants into one grant with a lower level of funding, which reduces federal aid for mass transit.

Airport Grants-in-Aid. Each year, the Federal Aviation Administration (FAA) provides airports with grants for expanding capacity and improving terminals. Recent trends in aviation have increased the importance of larger airports (as measured by the number of embarking passengers). Such airports would have little trouble financing capital improvements from the fees collected or additional bonds issued if the airport grants were eliminated.

In 1991, Congress passed legislation allowing airports to levy passenger facility charges of up to $3 per passenger to supplement revenues received from concessionaire rents, landing fees, and airline lease payments. In addition, revenues from the passenger facility charges, unlike federal grants, can be used to pay the interest on bonds issued by the airport. In light of the ability of airports to generate funds, this Task Force proposal calls for reducing airport grants-in-aid by 25 percent and for funding capital improvements through collected fees and bonds.

Airport Takeoff and Landing Slots. The FAA has established capacity controls at four airports: Kennedy International and La Guardia in New York, O'Hare International in Chicago, and Washington National in the District of Columbia. The Task Force proposal establishes permanent charges for airport takeoff and landing slots at those four airports. The airports could generate receipts by auctioning the slots among the commercial airlines that use the airports.

Since the slots reflect the right to use scarce public airspace, airports, and air traffic control capacity, the Task Force believes that private firms and individuals should not receive all the benefits of this scarcity but should share it with the public owners of these rights. Further, the charges would serve as incentives to put these scarce resources to their best use.

Essential Air Services Subsidy. The Essential Air Services program subsidizes air service for 125 small communities, thirty-three of which are in Alaska. Because rural communities are adequately served for reasonable prices by private carriers, they no longer need such a service. In many cases, service has improved since deregulation of the industry, and in many communities, the per-passenger subsidy is as high as $500. In addition, the government subsidizes alternative air service as a means of transferring air traffic from larger airports to smaller ones to avoid congestion during peak travel times. For example, the federal government pays National Capital Airways, a commuter airline and jet express, a total of $792,000 per year to fly travelers to the Homestead, a luxury resort in Hot Springs, Virginia.[2] The Task Force provision eliminates the Essential Air Services subsidy.

Rural Electrification Administration. Created in 1935 when only 10 percent of rural America had electricity, the Rural Electrification Administration (REA), an agency within the Department of Agriculture, provides financial assistance to electric and telephone utilities that serve rural areas. With 99 percent of farmers having electricity and 98 percent having phones, it is time for the REA to go.

While the REA has largely fulfilled its original goal, many borrowers continue to rely on federal loans to maintain and expand facilities, and many believe the subsidies continue to keep their services and utility rates competitive with urban areas. They argue that without these subsidies rural facilities may have to raise their utility rates, although many rural utilities already have obtained private financing for capital improvements. Furthermore, while rural utility rates may increase slightly during the transition from public control to market control, those rates will level out at a rate that is equitable for both providers and consumers.

The Task Force provision eliminates the Rural Electrification Administration by phasing out the direct loan program by 1995, phasing out all REA loan activity within five years to nonrural areas, raising interest rates on federally guaranteed REA loans from 5 percent to the Treasury Bill rate (if it is higher), and selling REA loans to private investors.

Hydroelectric Power Sold by Power Marketing Administrations. The Department of Energy (DOE) is America's largest seller of electricity. It manages five Power Marketing Administrations (PMAs), operated by the Bureau of Reclamation and the Army Corps of Engineers, and which sell at a wholesale rate 6 percent to 8 percent of all of America's electric power.

As federally owned businesses, the PMAs are required to charge the lowest possible rates consistent with "sound business principles," which means they should recover their operating and capital costs through power sales. In fact, the PMAs require subsidies from the federal treasury, primarily through low-interest loans. The Task Force provision would require charging market prices for hydroelectric power sold by Power Management Authorities. Such a charge would cover the government's true cost of delivering electric power by raising the level and schedule of the PMAs' debt repayments to the federal government. This proposal also would eliminate the requirement to offer PMA power first to preferred customers and would allow the PMAs to sell to the highest bidder.

Hetch Hetchy Power Facility in Yosemite National Park. The 1913 Raker Act authorized the City of San Francisco to build water and power facilities within the boundary of Yosemite National Park. Over the past 10 years, the city has realized profits of $275 million from the sale of water and power from these facilities while paying the government the required $30,000 annual fee. To keep utility rates down, the Raker Act requires the City of San Francisco to establish municipal utilities to distribute water and power directly to city residents without realizing a profit. Because the city has failed to comply with the directives of the Act, the Task Force proposes to assume government control of the Hetch Hetchy Power Facility in Yosemite National Park.

Tennessee Valley Authority. Although the Tennessee Valley Authority (TVA) was established in 1933 to generate electric power for the Tennessee Valley region, the TVA also engages in many nonenergy-related activities such as managing locks, dams, and recreational facilities in the region; funding the National Fertilizer Development Center in Muscle Shoals, Alabama; and funding economic development projects. These activities clearly are beyond the original purpose of the TVA and should not be federally supported. In addition, they duplicate the services of numerous other economic development and resource management agencies. The Task Force provision reduces fertilizer and environmental funds from the Tennessee Valley Authority.

Waste Infrastructure and State Revolving Funds. According to the Congressional Budget Office, federal support for the construction of local facilities for wastewater treatment is projected to continue at the 1994 level of $2.5 billion. This program was intended to be temporary but may have replaced, rather than supplemented, state and local funding. This Balanced Budget Task Force proposal calls for eliminating new federal grants for waste infrastructure and revolving funds after 1994.

Rural Development Association Direct Loans and Grants. Rural Development Association (RDA) programs assist rural development through programs that provide loans, loan guarantees, and grants for rural water and waste disposal projects, community facilities, rural development, and fire protection. Federal funds should be targeted toward activities whose benefits are national in scope, and state and local governments should fund rural development. Moreover, research shows that the two largest programs — water and waste disposal and business and industry programs — are not well targeted toward low-income or distressed communities.[3] The Task Force proposes to eliminate the Rural Development Association direct loans.

National Institute of Justice. The National Institute of Justice was created in 1984, under the Justice Assistance Act as an agency of the Office of Justice Programs to restructure the criminal justice research and statistics units of the Department of Justice. Its aim is to improve the efficiency of state courts by funding demonstration projects and research on crime, criminal behavior, and crime prevention, as well as distributing information about effective ways to administer justice. Because the Institute has no clear federal purpose and since termination would have little impact on services, the Task Force agreed with the Clinton Administration in calling for the elimination of the National Institute of Justice.

Corporation for National Service. Under current law and through the Corporation for National Service, the government provides qualified students with education stipends. The students, in exchange, agree to serve as volunteers in a variety of community-oriented capacities. Paying Americans to "volunteer" in a government program will not reinvigorate nongovernmental institutions. Volunteerism in America is booming; National Service's 20,000 paid "volunteers" hardly make a difference. Furthermore, AmeriCorps, a subdivision of the National Service Program, has provided funding for some questionable activities. Although the program's motto is "Getting things done," so-called volunteers spend one-fifth of their time in "training, education, and non-direct service activities." Such activities run from self-esteem classes to GED training.

The Corporation for National Service duplicates most private volunteer efforts and places an official government benefit on some forms of service and not others. The Task Force, which supports the spirit of true volunteerism and is aware of the country's reliance on an all-voluntary military, proposes to abolish the Corporation for National Service.

Health Care Block Grants. The federal government provides funds to states through block grants for programs to pay for preventive care, prenatal care, rehabilitation services for blind and disabled children, immunization, hypertension control, dental health, and other social programs. Funded through the Public Health Service, block grants allow states considerable flexibility in choosing the programs to fund within the specified areas. Generally, the grants do not restrict eligibility to a particular group of recipients, such as low-income Americans, and so the funds are available to citizens of all income groups.

The Balanced Budget Task Force proposes to consolidate block grants for substance abuse, mental health, preventive services, and maternal and child health. By cutting 5 percent in 1995 and 1996 and freezing spending at 1996 levels for subsequent years, the Congressional Budget Office estimates the federal government will save almost $2 billion over five years.[4] Other federal programs, such as Medicaid, which ensure access to health services, would more than compensate for a proposed 5 percent reduction in funding of these programs. For example, funding for Medicaid's coverage of low-income women and young children has been expanded in various ways. States are now required to provide Medicaid coverage to pregnant women and to children under age 6 in families with incomes below $19,000. Thus, block grants will not be essential for ensuring access to health services for those individuals.

Social Service Programs. Social service programs are provided to many individuals and families through an array of programs, each with its own rules and regulations. Those programs may be administered at both the federal and state levels by separate agencies, even though they serve the same or a very similar clientele. In recent years, the number of separate programs has grown, particularly in child care, which has seen five new programs enacted since 1988.

If social service programs are consolidated into one or more block grants for a certain group of recipients (for example, families with children or the elderly), localities could provide social services more efficiently. Because rules and regulations would be simpler with a consolidated program, duplicate services would be eliminated, administrative costs would decline, and savings would be realized through a reduction in administrative personnel. States and localities would have more freedom to tailor programs to local needs. Moreover, different services provided to the same individual or family could be coordinated more easily, improving service delivery from the client's perspective.

The Task Force proposes consolidating the following social service programs into one block grant and reducing the funds by 5 percent: social services, community services, child care and development, and dependent care planning and development.

Economic Development Administration. The Economic Development Administration (EDA) was formed under the Public Works and Economic Development Act of 1965 as an agency of the Department of Commerce to provide federal assistance to state and local governments in the form of grants that can be used for public works, technical assistance, defense conversion activities, job programs, and even loan guarantees to firms for business development. Originally created to support economic growth in some of this country's neediest areas, the EDA, through years of bureaucratic growth and political maneuvering, has outgrown its purpose and outlived its usefulness. Over the years, EDA funding has been poured into thousands of politically connected schemes that have invested in shopping centers, hotels, boating marinas, amusement parks, and numerous loans that went bad. The most notorious EDA grant, given in 1985, earned the EDA former Wisconsin Senator William Proxmire's Golden Fleece award for spending $200,000 to build a limestone replica of the Great Wall of China in Bedford, Indiana. That boondoggle followed a $500,000 grant to build a ten-story model of the Great Pyramid of Egypt.[5] Clearly, federal tax dollars can be better used.

According to the Congressional Budget Office, "EDA programs have been criticized for substituting federal credit for private credit and for facilitating the relocation of businesses from one distressed area to another through competition among communities for federal funds. The EDA also has been criticized for its broad eligibility criteria, which allow areas containing 80 percent of the U.S. population to compete for benefits, and for providing aid with little proven effect compared with other programs having similar goals."[6] Because of the competitive nature of EDA programs, local governments do not incorporate this type of aid into their budget plans. Therefore, eliminating future EDA funding, effective immediately, would not impose unexpected hardships on communities.

While the EDA once funded on a "greatest need" basis, today the decisions have become highly politicized with need apparently no longer the priority. The Task Force agrees with the Reagan and Bush administrations, the Congressional Budget Office, and the General Accounting Office and proposes to eliminate the EDA.

Appalachian Regional Commission. The federal government appropriates almost $200 million annually for the Appalachian Regional Commission (ARC) to fund activities that promote economic growth in the Appalachian counties of thirteen states. Critics argue that the programs supported by the ARC duplicate the activities of other agencies, such as the Department of Transportation's federal highways program and the Department of Housing and Urban Development's Community Development Block Grant program. The Task Force provision eliminates the Appalachian Regional Commission.

Community Development Block Grants. The Community Development Block Grant (CDBG) program provides grants to cities, urban counties, and states to support community and economic development. The CDBG program has been criticized for mismanagement, misuse of funds, and failure to target grants toward those truly in need. A recent House of Representatives report cited examples of municipalities unable to show that CDBG business loans had created jobs for low-income people, loans awarded to firms with links to county board members, and use of $1 million in CDBG funds for Broadway show tickets, banquets, gifts, dry cleaning bills, and promotional materials for attracting tourists to the county.[7]

Because federal funds should be targeted toward programs whose benefits are national rather than local, the CDBG, which generate primarily local benefits, should be funded by state and local governments. Moreover, to the extent that local jurisdictions use CDBG funds to help them compete against each other to attract business, benefits are shifted away from local jurisdictions to private firms. The Task Force provision eliminates Community Development Block Grants.

State Bank Examination Fee. The Office of the Comptroller charges examination fees. The Federal Deposit Insurance Corporation does not directly charge state charted banks an examination fee. The Task Force supports the 1994 proposal by the Clinton Administration to charge state bank examination fees to provide parity with federally chartered banks.

Minerals Management Service. The Minerals Management Service was largely established to assist in the sale of Outer Continental Shelf (OCS) leases. Because the amount of activity on this front has greatly diminished over the years and the time has come to roll back this overextensive authorization, the Task Force proposal would sharply downsize the Minerals Management Service. All OCS regional offices would be closed, except New Orleans. The future royalty streams of existing federal offshore leases would be sold, thereby eliminating many problems and unnecessarily large expenses associated with federal collection of the royalties. The mineral development rights for OCS areas with marginal development prospects would be transferred to nearby states. The federal government would retain an overriding royalty on any development of these resources that might occur in later years.

Three State Energy Conservation Grant Programs. Since the late 1970s and early 1980s the Department of Energy has administered three state energy conservation grant programs: Weatherization, State Energy

Management Conservation, and Institutional Conservation. The state grants for Weatherization assist low-income householders in making their homes more weather resistant. The states have reported to the DOE that about 4 million homes have been weatherized since 1977 when the program began. State Energy Management Conservation grants provide funds for state offices and officers for information on energy programs. The Institutional Grant Program helps reduce the use of energy in educational and health-care facilities by adding federal funds to private and local spending to encourage local investment in building improvements. All three of these state grant programs are independent of a related block grant program, the Low Income Energy Assistance Program, administered by the Department of Housing and Urban Development.

All of these grant programs were created to help states deal with a decontrolled oil market and were intended to help states promote conservation and lower consumption of energy. Now that the energy crisis has subsided, the pressing need for these state grants has diminished. The Balanced Budget Task Force reiterates the Reagan Administration's original call to terminate the three state energy conservation grant programs.

Superfund Cleanups. The Environmental Protection Agency (EPA), established in 1970 to protect the environment and maintain it for future generations, manages the Superfund program that was initiated in the early 1980s in response to Congress's passage of the Comprehensive Environmental Response Compensation and Liability Act (CERCLA). The Superfund program enforces regulation of the 1976 Toxic Substances Control Act by providing EPA oversight and financial resources for responding to and cleaning up hazardous substance emergencies and abandoned uncontrolled hazardous waste sites.

Estimates of the size of the nation's hazardous waste problem and of the resources required to resolve it have grown substantially since the Superfund program was established. This proposal calls for changing the mix of methods used to protect health and the environment at Superfund sites. The present statutory preference for permanent treatment technologies would be dropped in favor of an emphasis on institutional controls and containment methods. Preferred institutional controls and containment methods would include such things as caps, slurry walls, and surface water diversion. Less stringent cleanup standards could be chosen when they were consistent with the expected use of the land in the future.

An unpublished EPA analysis estimated that a set of similar changes proposed by the Clinton Administration in 1994 would reduce annual cleanup costs in the Superfund by 19 percent. A University of Tennessee study estimated that a judicious shift toward these measures could reduce remediation costs by 40 percent, without sacrificing health or environmental protection. Such a shift would reduce federal expenditures on enforcement, as well as on direct cleanup, since it would decrease the incentive for private parties to contest their hazardous waste liabilities.[8]

In light of these studies, the Task Force proposes de-emphasizing the permanence in Superfund cleanups. This change would result in fewer federal dollars being poured into often bottomless projects, as well as prevent further spreading of hazardous waste.

National Coastal Zone Management Grants and National Sea Grants College Programs. The Coastal Zone Management Act (CZMA) of 1972, as amended in 1990, was enacted to "preserve, protect . . . and . . . enhance the nation's coastal zone" by making grants to state governments to cover the costs of developing state plans designed to protect coastal resources. Examples of such plans include reducing pollution along America's coasts, preventing beach erosion, and managing fisheries. After completion of the state plan, a different federal program assists in its administration. The National Sea Grants College Program was established in 1966 to develop a network of colleges, universities, and institutional programs throughout the coastal states for research and education on coastal resource development.

The objective of the Coastal Zone Management Grants program has been achieved. Currently, most of the thirty coastal states have federally approved management plans covering 94 percent of the nation's coastline. Similarly, the National Sea Grants College program objective has been accomplished. More than 135 institutions have strengthened their academic and outreach programs, ending the need for expanded research capacity. Congress uses the college program as an indirect source of funds for additional staff. Every year, graduate students are hired for one-year positions using college program funds. These graduate students, however, perform constituent work for members of Congress. The Task Force believes this practice should end and proposes to eliminate the Coastal Zone Management Grants program and the National Sea Grants College programs.

States and Communities	Savings Over 5 Years (in dollars)
Reform health care block grants	81,960,000,000
Eliminate community development block grants	15,650,000,000
Eliminate new federal grants for waste infrastructure and state revolving funds	7,115,000,000

States and Communities	Savings Over 5 Years (in dollars)
Consolidate and reduce highway and mass transit grants	6,880,000,000
Reduce airport grants-in-aid by 25 percent	6,260,000,000
Charge market prices for hydroelectric power sold by PMAs	4,800,000,000
Eliminate highway demonstration grants	2,378,000,000
De-emphasize permanence in Superfund cleanups	1,940,000,000
Eliminate Rural Development Association direct loans and grants	1,930,000,000
Abolish the Corporation for the National Service	1,674,000,000
Establish charges for airport takeoff and landing slots	1,500,000,000
Impose state bank examination fee	1,350,000,000
Reduce NASA support	1,348,000,000
Eliminate funding for the watershed and flood prevention operations	1,245,000,000
Terminate three state energy conservation grant programs	1,143,000,000
Eliminate the Economic Development Administration	1,140,000,000
Consolidate social service programs and reduce by 5 percent	1,120,000,000

States and Communities	Savings Over 5 Years (in dollars)
Phase out the ACTION Agency as a federal program	1,115,000,000
Eliminate the Appalachian Regional Commission	780,000,000
Downsize the Minerals Management Service	465,000,000
Reduce Disaster Loan Program account	461,000,000
Eliminate National Coastal Zone Management Grants and the National Sea Grants College Program	413,000,000
Terminate the Bureau of Justice Assistance	412,000,000
Reduce flood control/coastal emergencies	327,000,000
Restructure community services block grants	309,000,000
Cut the Boat Safety Program	307,000,000
Reduce state and private forestry	292,000,000
Eliminate the Rural Electrification Administration	260,000,000
Flood control/Mississippi River and tributaries	226,000,000
Eliminate the Essential Air Services subsidy	173,000,000
Reduce fertilizer and environmental funds from the TVA	152,000,000
Assume government control of the Hetch Hetchy Power Facility	125,000,000
Terminate local freight assistance	77,000,000

States and Communities	Savings Over 5 Years (in dollars)
Terminate the National Institute of Justice	56,000,000
Eliminate Advisory Commission on Intergovernmental Relations	5,000,000
Restructuring Programs that Affect States and Communities TOTAL	**145,388,000,000**
Running Total of Savings	**681,229,000,000**

1 Congressional Budget Office. "Reducing the Deficit: Spending and Revenue Options," *Report to the Senate and House Committees on the Budget*. Washington, DC: U.S. Government Printing Office, February 1995, page 145.

2 "Federal Program Subsidizies Flights to Homestead Resort," *The Washington Post*. November 19, 1991, page A-1.

3 "Reducing the Deficit: Spending and Revenue Options," page 155.

4 Congressional Budget Office.

5 Donald Lambro. "EDA's Way of Serving Pork," *Washington Times*. February 26, 1995.

6 "Reducing the Deficit: Spending and Revenue Options," page 156.

7 The Concord Coalition. *The Zero Deficit Plan*. 1994, page 53.

8 House Budget Committee.

CHAPTER FOURTEEN

The Justice System

The proposed Republican Budget upon which we based our Task Force proposal contained an initiative to fight crime and enhance law enforcement. The Task Force believes in the importance of supplying state and local governments with the necessary resources to fight crime effectively. As a result, we included the Republican Crime Prevention and Law Enforcement Bill in the Task Force proposal, which included the following specific reforms:

Area of Concern	Proposed Reforms in the Justice System
Protection of neighborhoods, families, and children	• $500 million over the next five years in grants to schools for security measures, including additional police patrols, metal detectors, and closed-circuit cameras; for increased penalties for drug trafficking on school grounds and near public housing and for gun possession on school grounds; for making drive-by shootings and gang participation criminal offenses • $2 billion over five years in grants for additional police and improved efforts between police departments and their communities

Area of Concern	Proposed Reforms in the Justice System

- Increased penalties for crimes against children
- $10 million over five years for registering convicted child abusers
- $250,000 additional for training and educational programs on parental child abduction

Equal protection for victims

- Life imprisonment or death as penalties for retaliatory killings of witnesses
- Permission to use evidence from previous similar crimes in sexual assault and child molestation cases
- Prohibition of the use of an appeal to racial prejudice before a jury

Protection of women

- Making it a crime to travel across state lines for the purpose of stalking or committing spousal abuse
- For victims of sexual assault and exploitation, restitution for all necessary expenses, including loss of income, for victim's participation in investigations or proceedings
- Pretrial detention in serious sex offense cases if no other method can be used to prevent flight or harm to others

Prevention of terrorism

- Membership in a terrorist organization established as reason for denying entrance into the United States
- Establishment of a National Task Force on counterterrorism to monitor and react to terrorism
- Extension of the statute of limitations and increase of penalties for terrorist acts

Criminal aliens and smuggling

- $1.137 billion over five years for an additional 3,000 border patrol agents and 1,000 Immigration and Naturalization Service (INS) investigators to prevent illegal aliens and alien smuggling

Area of Concern	Proposed Reforms in the Justice System
	• Requirement for aliens on criminal probation or parole to register with the INS
Taking criminals off the streets	• $3 billion over three years for federal-state cost-sharing partnerships for new prisons • Making funding contingent on states' following an 85 percent truth-in-sentencing policy, mandatory minimum sentences of 10 years for serious felonies, pretrial detention, and challenges to court decrees limiting prison populations
Punishment and deterrence	• $21 million for establishing an instant background check for the purchase of handguns • Required life imprisonment for a federal violent felony committed by an individual with two previous violent felony convictions • Imposed mandatory minimum prison sentence of five years for possession of a firearm by an individual with a previous conviction of a violent felony or serious drug offense
Elimination of delays in carrying out sentences	• One-year limitation for filing habeas corpus petitions after a conviction in state court • Two-year limitation for filing for collateral relief by federal prisoners
Public corruption	• Establishment of fraud in local, state, and federal governments as an offense deserving punishment • Stiffening of penalties for offering bribes to public or nonpublic officials in dealing with any controlled substance

In addition to increasing funding for certain programs related to fighting crime, the Task Force also proposed reducing spending or reforming certain other programs within the departments of Justice and Treasury. Our justice system requires that our limited fiscal resources be targeted to programs that have produced real results and that have succeeded in producing a better society.

U.S. Marshall Service. The Task Force provision reforms the U.S. Marshall Service by eliminating the political appointment process and instead promoting professionally trained deputies to be U.S. Marshalls. This would reduce the service by seventy positions. This concept has been discussed since the Truman Administration and was proposed in Vice-President Al Gore's *National Performance Review.*

Public Safety Officers Benefit. The Victims of Crime Act of 1984 established a special fund in the Treasury, "The Crime Victims Fund." This fund is credited with criminal fines that are collected from people convicted of offenses against the United States. Annual grants are made to eligible crime victims' compensation and assistance programs.

The Task Force proposal funds the Public Safety Officers Benefit through the Crime Victims Fund. It places the provision of the financial benefit to the family of a slain public safety officer under the jurisdiction of this fund. Although this provision is to be a funding priority of the Crime Victims Fund, measures would be taken to ensure that existing programs funded through this fund are not unduly burdened by this new task.

Legal Services Corporation. The Legal Services Corporation (LSC) pays grants to state and local programs to provide legal assistance to the poor in civil matters. About 300 state and local agencies receive LSC grants annually. In addition to federal money, the LSC is funded through private sources and interest on escrow accounts. What began as a program to assist certain underprivileged areas now reaches the entire United States.

Local legal aid programs would be better supported by social services block grants that let localities tailor the programs to their needs. The sixteen national support centers spend much of their time engaging in political activities rather than extending legal services to the poor. Moreover, too often LSC lawyers focus on advancing social causes rather than assisting with people's true legal problems, which in any case should be the responsibility of localities.

Since its inception in 1974, the LSC has been the subject of controversy, including matters of stealing and embezzling tax dollars.[1] But supporters of the LSC believe that oversight and definition of permitted activities would curtail activities that some find objectionable. The Task Force agrees with the Reagan Administration and proposes to eliminate the Legal Services Corporation.

Civil Judgments. The Task Force proposal places an enforceable 15 percent surcharge on judgments for civil debt collected by the Justice Department. For example, if the Justice Department were called upon to enforce payment of child support in a particular case, the person owing the money would be charged an additional 15 percent to cover the cost to the department for that activity. This proposal also was recommended by the Clinton Administration.

FBI Fingerprint Laboratory in West Virginia. Funding for hiring an additional 500 new employees for the FBI fingerprint laboratory in West Virginia was appropriated through the Emergency Supplemental Appropriation Bill. This project is unrelated to the 1994 Los Angeles earthquake, for which the bill was created, is not authorized by law, and is not an emergency. Any funding for this project should be allocated through the regular budget process and be subject to proper authorization. The Task Force provision rescinds appropriations for the FBI fingerprint laboratory in West Virginia.

The War on Drugs. The federal government currently spends $13 billion a year in the war on drugs. I have long believed that the use, supply, and distribution of drugs must be drastically curtailed and reduced and that the federal government has an important role in this crackdown. However, I also believe that the federal government could coordinate its efforts more effectively to maximize the effect of the programs while minimizing costs. The Task Force adopted several proposals that reduce funding for some drug-related programs, such as the Byrne antidrug grants and P-3 drug interdiction, and consolidate funding for other programs, such as Organized Crime Drug Enforcement.

The Justice System	Savings Over 5 Years (in dollars)
Eliminate the Legal Services Corporation	2,113,000,000
Terminate Byrne antidrug grants	1,912,000,000
Consolidate Organized Crime Drug Enforcement	357,000,000
Improve compliance of harbor maintenance	285,000,000
Fund the Public Safety Officers Benefit through the Crime Victims Fund	174,000,000
Reduce Legal Services Corporation	163,000,000
Reduce deposits into the Department of Treasury forfeiture fund	159,000,000
Reduce P-3 drug interdiction	147,000,000

The Justice System	Savings Over 5 Years (in dollars)
Place a surcharge on civil judgments	145,000,000
Freeze certain judges' pay	113,000,000
Reduce air and marine drug interdiction procurement	95,000,000
Reform the U.S. Marshall Service	25,000,000
Rescind appropriations for FBI fingerprint laboratory in West Virginia	20,000,000
Eliminate the Administrative Conference of the United States	10,000,000
Increase funding for Crime Prevention and Law Enforcement activities	(7,398,000,000)
Restructuring Programs that Affect the Justice System **TOTAL**	**(1,680,000,000)**
Running Total of Savings	**679,549,000,000**

1 Congressional Budget Office. "Reducing the Deficit: Spending and Revenue Options," *Report to the Senate and House Committees on the Budget.* Washington, DC: U.S. Government Printing Office, February 1995, page 203.

CHAPER FIFTEEN

The Federal Government

B alancing the budget for the long haul will require a substantial restructuring of the federal government. Only by reshaping the infrastructure of the government at the federal level can we even attempt to roll back its expansion. The American people need to see dramatic systemic change to believe that business as usual is over in Washington.

Such change will become apparent as the government alters how it collects, spends, and saves money and how it uses resources through restructuring, reorganizing, and closing agencies in the government. The American people will become believers when they see the Congress cut back funds for doing business in the Legislative and executive branches of the federal government.

Changing How the Federal Government Deals with Money

When it comes to handling money, we in the federal government need to see ourselves as a business that carefully decides how to collect, spend, and save money. We need to examine how to reduce the amount of money we accrue in interest payments. We need to be more efficient in collecting money that is owed to us for services. We need to look at

overhead, salaries and expenses, and outdated resources. We need to become the kind of organization that handles itself so well that our investors — the American taxpayers — trust us with great sums of money
that we will turn into profits such as a healthy economy, a safe and secure country, and a satisfied population.

*Interest Payments Saved Due to Spending Reductions — Net
Interest.* Reducing the amount of projected government spending results in a decrease in the amount of projected spending for interest on
the debt. Consequently, the Balanced Budget Task Force proposal ensures
that all interest savings derived as a result of the spending reductions
contained in this package are dedicated to reducing the deficit.

Federal Employees' Parking. The federal government leases and owns
more than 200,000 parking spaces, which it allocates to its employees
— in most cases, without charge. Requiring employees of the federal government to pay commercial rates for their parking could reduce the deficit. Therefore, the Task Force proposes to charge federal employees for
parking.

Operating Subsidy for Amtrak. Discussion in the Task Force meetings regarding the operating subsidy for Amtrak drew hot debate. Some
members felt strongly that the government should not be "workin' on
the railroad." Others argued that government involvement was essential to the provision of passenger rail service for certain rural areas of the
country. After all opinions were on the table, the Task Force agreed on a
compromise.

When Congress established Amtrak in 1970, it expected to provide
subsidies for only a limited time, until Amtrak could become self-sup-
porting. In the early 1980s Amtrak's federal funding was substantially
reduced; it then raised fares and reduced costs. Amtrak technically is not
a federal agency, but the Department of Transportation owns almost all
Amtrak stock and the federal government appoints all Amtrak directors.
The federal government should not subsidize passenger rail service, particularly trips of well-paid travelers and vacationers. Passenger rail service should compete on a level playing field with other modes of
transportation — without the advantage of federal subsidies. Because the
federal government should not be running a railroad in times of $4
trillion debts and hundreds of billions in yearly deficits, the Task Force
proposes reducing the operating subsidy for Amtrak.

Overhead for All Departments. The federal government could reduce expenditures by about 7.5 percent for various overhead activities
such as printing and reproduction, travel, and shipping, an amount that
would not impair the essential functions of the agencies.[1] The Task Force
proposes to reduce overhead for all federal departments and agencies.
Under this proposal, cabinet secretaries and agency heads would retain
discretion to distribute the required savings as they saw fit.

Salaries and Expenses. Almost every department, agency, and program listed as a line item in the federal budget contains an account labeled "salaries and expenses." This is the revenue source for salaries of employees, business travel, promotional activities, and a variety of other nonspecific expenses of a particular agency. These accounts have been "padded" over the years and often have been used to fund "extra" agency activities. The Task Force provision reduces the salaries and expenses line item for most departments, agencies, and programs. Because salaries and expenses is a nonfixed cost, most agencies should easily be able to withstand a reduction in funding for that line item without requiring a reduction in services. Restraining the funds available for operating government agencies should be seen as a necessary incentive toward innovations that lead to more efficient practices.

Government Employee Buyout. The Republican Budget proposal contained an excellent provision calling for a reduction in the general government work force, which the Task Force readily accepted. This budget initiative calls for a general work force reduction in nondefense executive branch agencies of 162,472 over five years. All reductions will occur in civilian agencies only, not in the Department of Defense. These reductions should be readily achievable within the normal attrition rate (roughly 4 percent to 8 percent a year), even after excluding Pentagon personnel and accounting for work force reductions from other agency restructuring proposals in this budget.

SBA Tree Planting Grants. Taxpayers should wonder why the Small Business Administration (SBA) grants millions of tax dollars — as if money grows on trees — for tree planting. In fiscal year 1995 appropriations, the administration questioned the validity of this program and suggested its termination, and the Senate concurred. The House, however, included $16 million for tree planting grants. The final bill, PL 103-317, included $15 million for this program. There are powerful interests who protect this little project, which received $18 million to plant trees in Iowa in the 1994 Earthquake Relief Bill — and the earthquake was in California, not Iowa. The Task Force provision terminates the SBA tree planting grants program.

SBA Earmarks. This Task Force proposal eliminates Small Business Administration earmarks that were not awarded competitively, not authorized, or not part of SBA's overall SBA mission. This proposal was a recommendation by the Clinton Administration's FY 1995 Budget.

Saving Money Through Reorganization and Closure

Government management involves a wide range of areas including personnel, administration, regulations, and loan programs. No matter what activity the federal government is involved in, government officials should strive at all times to achieve the greatest possible efficiency with the public dollars for which they are responsible. This fiscal mandate may require the government either to change its approach in managing an activity or to get out of a particular business altogether. The Task Force recognized this reality when making the following recommendations for reorganization and closure.

Financial Institution Regulators. The Clinton Administration proposed consolidating the four federal financial institution regulators[2] into one super regulator to achieve efficiency and reduce the paperwork burden for federally insured financial institutions. Implementing the administration's proposal would result in substantial direct savings to the federal government. In addition, it is estimated that the financial institutions would gain $1 billion a year in lower compliance costs, and direct savings would be generated because of the consolidation at the federal level. Rather than rebate all resulting government savings to the financial institutions (technically, reduce bank examination fees and deposit insurance premiums), this proposal would dedicate the direct federal government's savings to deficit reduction. The Task Force supports this provision, which also includes credit unions.

Army Corps of Engineers. The face of the Army Corps of Engineers has changed over the years. It is the principal engineering component of the United States Army and dates from June 16, 1775, when the Continental Congress authorized a chief engineer and two assistants for the army to prepare fortifications for the Battle of Bunker Hill. The engineers were permanently organized into a corps in 1802.

The Corps of Engineers carried out strictly military duties until the scarcity of trained civil engineers prompted Congress to pass the General Survey Act in 1824. The act allows army engineers to undertake nonmilitary duties, such as canal, road, and railroad surveys; lighthouse construction; and river and harbor improvement. Over the years, the Corps contributed to the building of the nation and left its mark throughout the country. It planned and built important public buildings in Washington, DC, including the Capitol of the United States, the Lincoln Memorial, the Library of Congress, and the Washington Monument. Its chief engineer and many aides contributed to the construction of the Panama Canal. During World War II, the Corps built the Alaska Highway and was involved in the construction of the nuclear production plants used in the Manhattan Project's work that led to the first atomic bomb.

Today, the Corps of Engineers continues to play an important role in the ongoing process of building a nation. Civil programs focus on development of water resources, including navigation improvements, hydroelectric power, flood control, recreation, and conservation of fish and wildlife. In addition, the Corps is ready to provide emergency assistance during disasters such as floods.

The role of the Corps of Engineers has changed over time, and the Task Force believes its functions can be exercised effectively through a more centralized bureaucracy. Vice-President Al Gore's *National Performance Review* proposed streamlining and reorganizing the Corps of Engineers by reorganizing the headquarters offices, reducing the number of division offices, and restructuring the district functions to increase the efficiency of the Corps. The Task Force proposal accepts the recommendation to reorganize the Army Corps of Engineers.

Air Traffic Control. Air traffic control (ATC) is one of the functions of the Federal Aviation Administration (FAA), an arm of the Department of Transportation (DOT). This function develops and operates ATC and navigation systems for civilian and military aircraft.

The Task Force proposes to create an air traffic control corporation by spinning off the FAA's air traffic control function into a private corporation. Because the ATC function of the FAA includes developing and operating ATC and navigation systems for both civil and military aircraft, the military would contract with the new corporation for this assistance, or those functions might be partially absorbed by the military itself, depending on where the need exists. The corporation would raise capital for control modernization by selling stock to users — airlines and airports — and would charge users' fees to generate operating revenue. Under this proposal, the safety and regulatory functions of the Federal Aviation Administration would remain within the Department of Transportation, although the FAA itself would no longer exist. Currently, the federal government pays for nearly 25 percent of FAA costs, totaling about $12 billion over five years.

The FAA has been "reinvented" more than twenty times in the past decade, and the system is still run on technology that is, in some cases, a half-century old. Privatizing ATC services will allow for real reinvention, as well as substantial capital investment and technological improvements.

Air Traffic Control User Fees. The Federal Aviation Administration manages the air traffic control system that serves commercial air carriers, military planes, and much smaller users such as air taxis and private planes. Its services include air traffic control towers that assist planes in takeoffs and landings, air route traffic control centers that guide planes through the nation's airspace, and flight service stations that assist smaller users. The FAA has more than 17,000 air traffic controllers, as well as sophisticated software, to perform these tasks. The total cost of operating, maintaining, and upgrading the ATC system was about $5.6 billion in 1993.[3]

Currently, one-half of FAA operations is financed through annual appropriations from the general fund, whereas revenues from aviation excise taxes are used for a variety of purposes, such as facilities and equipment, research, engineering and development, and such non-ATC activities as airport improvement. If users paid the marginal costs that ATC incurs on their behalf, the deficit would be reduced by about $7 billion over five years. Users would be charged according to the number of facilities they used on a flight and the marginal costs of their usage at each facility. Levying efficient fees presumably would oblige users to moderate their demands. An additional benefit of efficient fees is that, on the basis of users' response, planners can judge how much new capacity is needed and where it should be located. The Task Force proposal imposes air traffic control users' fees and directly correlates with the proposal to privatize air traffic control into an air traffic control corporation.

Close the Interstate Commerce Commission. The now-obsolete Interstate Commerce Commission (ICC) should be retired. At 105, the ICC is the nation's oldest regulatory commission. It was created in 1887 to oversee federal regulation of the railroad industry, but its jurisdiction now includes trucking, barges, buses, and other surface transportation.

In the past decade — thanks to deregulation — the ICC's role has diminished considerably. Now it primarily processes the paperwork it requires from trucking companies. With trucking deregulation, however, most of this paperwork serves no purpose. Trucking prices and service levels are set by the market, not the ICC.

The ICC's rail regulatory functions should be shifted to the Department of Transportation, while its consumer-protection functions should be handled by the Federal Trade Commission (FTC), which is commissioned to promote free and fair trade competition. Last year, the House of Representatives approved the elimination of the ICC during consideration of the FY 1995 Transportation Appropriation Bill, but a 30 percent reduction in funding for the commission was all that was actually passed by Congress. This Task Force proposal calls for the completion of this reduction, which would result in closing the Interstate Commerce Commission.

Restructure the Department of the Interior

The Department of the Interior is the accumulation of 200 years of public land history. It has been riddled with added extras and outdated programs since its creation. As a result, many of its functions could be more effectively performed by state or local governments or by the private sector. The Task Force believes this department should be restructured to preserve its original intent, while eliminating functions that are no longer necessary or are inefficient.

Federal Land Purchases. Federal land ownership in this country now totals 650 million acres, or 30 percent of the country. According to the House Committee on Resources, by comparison, the government of France owns 7.1 percent of the land in that country and the government of

Germany owns just 2.2 percent of that land. A 1995 General Accounting Office Report found that federal land ownership in the lower forty-eight states has increased by 19 million acres in the last thirty years. This is an area the size of Maine.

Some of the federally owned land, such as the interstate highway rights-of-way, national parks, and military bases clearly serve legitimate purposes. Other land, however, is not used for any purpose of the federal government or is clearly in excess of the government's needs. Nevertheless, the federal government spends nearly $300 million annually acquiring additional land.[4]

Adjusting the federal land base could be accomplished easily through exchanges or acquisition with funds generated through the sale of excess lands. The Balanced Budget Task Force provision imposes a moratorium on federal land purchases, establishes a revolving fund to pay for all land acquisitions, and sets up an agency within the Department of the Interior to manage the acquisition and sale of land for the entire federal government.

Federal Land Management. In the United States, four federal land management agencies — the National Park Service, the Bureau of Land Management, the Fish and Wildlife Service, and the Forest Service — manage 95 percent of the federal land. Lands under federal ownership are not only permanently removed from the tax base, they are increasingly locked up from any economic use. Things must change.

The Task Force proposal would consolidate federal land management functions into a single agency to manage lands of national significance. These lands include most units of the National Park Services, wilderness areas, wild and scenic rivers, Special Management Areas (such as environmentally sensitive areas and special wilderness preserves), and most existing wildlife refuges. This approach will facilitate integrated resource management. Savings are achieved by eliminating duplicate field offices, reducing duplicate programs among the agencies, and eliminating nonessential functions.

Bureau of Mines. The Bureau of Mines (BOM) ensures that the nation has adequate mineral supplies and oversees and evaluates all aspects of minerals research. The Task Force proposal abolishes the Bureau of Mines. Legislation phasing out the Mineral Institutes Program, a relatively small part of the BOM, has already been proposed by the Clinton Administration and has passed a vote by the House of Representatives. Other agencies have taken over many of the bureau's original functions. The Department of Energy, for example, collects data on minerals used for generating energy.

The BOM is limited to gathering information on hard-rock minerals and conducting research on mining techniques. Opponents of this proposal argue that BOM also gathers information about environmental and physical conditions at current and abandoned mining sites. To address these concerns, other agencies will undertake health and safety research that justifies a federal involvement.

Geological Survey. The U.S. Geological Survey was established in 1879 as a bureau within the Department of the Interior as a permanent agency to conduct systematic and scientific classification of public lands. The Task Force proposal abolishes the Geological Survey. The basic research functions, which include water resources investigations, ecosystem research, and geologic and mineral surveys, would be assumed by the National Science Foundation. Mapping would be eliminated, since that can be provided by either private operators or the Department of Defense, when national security is involved. The federal-state cooperative program of water division would be eliminated, since states can purchase water studies from private consultants. The Environmental Protection Agency would assume any necessary role in stream monitoring.

Bureau of Indian Affairs. The Bureau of Indian Affairs (BIA) promotes and provides for the welfare of American Indian reservation communities. It administers government programs to help Native Americans living on federal Indian reservations to use their land productively. It brings industry and jobs to the reservations, helps job-seekers with employment assistance, and provides child- and adult-education programs. Established in 1824 as part of the War Department, it became part of the Department of the Interior in 1849.

Many now believe the federal government should accelerate the trend toward self-determination for Native Americans, as suggested by the Grace Commission.[5] Such a move transfers direct management of tribal communities to the tribes themselves and phases out government financial assistance for management costs. The reinvented BIA will provide block grants (as is already being done under an experimental "self-governance" program), rather than engaging in the direct provision of services or the direct supervision of tribal activities.

The Task Force proposes to consolidate the Bureau of Indian Affairs, thus centralizing more of its bureaucratic anatomy. In addition, federal subsidies will be eliminated from tribes that are economically self-sufficient.

Office of Territorial and International Affairs. The Office of Territorial and International Affairs manages the Trust Territory of the Pacific Islands — 2,100 islands and atolls, including the Marshall, Caroline, and Mariana islands, except Guam, which is a U.S. territory. The trust islands, the only remaining of the eleven trust territories created after World War II by the United Nations, were taken from Japan during the war; Japan had taken them from Germany during World War I. The Department of the Interior is responsible to the United Nations Trusteeship Council for the administration of the islands.

The Task Force proposes to restructure the Office of Territorial and

International Affairs by transferring the administration and termination of the Trust Territory of the Pacific Islands and the implementation of the Compact of Free Association to the Office of Pacific Island Affairs in the Department of State; transferring technical assistance and operations and management assistance to the Department of Commerce; and eliminating the position of Assistant Secretary for Territorial and International Affairs.

Reduce Legislative and Executive Branch Costs and Reform Specific Executive Programs

Throughout this budget blueprint, the American taxpayer has been asked to do more with less. But, if this is truly a plan for all Americans, then *every* American must sacrifice, which means that any realistic and honest plan to restructure the federal government must involve reductions on the front lines of both the legislative and executive branches.

Legislative Branch Appropriations. The legislative branch appropriation last year was approximately $2 billion. The money appropriated funds the operations of Congress itself and legislative agencies, including the Library of Congress, the Government Accounting Office, the Government Printing Office, and the Architect of the Capitol.

Committee and personal staffs are oversized at 17,000, triple the number in 1960. That averages out to about sixty staffers for each Senator and twenty-six for each member of the House. The proliferation of committees, committee staff, and personal staff is excessive. Sacrifice must start with government. Therefore, the Task Force proposes a 25 percent reduction in legislative branch appropriations.

Congressional Frank. The vice-president and members of Congress use the franking privilege to mail official correspondence, public documents, the Congressional Record, and reports. The sender puts his or her name (or its facsimile) on each piece of mail instead of a postage stamp, and Congress appropriates money to pay the U.S. Postal Service directly for the mailing privilege. The 1991 Legislative Appropriation Act established an "Official Mail Allowance" to pay the postage costs of all franked mail in the House of Representatives, although it is almost unlimited in what it can be used for. (The Senate has always decided its own restrictions for its mail allowances.) Each congressional office is allotted a different amount for the mail allowance based on a formula of postal costs, number of households in a district, and the frequency of mailing to those households. The 1994 franking allowance for members of the House was $40 million. The Task Force proposes reducing the congressional frank by 50 percent.

House Members' Pay. This Task Force proposal calls for a five-year freeze at existing levels of pay for the members of both the House and the Senate. The decision for this highly controversial and sensitive issue emerges from the belief that sacrifice to balance the federal budget must be carried out by everyone, including the legislators. Because the benefits of a balanced budget will extend to all, all people must shoulder their share of the costs.

Limit Office Furniture Purchases by Departing Members. Since 1974, federal law has allowed departing members of Congress to buy their office furniture at significant discounts. This situation leads to new members coming in to empty offices and having to buy all new equipment, at substantial cost to the taxpayers. At the end of the 102nd Congress, some ninety-eight departing members bought a total of 3,971 pieces of used office equipment and furniture for roughly $67 per piece. This figure does not include the $13,000 that departing members paid for their own desks and chairs, sold at $100 each.[6] The Task Force provision repeals the first section of Public Law 93-462, thus limiting departing members' purchases of office equipment and office furnishings from their district offices.

Executive Office of the President Appropriations. Consistent with the expressed sentiments of the White House (and many in Congress), realistic budget cuts should include the executive branch, which has boomed in employee numbers and department budgets. As with appropriations for the legislative branch, the Task Force proposes a 25 percent reduction in appropriations for the Executive Office of the President.

Federal Building Construction. The General Services Administration (GSA), an independent agency of the federal government, manages property and records belonging to the federal government. Established by the Federal Property and Administrative Services Act of 1949, GSA is charged, among other things, with the construction and operation of buildings. It is directed by an administrator who is appointed by the president.

The Task Force proposal places a moratorium on construction and acquisition of new federal buildings. The vice-president's *National Performance Review* stated, in part: "Over the next five years, the Federal Government is slated to spend more than $800 million a year acquiring new federal office space and courthouses. Under current conditions, however, those acquisitions don't make sense." The review recommended that the GSA place a hold on its acquisitions and begin aggressive negotiations for existing leases and new leases to reduce costs further. This proposal would place a moratorium only on projects not in the design phase; construction and acquisition projects for which funds already have been authorized would not be affected.

Political Appointees. The term "political appointee" refers to employees of the federal government who are appointed by the president, some with and some without confirmation by the Senate, and to certain policy advisors. Total employment in such positions will average about

2,900 over the next five years. The Congressional Budget Office (CBO) estimates that the average 1995 salary for political appointees is $68,000. The *National Performance Review* called for reductions in the number of federal managers and supervisors but made no effort to include those managers and supervisors who were political appointees, such as Schedule C employees, executive schedule employees in the top levels of government, and noncareer members of the Senior Executive Service. The National Commission on the Public Service (otherwise known as the Volcker Commission) called for limits on the number of political appointees. The Task Force proposal would cap the number of political appointees at 2,000.

The Federal Government	Savings Over 5 Years (in dollars)
Save interest payments by reducing spending	73,432,000,000
Continue government employee buyout	34,838,000,000
Reduce government agency overhead	33,554,000,000
Impose air traffic control user fees	7,000,000,000
Reduce salaries and expenses	5,638,000,000
Consolidate federal land management	3,905,000,000
Reorganize the Army Corps of Engineers	3,274,000,000
Abolish the Geological Survey	3,261,000,000
Reduce the operating subsidy for Amtrak	2,840,000,000
Reduce legislative branch appropriations by 25%	2,743,000,000
Freeze FAA operations and safety work force	1,910,000,000
Reduce Corps of Engineers construction	1,898,000,000
Limit federal building construction	1,833,000,000

The Federal Government	Savings Over 5 Years (in dollars)
Remove 1994 automation investment from the 1994-2000 baseline	1,516,000,000
Reduce NASA support	1,348,000,000
Impose a moratorium on federal land purchases	1,066,000,000
Abolish the Bureau of Mines	873,000,000
Reduce Corps of Engineers operation and maintenance	800,000,000
Consolidate financial institution regulators	750,000,000
Institute IRS fees	730,000,000
Charge federal employees for parking	530,000,000
Reduce the operation of Indian programs	470,000,000
Reduce Treasury (other than IRS)	463,000,000
Downsize the Bureau of Reclamation	427,000,000
Reduce Bureau of Reclamation construction program	367,000,000
Reduce the number of political appointees	355,000,000
Reduce Corps of Engineers general investigations	339,000,000
Reduce District of Columbia, miscellaneous contributions	323,000,000
Reduce Executive Office of the President appropriations by 25 percent	286,000,000
Reduce Bureau of Indian Affairs construction	285,000,000

The Federal Government	Savings Over 5 Years (in dollars)
Charge penalty for early redemption of Savings Bonds	240,000,000
Cancel presidential checkoff on tax forms	239,000,000
Eliminate Territorial Affairs (Department of the Interior)	217,000,000
Consolidate the Bureau of Indian Affairs	215,000,000
Partially remove disability investment from 1998-2000 baseline	185,000,000
Close the Interstate Commerce Commission	170,000,000
Freeze general operating expenses of Veterans Affairs	157,000,000
Abolish the National Biological Survey	139,000,000
Reduce the Congressional frank by 50 percent	131,000,000
Use the proposed $1 coin	112,000,000
Eliminate SBA tree planting grants	75,000,000
Institute Corps of Engineers/regulatory program permit fee	54,000,000
Eliminate SBA earmarks	54,000,000
Freeze copyright office	50,000,000
Freeze pay of members of Congress	49,000,000
Freeze Postal Service fund payments	35,000,000
Reduce subsidies for future guarantees	31,000,000

The Federal Government	Savings Over 5 Years (in dollars)
Eliminate the Federal Information Center	20,000,000
Institute Bureau of Public Defender treasury securities fees	15,000,000
Restructure the Office of Territorial and International Affairs	10,000,000
Reform Office of the Inspector General	7,000,000
Terminate specific statutory boards and commissions	2,400,000
Limit office furniture purchases by departing members	500,000
Continue civilian, non-DOD personnel reductions	(4,869,000,000)
Create air traffic control corporation	(5,673,000,000)
Restructuring Programs that Affect the Federal Government **TOTAL**	**178,719,900,000**
Running Total of Savings	**858,269,000,000**

1 House Budget Committee.

2 Federal Deposit Insurance Orporation, Office of the Comptroller of the Currency, Office of Thrift Supervision, and Federal Reserve.

3 Congressional Budget Office. "Reducing the Deficit: Spending and Revenue Options," *Report to the Senate and House Committees on the Budget.* Washington, DC: U.S. Government Printing Office, February 1995, page 258.

4 House Committee on Resources.

5 See Glossary.

6 Citizens Against Government Waste, 1994.

CHAPTER SIXTEEN

International Affairs

The United States is the world's only super power and, as such, plays a key role in international affairs and diplomacy. As a lead nation in most international organizations, most notably the United Nations (UN), the United States also spends billions of taxpayers' dollars on foreign aid.

I have long preferred continuing those foreign aid programs that directly affect American security interests. Unfortunately, much of our foreign aid has been swallowed up by nation-building missions and global development campaigns. Despite billions of American tax dollars spent on assistance, the record of those missions has been mixed and some have shown no results. The Balanced Budget Task Force believes the federal government could achieve substantial savings in the area of international affairs without jeopardizing our national security interests.

Reduce Multilateral Development Bank Credit Assistance

The United States provides aid in the form of credit to development banks, which in turn loan money to "qualified" foreign borrowers. Such multilateral development banks include the World Bank, the Export-Import Bank, the Inter-American Development Fund, the Asian Development

Bank, the African Development Bank, and the European Bank for Reconstruction and Development. According to the Congressional Budget Office (CBO), those banks have grown over the years and now have assets of $220 billion and are owned by more than 177 member countries who serve as stockholders.

Export-Import Bank. The Export-Import Bank of the United States, an independent agency of the federal government, was created in 1934 as a District of Columbia banking corporation and became an independent government corporation after an act of Congress in 1945. Designed to supplement and not compete with private capital, the bank aids in financing and facilitating exports and imports and the exchange of commodities between the United States and any foreign country.

Eximbank, as it has been known since 1968, makes direct loans with below-market interest rates and provides guarantees of private lending without receiving full compensation for the contingent liability of future losses. The 1945 act states explicitly that the loans should be for specific purposes and should offer reasonable assurance of repayment. The bank, authorized to have capital stock of $1 billion, may have a total of $40 billion in loans, guarantees, and insurance outstanding at any one time. It has helped finance sales of a wide range of American equipment, including fertilizer plants, bridges, jet aircraft, and locomotives, to foreign buyers. Eximbank is managed by a bipartisan board of five directors appointed by the president with the advice and consent of the Senate.

The Balanced Budget Task Force provision reduces the Eximbank credit by 50 percent, allowing the government to realize substantial savings by increasing risk-related fees, cutting the bank's projected subsidy by one-third, and directing the remainder to the private sector in middle-income countries that pose a moderate credit risk and whose economies have the potential to grow. By not agreeing to new stock purchases or contributions, we would realize a savings while still fulfilling our currently authorized commitments.

Capital Contributions to Multilateral Development Banks. The Task Force provision reforms new capital contributions to multilateral development banks (excluding the International Development Administration). The proposal recommends that the United States withhold all new capital contributions to the World Bank, the Asian Development Bank, the Asian Development Fund, the International Finance Corporation, the European Bank for Reconstruction and Development, the Inter-American Development Bank, and the African Development Fund. However, the banks would be allowed to use their "reflows" or loan payments to make new loans. Particularly interesting is the case of the Asian Development Bank, which was established to improve the efficiency of Asian capital markets. Those markets are now very efficient, yet the United States continues to make contributions.

Unspent Foreign Economic Assistance. Foreign aid programs usually are funded in advance. For example, economic aid to country "X" for the next three years will be authorized and appropriated this year. At the end of each year, the president will have the authority to de-obligate any unspent funds and pull them back "out of the pipeline." The president would be authorized to waive this requirement on a case-by-case basis. The Task Force proposal calls for using any unspent funds and uses them to reduce the deficit.

International Development Administration. The International Development Administration (IDA) is financed out of the budget account entitled "Funds Appropriated to the President." A member of the World Bank Group, the IDA provides development financing on highly concessional terms to the world's poorest and least creditworthy nations. It is the largest source of multilateral lending extended on concessional terms to developing countries.

The Task Force proposal reduces funding for the IDA for fiscal year (FY) 1996 to the level proposed by the Senate for FY 1994 ($975 million) and does not reauthorize the program beyond that point. Despite numerous requests for funding decreases by both President Clinton and many members of Congress, spending in this program continues to increase. The Foreign Operations Bill for FY 1995, for example, contained an increase of more than $300 million.

U.S. Agency for International Development. The U.S. Agency for International Development (USAID) administers development-related projects and provides technical advice in ninety-two developing countries. Since the creation of USAID in 1961, the United States has spent $114 billion on development assistance. USAID has been criticized for waste and ineffectiveness and, as documented by both the President's Commission on the Management of AID Programs and the President's Commission on Development and the National Interest, has too many objectives and supports projects in too many countries.

Under the Bush Administration, the President's Commission on the Management of AID Programs recommended that USAID be merged into the Department of State, which would enable it to respond flexibly and accurately to U.S. foreign policy and strengthen USAID's ability to establish and hold to a clearly defined set of priorities and objectives. The Task Force proposal restructures the U.S. Agency for International Development by reducing the size of USAID and the programs it administers, thus allowing the agency to focus on more realistic goals in the countries most likely to benefit from United Nations development assistance. The proposal also recommends focusing the agency's funding on programs that emphasize alleviating poverty and promoting economic development.

U.S. Contributions to the United Nations. This Task Force provision limits assessed and voluntary U.S. contributions to the United

Nations to an amount that bears the same ratio to the total budget of
the UN as the population of the United States bears to the total population of all the member states of the United Nations. In 1992, the United
States paid 25 percent of UN operating costs and 30.4 percent of the
costs of UN peacekeeping operations. Those percentages are significantly
more than any other nation is asked to contribute. Japan contributes
only 12 percent of the UN budget, and the next highest contributor is
Great Britain with only 5 percent of the funding. In fact, the U.S. contribution to UN peacekeeping missions is becoming the fastest-growing
account in the State Department's budget.

While appreciating the critical role the United Nations has played
in recent international crises, the United States should not be called upon
to pay an unduly large share of UN expenses each year while other nations pay relatively little. This proposal would not minimize the efforts
or effectiveness of the United Nations but would create a more equitable
contribution formula, one that would save the U.S. Treasury much-
needed revenue.

Economic Support Fund. The Economic Support Fund (ESF) has been
used to provide economic and counternarcotics assistance to selected
countries in support of U.S. efforts to promote stability and U.S. security
interests in strategic regions of the world.

The Task Force proposal reduces the Economic Support Fund. Under
this provision, cash payments to Israel would equal the annual level of
loan repayments by Israel ($1.1 billion in 1995). At present, ESF for
Israel exceeds the amount needed to repay outstanding loans and loan
guarantees by $70 million in 1995 and nearly $1.3 billion over the next
five years. ESF for Egypt would be cut in proportion to the cut in aid to
Israel. This proposal goes beyond the CBO option in accepting the
president's proposal to terminate ESF to countries other than Israel and
Egypt.

Bilateral Development Aid. The federal government provides foreign economic and bilateral development aid to a number of nations
through a variety of foreign aid programs. The Task Force proposal
reduces and consolidates bilateral development aid to assume a global
USAID long-term development program that is no larger than the
current USAID program in Africa ($800 million). This provision assumes
that the number of countries currently served by USAID, now ninety-
two, would be reduced drastically, leaving fewer than forty USAID
missions, mostly in Africa.

Reduce Foreign Aid Direct Assistance

Occasionally, American security interests require close monitoring
of the foreign aid received by certain countries. Such concerns arise be-

cause of complications in the delivery of aid, the perceived misuse of funds, or the souring of relations between the United States and a particular nation. Consequently, the federal government can limit or even prevent foreign aid from being delivered to these nations in question.

Aid to Eastern Europe and Russia. This Task Force provision reduces aid to Eastern Europe and Russia by 50 percent of the FY 1994 level by FY 2000. The proposal provides $380 million for assistance for Central and Eastern Europe, as proposed by the Senate for FY 1994, and reduces future funding in absolute terms by 50 percent. The head of Poland's aid distribution network has stated that foreign aid has not affected the pace of Polish reform and that the country would have progressed this far without it. According to the House Budget Committee, internal economic policies, and not foreign aid, will determine the outcome of postcommunist transformations.

Aid to Russia. The Task Force proposal conditions all unexpended bilateral assistance to Russia. Pending certification by the president regarding Russian compliance with a number of security, free market, and democratic reforms, aid to Russia would be withheld. Tens of billions of Western aid to Russia in recent years have had no noticeable positive impact. Reformers have been ousted and the Russian government has done next to nothing of late to implement structural economic reforms. Russian foreign policy also has become more aggressive recently, making their commitment to the sovereignty of the former Soviet countries questionable.

Reduce Humanitarian Assistance Programs

Through various international development programs, the United States participates substantially in humanitarian efforts abroad. Most notable are those in Ethiopia in the 1980s and Somalia in the 1990s. Despite the large amounts spent, these perhaps worthwhile missions do not always work out as intended.

Refugee Assistance. The Task Force provision accepts the Clinton Administration's FY 1995 proposal to reduce refugee assistance and migration. Such assistance is designed to provide funding for unexpected and emergency relief work. Unfortunately, the assistance often becomes a slush fund for special untargeted, and often inefficient, programs. Spending for FY 1995 would be reduced by $47 million to $633 million.

International Peacekeeping. Traditionally, the United Nations has involved itself in peacekeeping activities in which fighting in a country has ended and all parties to a conflict have agreed to the presence of lightly armed UN forces during efforts to negotiate an enduring settlement. Funding for UN peacekeeping has surged since 1990, however, because the United Nations increasingly has become involved in nontraditional peace-enforcement missions.

The Task Force proposal returns international peacekeeping to its traditional role, freezing funding for international peacekeeping at 75 percent of its FY 1994 level.

The proposal also rejects the concept of "assertive multilateralism," which requires the United States to subordinate its national security responsibilities to the United Nations. U.S. armed forces should always remain under U.S. command and should not be loaned to international operations with ambiguously defined objectives. The United States should not cede this responsibility to an organization with an uncertain agenda.

Peace Corps. The Peace Corps was created by executive order in 1961 to promote world peace and friendship by training American volunteers to perform social and humanitarian service overseas. Originally an agency of the Department of State, it became an independent government agency in 1981. The Task Force proposal freezes Peace Corps funding at the FY 1994 level of $220 million for five years. Although the proposal supports the goals of the Peace Corps, it recognizes that funding for the Peace Corps has increased rapidly since 1990.

Educational and Cultural Exchange Programs. Since 1949, with the aid of the Fulbright Scholarship, more than 100,000 students from countries around the world have visited the United States, and Americans from every state and territory have studied, taught, or conducted research abroad. This scholarship was made possible by the 1946 Fulbright Act, introduced by Senator J. William Fulbright (D-Arkansas), which financed grants for international student exchanges through the use of U.S.-owned foreign currencies obtained from the sale of post-war surplus military equipment.

The United States Information Agency (USIA) account funds international exchanges such as the Fulbright, Humphrey, International Visitors, and Muskie programs. Because of additional appropriations, the account more than doubled during the 1980s and since 1990 has grown by an additional 45 percent. Because the USIA exchanges account should not be immune to cost savings in the government-wide reallocation of foreign affairs resources in response to the end of the Cold War, the Task Force proposal reduces aid to educational and cultural exchange programs by 25 percent.

International Security Assistance Funding. The Task Force provision freezes international security assistance funding for all countries. Under this proposal, Egypt will receive $1.3 billion annually in military grants and $.8 billion annually in economic grants. Likewise, Israel will receive $1.8 billion annually in military grants and $1.2 billion annually in economic grants. Those allocations maintain the current level of funding for both Israel and Egypt. This assumes, however, that the funding cuts proposed under the Economic Support Fund will be frozen at their reduced levels for five years and foreign military financing will be frozen at their FY 1994 levels. Finally, the Task Force recommends that Congress permit countries receiving ESF funding to use those funds at their discretion to retire portions of their outstanding debt with the United States.

Public Law 480 (Food for Peace Program). President Franklin D. Roosevelt believed that foreign aid should be held to exacting standards. To prevent a widespread loss of life following World War II, for example, the United States urged the United Nations to organize a Relief and Rehabilitation Agency (UNRRA). Because it was understood that the danger of postwar famines was a temporary problem, UNRRA's mandate was explicitly limited. UNRRA stressed its intentions to withdraw after the first adequate harvest in an afflicted country — and kept its word. The Agricultural Trade and Assistance Act of 1954, however, was enacted when the inconvertibility of foreign currency and the lack of foreign exchange held by potential customers limited commercial exports of domestic agricultural commodities. Sales in exchange for foreign currencies, concessional credit, and grants provided a mechanism for developing markets, disposing of surplus commodities, and furthering U.S. interests.

According to the Congressional Budget Office, because of changes in the world over the past forty years, the program may be obsolete. The Task Force proposes to restructure Public Law 480 — the Food for Peace Program.

Foreign Claims Settlement Commission. The Foreign Claims Settlement Commission adjudicates the claims of American citizens concerning their naturalization or expropriation, or the taking of their property by a foreign government. The commission, which works in conjunction with the departments of State and Treasury, currently is involved in the expropriation of U.S. property in Vietnam. The Task Force provision eliminates the Foreign Claims Settlement Commission, whose responsibilities could be absorbed by existing offices and personnel at the State Department without jeopardizing its mission.

Reform the Administration of Programs

The Task Force examined the United States' role and expenditures in foreign assistance and concluded that, with so many foreign assistance programs, we can realize substantial administrative savings by eliminating overlapping functions, jurisdictions, and responsibilities.

The State Department. The Department of State promotes U.S. foreign policy interests abroad. In 1994, it received about $2.6 billion to administer its foreign affairs programs. In the 1980s, this portion of the department's budget averaged $1.6 billion. Inflation has been responsible for some of the increase since then, but the funding added to provide security for diplomats and to establish new posts in the republics of the former Soviet Union also contributed. Even when funding for added security and new posts is included, however, real growth from the 1980s through 1994 amounts to about 10 percent real annual growth. The increases in funding mainly reflect growth in salaries and related expenses and in rental and acquisition costs of residences and office space.

The State Department is not the only federally funded organization that works in foreign affairs activities. Smaller agencies such as the U.S. Institute of Peace, the Asia Foundation, the East/West Center, and the North/South Center, which are independent but under the guidance of the State Department, perform functions that could be eliminated without directly affecting U.S. foreign policy. These agencies, with combined annual budgets of about $60 million, conduct research and work to build better relations between the United States and various foreign countries.

The Task Force provision restructures the State Department. The proposal keeps State Department funding at its 1994 level from 1995 to 1997. By 1997, State Department funding (excluding the cost of security improvements and new posts in the former Soviet Union) would return to its average real level of the 1980s. The department would accommodate these cuts by eliminating or consolidating posts in less important areas of the world, by reorganizing the department's bureaucracy, and by reducing the number of senior foreign service officers. This proposal also eliminates funding for the smaller agencies dealing in foreign affairs.

Reform Treasury Exchange Stabilization Fund. The Secretary of the Treasury is authorized to deal in gold and foreign exchanges of credit as necessary to fulfill U.S. obligations in the International Monetary Fund (IMF) regarding orderly exchange agreements. An Exchange Stabilization Fund, with capital of $200 million, is authorized for this purpose. The Task Force proposal reforms the Exchange Stabilization Fund by requiring it immediately to return part of its interest earnings to the General Fund of the Treasury. In 1996, the fund would begin repaying its initial federal capitalization, part of which is derived from windfall profits realized when the United States went off the gold standard in 1933. At present, all interest and earnings accruing to the fund are available only for foreign exchange transactions.

Overseas Broadcasting. Several entities provide overseas broadcasting for the United States. Radio Free Europe and Radio Liberty broadcast country-specific news to Eastern Europe and the former Soviet Union, respectively. The Voice of America (VOA) overseas radio broadcasts provide news and U.S.-related information to audiences worldwide. The United States Information Agency overseas television broadcasting services are similar to radio broadcasts of VOA. USIA also manages broadcasting to Cuba.

The Clinton Administration has called for consolidating funding for Radio Free Europe, Radio Liberty, and the Voice of America. Such a consolidation results only in the merger of the funding, not of the agencies themselves. The Task Force agrees with the Clinton Administration's proposal to consolidate overseas broadcasting.

U.S. Travel and Tourism Administration. The U.S. Travel and Tourism Administration (USTTA), an agency of the Department of Commerce, promotes foreign travel to and within the United States. Since 1961, USTTA has been promoting the United States as a tourist destination for foreign travelers; it also works with government officials to reduce barriers to international travel and maintains field offices in eight cities around the world.

The Task Force believes tourism advice is best left to the firms and industries involved, rather than to the USTTA. Because USTTA's activities do little or nothing to improve the nation's current-account balance, the Task Force provision eliminates this agency immediately.

International Trade Administration. The International Trade Administration (ITA) promotes American industries and interests abroad and works in tandem with the U.S. Travel and Tourism Administration. The ITA, established in 1980 as an agency of the Department of Commerce, has among its duties export promotion, marketing, and counseling. The Task Force proposes to reduce the International Trade Administration by eliminating its trade promotion activities. Such a reduction would have reduced outlays by $120 million in 1994 alone.

Arguments have been made that such activities are better left to the firms and industries involved rather than to the USTTA and ITA. To the extent that the beneficiaries are not charged the full cost, ITA's and USTTA's activities effectively subsidize the industries involved. Such subsidies are an inefficient way to help U.S. industries because benefits go in part to foreigners in the form of lower prices for U.S. goods and travel.

Customs Tonnage Duty Fees. This Task Force proposal increases by 150 percent the existing customs tonnage duty fees paid by commercial shippers to offset the costs of services provided to the maritime industry by the U.S. Coast Guard. The Omnibus Reconciliation Budget Act (OBRA) of 1990 enacted customs tonnage duty fees through 1998. OBRA 1990 increased the duties from 2 cents per ton to 9 cents per ton (to a maximum of 4.5 cents per ton per year) on vessels entering the United States from the western hemisphere. The per-ton duties were increased from 6 cents to 27 cents (to a maximum of $1.35 per ton per year) on vessels entering the United States from other foreign ports.

International Affairs	Savings Over 5 Years (in dollars)
Reduce bilateral development aid	4,516,000,000
Condition unexpended aid to Russia	3,000,000,000
Reduce aid to Eastern Europe and Russia by 50 percent	2,927,000,000
Reform Treasury Exchange Stabilization Fund	1,885,000,000
Freeze international security assistance funding	1,870,000,000
Reduce the Economic Support Fund	1,812,000,000
Limit U.S. contributions to the United Nations	1,762,000,000
Restructure Public Law 480 (Food for Peace Program)	1,676,000,000
Reform the International Development Administration	1,663,000,000
Restructure the U.S. Agency for International Development	1,310,000,000
Restructure the State Department	1,170,000,000
Consolidate overseas broadcasting	1,161,000,000
Return unspent foreign economic assistance	1,141,000,000
Reduce Export-Import Bank credit by 50 percent	893,000,000
Return international peacekeeping to its traditional role	782,000,000
Reduce International Trade Administration	735,000,000
Reform new capital contributions to multilateral development banks (excluding IDA)	705,000,000

International Affairs	Savings Over 5 Years (in dollars)
Increase customs tonnage duty fees by 150%	500,000,000
Reduce refugee assistance to president's FY 1995 request	463,000,000
Reduce aid to educational and cultural exchange programs by 25 percent	170,000,000
Freeze Peace Corps funding	86,000,000
Eliminate U.S. Travel and Tourism Administration	85,000,000
Terminate annual direct assistance to the Marianas	84,000,000
Eliminate cargo preference	70,000,000
Eliminate the Institute of Peace	55,000,000
Reduce budget of the Export Administration by 25 percent	51,000,000
Institute a decommissioning fee	40,000,000
Collect fees for certification and surveillance of foreign repair stations	9,000,000
Eliminate the Japan-U.S. Friendship Commission	5,000,000
Eliminate the Foreign Claims Settlement Commission	5,000,000
Restructuring Programs Concerning International Affairs TOTAL	30,631,000,000
Running Total of Savings	888,900,000,000

CHAPTER SEVENTEEN

The Department of Defense

B ecause the budget of the United States serves as a blueprint for how our nation should operate, it also serves as a primary indicator of our nation's priorities. One of the most important duties of the federal government is to protect the citizens of this country. As such, the federal budget must reflect that our national security is the most important priority of the federal government, and efforts to balance the budget must ensure that our security is not threatened. In fiscal year 1996, the federal budget is projected to spend more money in interest payments on the national debt than it will on the Army, Air Force, Navy, Marines, and the entire federal bureaucracy at the Department of Defense (DOD). Defense spending based on budgetary necessity rather than strategy threatens the long-term security of our nation. Balancing the budget must reflect a dedication to the fundamental purpose of government — the protection of its citizens.

The Balanced Budget Task Force proposal asserts the need to maintain a sound national security policy to meet both predictable and unexpected emergencies. We believe that our limited resources require a thorough examination of every facet of the Defense Department. While our budget proposal calls for an increase in defense spending of almost $60 billion over five years, it also recommends the elimination or scaling back of certain nondefense spending or low-priority defense programs. My

friend and colleague, Bob Dornan (R-California), a fellow defense sup-
porter, was largely responsible for drafting this portion of our proposal.

Restore Defense Spending

Since the beginning of the Clinton Administration, the defense budget has been reduced by $127 billion over five years to satisfy other pri-
orities in the budget. Serious questions have been raised by independent
assessments about whether these funding levels meet the demands facing our military in the future. As recently as September 1994, according
to testimony before the Senate Armed Services Committee by Deputy
Defense Secretary John Deutch, the Department of Defense was "reviewing" the top weapon systems launched by the Pentagon in an effort to
find an additional $20 billion to meet a shortfall over the next six years.
This shortfall is needed to bankroll military pay raises, retirement funds
and housing, and Army readiness. The Task Forces provision restores
defense spending.

Defense Baseline Adjustment. The Balanced Budget Task Force provision addresses the issues of defense budget reductions and shortfalls
by increasing defense spending by $60 billion as follows:

- Restore the funds that the Pentagon lacks in its defense budget to
  carry out its mission in the post-Cold War era
- Provide cost-of-living increases for military pay
- Retain twelve Army divisions
- Restore two Air Force fighter wings and fifty bombers
- Increase funding for readiness-related procurement, training, and
  maintenance

Specific programs that should be considered for these slated increases
in program funding include the Ballistic Missile Defense Program, the
V-22 Osprey, and Sealift and Airlift capabilities.

The Task Force believes that the funding needed to restore those programs and overall defense readiness should come from other areas of
the budget rather than from existing funding for defense. The fiscal year
(FY) 1995 Defense Appropriation Bill calls for spending $244 billion. The
Balanced Budget Act of 1995 restores the level of defense spending necessary to meet our defense challenges efficiently.

Rescind Unused Funds of Selected Congressionally Mandated Defense Programs

Because of the expansive responsibility of the Defense Department,
programs that have not been officially requested by the Pentagon or without any direct impact on the ability of our nation to carry out its

security mission often are funded under the banner of defense spending. Most often the programs have been initiated by Congress without the approval of the Pentagon. The bipartisan Congressional Porkbusters Coalition has done a marvelous job of identifying those low-priority programs.

General Purpose Bombs. This appropriation provides for procuring and modernizing missiles, torpedoes, ammunition, and other weapons systems. The Task Force proposal rescinds funding for general purpose bombs in this way: $4 million appropriated to complete Phase II of the Rockeye Product Improvement Program (PIP). Phase II of the Rockeye PIP was completely funded with prior funds; therefore, the $4 million can be rescinded. The Navy's ability to accomplish its mission successfully would not be affected by this rescission proposal. The appropriation was opposed by the Pentagon and originally was proposed for elimination (as a rescission in 1991) by President George Bush.

Rescind Funding for Defense Nuclear Agency Material. This appropriation provides for the procurement of ship modernization equipment, other equipment, and materials for which provision is not made elsewhere. The Task Force provision rescinds funding for the Defense Nuclear Agency Material because of the cancellation of the Nuclear Depth Strike Bomb development effort, which eliminated the requirement for procurement funds. The Navy's ability to accomplish its mission successfully would not be affected by this rescission proposal. As a program, opposed by the Pentagon, this originally was proposed for elimination (as a rescission in 1991) by President Bush.

Reform Department of Defense Administration

One of the largest areas for program reform in any department is in the administration of its bureaucracy and personnel. The Defense Department should not be exempt from this reform. While I believe the defense of the nation is the most important function of government, and our men and women in uniform must be taken care of properly, I also believe the Defense Department can provide efficient services with less bureaucracy and less money.

Aviation Center Career Incentive Pay. This Task Force proposal reforms the Aviation Center Career Incentive Pay (ACIP) program by limiting payments to officers serving on regular and frequent flight duty assignments. DOD should eliminate ACIP, except for those individuals actually performing operational or proficiency flying duty required by orders. The ACIP payment schedule should be restructured for eligible recipients with more than twelve years of service. This proposal is another Grace Commission[1] recommendation.

Learning Resource Center Program. Learning Resource Centers provide a wide range of training intended to promote realistic career and

self-development activities and opportunities for both military and civilian personnel. Courses are provided to DOD civilian and military employees during and after business hours at no charge to the employee.
As the Grace Commission pointed out, there is little justification for such
an expenditure when funds are needed for the primary mission. The Task
Force proposes to reduce this program that provides nonessential training at taxpayers' expense.

DOD Recovery Procedures from Third Parties. According to the General Accounting Office, since 1949 more than twenty-two studies have
reviewed whether a central entity should be created within DOD for the
centralized management and administration of medical care among military departments. Currently, each department has its own administrative,
management, and operational functions. Departments currently perform
these functions through a vast array of nonspecific and bureaucratic
procedures that make the medical recovery process excessively expensive
and often difficult for patients.

Since 1979, the increase in dollar amounts of medical claim recovery
has not kept pace with inflation, so there is substantial room for improvement. Modifying the recovery process by providing promotional and
monetary incentives for effective cost recovery, establishing an independent unit responsible for claims recovery, and instituting needed changes
in the legal medical claim environment could produce an increase of
120 percent or more in claims recovered. The Task Force supports this
Grace Commission recommendation, which would improve DOD procedures for recovering the cost of medical care from third parties.

Reform Department of Defense Programs

The Balanced Budget Task Force believes certain current programs
could fulfill their purposes at a lower cost to taxpayers. We came up with
five specific reforms that will give us more defense for less money.

Intelligence Agencies. The overlap of roughly 20 intelligence organizations could be reduced. The Task Force proposes to reorganize the
intelligence agencies by eliminating inefficiencies, achieving a personnel savings of 25 percent over five years, and maintaining the nation's
ability to gather necessary and accurate intelligence information quickly.
According to the Congressional Budget Office (CBO), this change would
result in a five-year savings of more than $18 billion.

Second Seawolf Submarine (SSN-2). The Pentagon planned the construction of three Seawolf nuclear submarines. This Task Force proposal
suggests the cancellation of the SSN-2, the second Seawolf submarine,
currently under development by DOD. Since the first Seawolf is almost
completed and the third remains scheduled for construction, these two
submarines will sufficiently meet our defense needs and expectations for

the next five years. If at the end of this period it is necessary to build the SSN-2, construction of this defense project will remain an option.

Modernize Defense Stockpile. The Task Force proposal requires the president to dispose of defense stockpiles in precious metals that are either obsolete for military purposes or in excess supply.

Environmental Defense Fund. While DOD should be responsible for cleaning up environmental waste on DOD installations, the Task Force proposal to reduce the Environmental Defense Fund by 50 percent would in no way affect base closure or day-to-day base compliance with this responsibility. DOD compliance funding would not be affected by this proposal. This budget provision applies only to Superfund DOD sites where, currently, only approximately 20 percent of approved funds are obligated per year.[2]

Former Soviet Threat. While any reduction in the former Soviet threat is desirable, why should such funds come from the DOD budget? Consider, for example, what these funds are actually being used for: $10,000,000 for nuclear waste disposal by the former Soviet Union in the Arctic Region. The Task Force proposes to reduce the former Soviet threat reduction by at least 50 percent.

The Department Of Defense	Savings Over 5 Years (in dollars)
Reorganize the intelligence agencies	19,150,000,000
Modernize defense stockpile	4,600,000,000
Reduce Environmental Defense Fund by 50%	3,894,000,000
Cancel second Seawolf submarine (SSN-2)	900,000,000
Reduce former Soviet threat reduction by 50%	685,000,000
Reform Aviation Center career incentive pay	605,000,000
Improve DOD recovery procedures from third parties	149,000,000
Reform severance pay for nonpromotion discharges of officers	126,000,000
Reduce aid to Learning Resource Center program	35,000,000

The Department Of Defense	Savings Over 5 Years (in dollars)
Rescind funding for general purpose bombs	6,000,000
Rescind funding for C-12F aircraft	1,000,000
Rescind funding for Defense Nuclear Agency material	1,000,000
Rescind funding for P-3 upgrades	0
Increase defense baseline adjustment by $60 billion	(57,500,000,000)
The Department of Defense **TOTAL**	**(27,348,000,000)**
Running Total of Savings	861,452,000,000

1 See Glossary.

2 Congressional Budget Office. "Reducing the Deficit: Spending and Revenue Options," *Report to the Senate and House Committees on the Budget.* Washington, DC: U.S. Government Printing Office, 1994, pages 74-75.

Part III – The Solution

CHAPTER EIGHTEEN

Budget Process Reforms

T he Republicans say the Democrats are at fault. The Democrats say the Republicans did it. And so the conversation about debt and deficit degenerates into a "Who Done It." But we don't need a clue to find out if it was Colonel Mustard in the drawing room with a rope. There is no mystery about how we got to where we are. It's plain and simple: The federal debt and deficit are not partisan or political issues. Government irresponsibility by all parties has played a part in creating the problem. The cold, hard fact is that the debt and deficit are real. They loom ominously over the future of our children and grandchildren.

Just as we have discussed many of the tough choices we must make to balance the budget, we also must examine the system that has allowed us to get our country into this mess. Making the hard decision on how much money to spend, along with what to spend that money on, will always be the final and most important decision. But the procedural framework in which members of Congress actually make these decisions will have a fundamental impact on the outcome of those decisions. Too many times we have discovered Colonel Mustard hanging himself with the rope in the drawing room. The rules of the game allowed him to play out his own scheme at a high price.

So it is with the current budget system. It does not compel us to answer the tough questions. It encourages us to spend more. And, in the end, we hang ourselves, or find ourselves hanging by a thread.

Because balancing the budget will require many politically sensitive votes, it is imperative that the system be geared to assure that the tough questions are answered. Our current budget system too often allows members of Congress to duck such questions and get away with it. The system must require real answers to our budget problems or face the consequences.

The budget process currently makes it easier for (I would even say encourages) members to spend more and cut less. The days of spending taxpayers' dollars with an unlimited credit card must end, and budget process reforms are essential to providing this change in budget behavior.

I believe four fundamental reforms — passing the balanced budget amendment, instituting a line item veto, eliminating baseline budgeting, and prohibiting unfunded mandates — would go a long way toward restoring fiscal discipline in the United States government. I want to say at the outset that I do not believe any of these budget reforms will in and of themselves cut or even reduce spending. What I do believe is that these reforms will foster a procedural environment in which spending restraint will be the norm, not the exception.

Pass the Balanced Budget Amendment

In my sixteen years as a member of Congress, I consistently have been disappointed in the inability of legislators to control the government's spending habits. From the beginning I have strongly advocated placing limits on the total amount of taxpayer dollars the federal government can spend, or even take from citizens in taxes. One such way to limit the ability of Congress to spend money is to pass a balanced budget amendment to the United States Constitution.

Since I have been a member of Congress, the American people have seen the Congress attempt to control its own behavior through a number of proposals that annually limit how much Congress can spend. Every one of these Gramm-Rudman-Hollings-type[1] laws were statutory amendments to the Budget Act, which directs the entire budgetary process. Such statutes, initially passed by a majority of the House and Senate, later were waived by a majority of the House and Senate when the going got tough. Here's an example of how they played the game: Under Gramm-Rudman-Hollings, spending and deficit targets were set in law. If the law had been followed, Congress would have balanced the budget in the early 1990s. If Congress failed to meet the procedural requirements of the law, an automatic across-the-board cut of all funds would be triggered, bringing spending levels back down below the caps. When it appeared that Congress was going to violate the rules they placed on their own behavior, members waived the requirement and claimed they had averted a major fiscal calamity. What they did not say is that they had succeeded only in postponing a greater fiscal calamity.

With a statute, Congress can waive or change the law whenever it comes time to make tough decisions. With this budget mandate in the Constitution, in the form of a balanced budget amendment, Congress will no longer be able to duck the tough choices.

The Constitution is the backbone of our democracy. A balanced budget amendment to the instrument that keeps us upright and standing tall would give Congress and the president the political backbone to balance the budget and keep it balanced.

With the current system, when it comes to making the tough choices, Congress often acts as if it has no spine. The easiest choice for members of Congress to make when faced with constituents' demands for higher spending and lower taxes is to pay for spending by borrowing money. A balanced budget amendment would reverse that situation by making it more difficult to borrow money.

The amendment would require Congress to pass legislation implementing the details of how the amendment would work. The implementing legislation could be similar to the budget resolution and appropriation bills that would follow passage of such a tight resolution as offered by our Balanced Budget Task Force. Even if Congress did not pass implementing legislation, the amendment would be self-enforcing: It would force Congress and the president to take the action necessary to bring the budget into balance, and it would ensure that the budget remains balanced.

The amendment provides a "glide path" until 2002 before it will be effective as part of the Constitution. It took us several years to dig the hole we are in, and it will take several years to climb out. Congress will not be able to ignore the deficit during this period. The realization that there will be a point at which the rubber hits the road will prompt Congress and the president to take action to balance the budget before the amendment becomes effective. Indeed, our Task Force proposal calls for a balanced budget in the fifth year, thereby giving Congress and the economy time to adjust to the "radical idea" of having balanced budgets. By passing the amendment and sending it to the states for ratification, Congress will force itself, in cooperation with the president, to adopt an orderly deficit reduction plan and to balance the budget before the amendment takes effect.

It is impossible to predict every decision Congress and the president will make to comply with a balanced budget amendment. As I have stated before, the plan of the Balanced Budget Task Force provides only one blueprint of how the nation's accounts could be balanced. The amendment would force Congress and the president to set priorities within a balanced budget and force an honest debate about what decisions and trade-offs are necessary to balance the budget. The same bargaining that occurred in our Task Force meetings, pitting programs against one another and then reaching a conclusion based on the Task Force's — or in this case the Congress's — priorities would occur. We have accumulated $4.96 trillion in debt by refusing to set priorities.

Members of Congress support each other's spending programs and simply borrow money to pay for all of them. A balanced budget amendment would end this practice of logrolling and force Congress to decide which programs truly are priorities. Congress will be able to protect programs with high priorities, while reducing lower-priority programs.

Furthermore, the balanced budget amendment was carefully drafted to avoid creating loopholes and to prevent Congress from evading its requirements. The provisions of a balanced budget amendment are self-enforcing through the three-fifths majority required to authorize spending out of balance, as well as the requirement for a three-fifths vote to raise the debt limit, the limit on the amount of money the government can borrow. For the first time ever, a deficit would be accompanied by members of Congress explicitly voting for one.

The requirement for a three-fifths vote to allow the government to borrow money provides the teeth of the amendment. No matter what accounting gimmicks, timing shifts, or other political games Congress and the president use to try to get around the amendment, the government would shut down at the point where spending began to exceed revenues, unless three-fifths of the Congress had authorized a deficit. If the government runs a deficit, Congress would then, by a three-fifths vote, have to raise the debt limit to allow borrowing by the Treasury Department to finance the deficit and allow the government to continue operations.

Raising the debt limit is always a difficult task for Congress. Congress would do anything to avoid a situation in which three-fifths of the members would have to vote to raise the debt limit; they would even balance the budget. They would need to establish an "early warning system" to identify potential deficits before they occur to avoid the necessity of raising the debt limit. The debt-limit provision provides what the budget process currently lacks — accountability and real political consequences for deficits.

Once the amendment is in place, the president would be required to propose a balanced budget. Actually balancing the budget has not been done since 1969. As the nation's chief executive, the president also would be required to order that no funds be spent at the point in which spending would exceed revenues, unless a deficit was specifically authorized by a three-fifths vote of Congress. The president would not have discretionary authority to stop funding for certain programs while allowing funding for other programs to continue. He would be required to stop spending on all programs if he determined that the government did not have enough revenues to continue spending.

As an absolute last resort, the courts would have a limited role in enforcing this amendment. The courts would state whether a budget is in deficit, strike down any action that violated the amendment, and require Congress to take action. It would be up to Congress and the president to decide what they should do to bring the budget into balance.

When the balanced budget amendment is passed, we will have enshrined in the Constitution the fundamental principle that current generations should not be able to burden future generations with excessive debt. The public will hold accountable any official who ignores this Constitutional mandate, and it will be clear whether Congress and the president meet the obligations established by this amendment. I believe such accountability will provide the ultimate enforcement of the amendment.

Supporting the Case for the Amendment. Many of my colleagues do not agree with my position. Although the balanced budget amendment was approved by the House of Representatives, it was rejected by the Senate in March 1995. To understand the amendment, examine the following three opposing arguments.

First. Some critics of the amendment call it a budgetary gimmick, out of touch with the tough choices needed to balance the budget. They say the amendment is not needed, that Congress can balance the budget without it. I agree that an amendment would be only a requirement binding Congress to act in a particular fashion. However, I disagree that all Congress has to do is exercise the political will to balance the budget. Since Congress has balanced only 29 percent of the budgets in the twentieth century and 0 percent in the last 25 years, I cannot be persuaded that it will in and of itself miraculously vote to balance the budget. Furthermore, since 1969 there has been only one budget resolution that presented a specific, line-by-line accounting of how the nation's finances would be placed back in balance. As the primary sponsor of that budget, I am well aware of the political will and sacrifice necessary to propose and eventually pass a balanced budget. To my Democratic colleagues, I ask, "Why did you not balance the budget and where were your proposals to balance the budget when you controlled the House agenda for the past forty years?"

The fact that the Balanced Budget Task Force's balanced budget proposal, a proposal that actually shows line by line how to get there, received only seventy-five votes from both Republicans and Democrats on the House floor[2] is a telling sign. Where was the political will or courage then? Why didn't more members step up and either vote for this balanced budget proposal or offer one of their own?

The answer is simple: In the past, it has not been good politics to be honest about the budget or to be forthright about some of the detailed conclusions that must be reached. Here was one proposal that offered in detail what most members of Congress, as well as the American people, almost every day claim they support in the abstract — yet it was defeated.

Since 1969 Congress and the president have allowed continuous deficits, adding billions of dollars to the federal debt each year. Consequently, I believe a constitutional requirement is the only fail-safe mechanism that can force the passage of a balanced budget.

Second. Critics of our budget, and ultimately of the balanced budget amendment, claim balancing the budget would wreck havoc on the poor and the working class. Such criticisms are mere scare tactics devised to perpetuate the failed government fiscal philosophy that created our crisis in the first place. The Clinton Administration has even claimed the restraints of such an amendment would force Congress to balance the budget in ways that would maximize pain, namely through steep reductions in Social Security, Medicare, and defense spending, in addition to large tax increases. In response to this accusation I point once again to what our Task Force was able to put together in just a few weeks. We projected a balanced budget for at least three consecutive fiscal years with no tax increases and no cuts in Social Security benefits, restructured the Medicare and welfare systems, restored shortfalls in the defense budget, and began to pay down the debt.

Regarding the amendment's impact on the poor and working class, I would point to the debt. The federal debt currently places a burden of $19,100 on every newborn child, rich or poor. Continuing to pile bill after bill on top of this debt is akin to child abuse. What is so compassionate about continuing this policy? Balancing the federal budget by establishing priorities for limited spending is the only way our nation can ensure that spending for vital government programs can continue. Anything short of this approach is undeniably unrealistic.

We must keep in mind that balancing the budget does not require cutting every government program. In fact, many government programs may not even be touched under a balanced budget. Theoretically, the budget could be balanced thousands of different ways, involving a wide array of spending and revenue options. In fiscal year 1994, the federal government spent more than $1.4 trillion on millions of government programs. I believe, to our credit, that the Republican Contract With America established certain parameters for our proposal to balance the budget, enabling us to say, "We will not cut Social Security or earned veterans' benefits. We will increase defense spending and set defense priorities. We will not increase taxes." Cutting taxes may make our job more difficult, but it will not, as some have claimed, prevent the budget from being balanced. To balance the budget under a Constitutional amendment, we would have to adjust spending to make up for any lost revenues no matter what the proposal.

Third. Other critics claim that a balanced budget amendment should not be passed unless the authors spell out the specifics of how the budget would be balanced. While that is a laudable goal, I must question the intent of such assertions. Do these critics honestly wish to balance the budget, or do they seek to find the political pain involved in compliance so they can defeat the amendment? Again, I have to assume the latter because opponents seem to miss the point of the amendment's authors. During the balanced budget debate in 1994, Director of the Office of Management and Budget (now White House Chief of Staff and formerly a member of the House) Leon Panetta was quoted as stating, in reference to the amendment, that "No other country in the world would do this to themselves."[3] My response is that no other country would have allowed itself to get into this fiscal travesty in the first place.

I wholeheartedly agree with the critics that a balanced budget amendment will force most of us to make politically sensitive votes. Voting with courage is the only way out of our situation, and it may find some of us hanging with Colonel Mustard in the drawing room. But it is time for politically sensitive votes to become more common since almost every vote cast in Congress affects our limited pool of taxpayers' dollars.

Regardless of political sensitivity, the only way to ensure a balanced budget is to downsize the federal government to a level consistent with its incoming revenues. Without restraints on the spending side, revenues will be increased to keep pace with spending levels indefinitely. Government will always grow. It will always expand. A balanced budget amendment will force Congress not merely to reinvent government but to redefine what it can and, I would suggest, what it cannot do. Current government growth rates cannot continue without severely impeding the ability of the private sector to grow economically, without strangling the ability of citizens to exercise their rights to life and liberty, and without erecting a government leviathan so top heavy that state and local governments, the heart of our Constitution, are crushed under the strain of federal mandates.

I look forward to the day when Congress will debate numerous budget resolutions, based not on *whether* they balance the budget, but on *how* they balance the budget. I think that is what the American people voted for on election day in 1994 and that is the fiscal policy our forefathers intended.

Institute a Line-Item Veto

One of the first pieces of legislation I introduced when I came to Congress in 1979 was a bill granting the president authority to use a line item veto. Since that time the line item veto has been a frequent and controversial topic of debate. In public opinion surveys, most Americans consistently voice support for the line item veto, a budgeting tool that already is granted in some form to forty-three of the nation's governors. As such, it has been an effective tool for pruning wasteful spending from state appropriation bills. I believe we should give the president similar authority.

Every president in recent times has asked for this precision tool to cut out wasteful spending. I believe, regardless of the president's political affiliation, that Congress should grant that additional authority. The line item veto process would be entirely different from the existing process, which is based on the Congressional Budget and Impoundment Control Act of 1974. Look at the difference between how the line item veto would work and how the current system works.

Line Item Veto Process

- Congress passes a spending bill, which then proceeds to the president's desk for signing.
- After signing the bill the president, within a specified number of days, sends Congress a "rescission," or cancellation message, vetoing certain parts of that spending bill. This system allows the president to sign the bill and then reach in and pull out those items that warrant further scrutiny.
- If Congress *disagrees* with the cancellation, it passes a resolution of disapproval that, if signed by the president, forces the money to be spent.
- If Congress does not act to disapprove the cancellation, the money is automatically cut.

Current Process

- Congress passes a spending bill, which then proceeds to the president's desk for signing.
- The president submits cancellation messages to Congress for approval.

- If Congress *agrees* with the cancellation message, it must approve the cuts within a certain period of time before spending is actually reduced.
- If Congress fails to approve the rescission, then the spending automatically goes into effect.

The line item veto process would tilt the scales in favor of spending restraint rather than spending freedom. The current system, on the other hand, allows Congress to choose not to act on the rescission message, which by delay or inaction allows the money to be spent freely and perpetuates deficit spending.

Some argue that granting the president so much authority over spending bills may result in his abusing this power by canceling spending for important programs. Unfortunately, the abuse of power is built into the very nature of politics. Our Founding Fathers recognized this fact when they created a federal government based on a system of checks and balances, limiting the unbridled use of government power by any one individual. I would like to believe that the president would seek a higher level in this regard. One of the benefits of placing the spending review responsibility in the hands of the chief executive is that the president can take a national view of a program rather than the parochial view often taken by members of Congress.

Regarding concerns that the president will cancel funding for important programs, it is useful to point out some of the more egregious items included in spending bills from the Congress. Here is just a sampling from the 103rd Congress:

- $34.6 million for screw worm research in Mexico
- $5 million for honeybee research
- $19.6 million for the International Fund for Ireland (which has been used for golf videos and pony trekking centers)
- $1 million to conduct chiropractic demonstrations in Iowa
- $.2 million for locoweed research

Those spending line items are prime examples of what is commonly referred to as "porkbarrel" spending. Such items usually are unauthorized by any law, are earmarked funds for a specific purpose, and are not subject to any competitive bidding process. Members of Congress slipped those provisions into omnibus spending bills when the taxpayers weren't looking. As long as this type of wasteful spending is allowed to permeate our appropriation bills, the budget system is failing. Such misuse of the process happens because the system is biased toward spending free-for-alls.

Under current law, when the president is presented with such a bill for signing, he is faced with the choice of vetoing the entire bill or allowing those outrageous spending items to flow out through the treasury, because the Constitution gives the president the power to veto the entire bill but not just one item. Often the omnibus spending bills contain funds for vital functions of our government. To veto those bills might mean shutting down entire services, such as the national defense or the Postal Service. When our Founding Fathers wrote the Constitution, omnibus spending bills fit on one side of one piece of paper — handwritten. Today's bills cover hundreds of pages and are accompanied by long reports providing further detail about how those funds will be spent. The line item veto would enable the president to set priorities on limited taxpayers' dollars, giving high priority to the most important programs.

I think it is important to note again that I do not believe that an effective line item veto will in and of itself balance the budget. However, I do believe that it will have a deterrent effect on spending by discouraging members of Congress from slipping pork into our appropriation bills in the first place. A president with the line item veto is similar to an inspector looking for flaws in an otherwise good document. If a flaw is found, the individual responsible for writing that document is held responsible for fixing it. Look at this example from a January 1992 General Accounting Office (GAO) report.

> *Since 1974, presidents requested 1,019 individual rescissions of appropriations. Congress has "approved" only 354 of them — less than 35 percent — which amounts to 30 percent of the dollar volume of the proposed rescissions. Excluding 1981, Congress has approved less than 20 percent of the dollar volume of rescissions proposed by presidents. Furthermore, Congress has simply ignored $48 billion in rescissions proposed under Title X of the 1974 Budget Act, refusing to take a vote on the merits.*[4]

That same GAO report concluded that although the effectiveness of a presidential line item veto could vary by administration and spending areas of the budget,

> *If presidential line item veto/line-item reduction authority had been applied to all items to which objections were raised in the Statements of Administration Policy during fiscal years 1984 through 1989, spending could have been reduced by amounts ranging from $7 billion in 1985 to $17 billion in 1987, for a six-year total of about $70 billion. This authority would have reduced federal deficits and borrowing by 6.7 percent, from the $1,059 billion that actually occurred during that period to $989 billion.*[5]

Clearly, this type of fiscal discipline would have a significant effect on spending. Given that Congress has balanced only twenty-seven federal budgets since 1901, this fiscal tool, which was first introduced in the House in 1876, is fundamentally important to all efforts to regain control of the budget.

As the new Chairman of the House Rules Committee, which has some jurisdiction over the budget process, I was elated when 300 members of the House of Representatives, both Republican and Democrat, voted for the line item veto during the first few months of the 104th Congress. Perhaps some semblance of fiscal reality has finally hit Washington, and maybe the Congress will start to turn our country around.

Eliminate Baseline Budgeting

Over the past few years newspapers have been covered with headlines such as "Congress Cuts School Aid" or "President Calls for Less Money for Seniors." In the minds of most people around this country, such rubrics set off alarms. They think the government is going to spend less money on a program that affects them. If taken at face value, those headlines can be very misleading.

When discussing the federal budget the American people deserve an explanation based on accuracy. If the taxpayer wants to know how much was spent on a particular program last year and what will be spent on the same program next year, the federal government must admit that, "gobbledygook" aside, it cannot actually tell the taxpayer what that amount is. The truth is, there are no regularly kept accounts of these numbers. The government deals in projections and inflationary "baselines," not with bottom lines. Can you imagine how confusing your personal or family budget would be if you spent your money on projections? Family budgets usually consist of set bills such as a mortgage payment, a telephone bill, and an electric bill. If a family budgeted its money based on what it expected the bills to be next month after adjusting for inflation and an increased use of the home (whatever that may be), its budget would become so unwieldy that the family would never know how much it is actually spending, only that it is spending too much. Herein lies the problem.

Current law requires budget proposals to be measured against a "current services baseline" — which includes an automatic adjustment for inflation and eligible population growth — rather than against actual spending levels.[6] Against this baseline, any effort to slow down spending growth is shown as a cut, even if spending for the program would actually be higher than in the previous year. Professor Allen Schick of the University of Maryland, an expert on Congressional budgeting, explains the process in his book, *The Capacity to Budget*:

> *The baseline assumes that existing programs will continue without policy change. It adjusts projected expenditures for estimated inflation and mandated workload changes. A simple example will show how a baseline is constructed and used. A program spending $100 million a year and projected to have an annual 5-percent increase in participants and a 5-year inflation rate would have approximately a $110 million baseline for the next year, a $121 million baseline for the second year, and a $133 million baseline for the third year. These hypothetical extrapolations are highly sensitive to the assumptions underlying them. Any action projected to reduce spending below these hypothetical levels would be scored as a cutback, even if spending would still be above the previous year's.[7]*

Under this process, budget makers try to forecast the level of spending needed to maintain next year's services at this year's level. That forecast includes assumptions about growth in the economy, inflation, and beneficiary population. Such economic and demographic factors are rather easy to measure and follow, but other elements involved in those assumptions are subject to manipulation. Forecast assumptions and budget terminology can be misused to create a bias toward higher spending.

For example, if budget forecasters overestimate the rate of economic growth, then revenues forecast from the growth will be higher on paper, allowing the spending baseline to grow. Typically, the spending based on the assumption of higher growth takes place, but the revenues fail to materialize. As a result, the process allows Congress to spend more money than it receives in revenue. Regardless of whether baseline budgeting should even be used, it distorts perceptions of what is really happening.

The baseline serves as a benchmark for measuring the budgetary effects of proposed changes in revenues or spending. The various estimates on which baselines depend make budgeting against the baseline a tricky proposition, regardless of how carefully the projections are developed. But the most important problem is the one that Professor Schick notes: To the extent that baselines generally assume increases for inflation and other factors, they build a higher-spending bias into the budget process itself. This bias is more than rhetorical, because a spending "cut" in a program may amount to no more than limiting the amount of inflation increase the program receives. As a result, it becomes almost impossible to reduce a program significantly by cutting into its base.

Our Task Force budget was measured by the Congressional Budget Office against the baseline to determine how much deficit reduction would result from our proposed program changes. I would have preferred to have our budget scored from year to year on the basis of actual spending differences rather than projected spending differences, but current law required that it be scored from the baseline. Furthermore, this form of scoring apples with apples allows members the ability to compare on an equal footing the Task Force budget with other budget proposals.

Measured against previous years' spending levels, the Task Force balanced budget shows that despite the fact that we are cutting more than $800 billion in government spending, overall government spending continues to increase. In relation to the previous year's spending level, only the first year would result in an actual "cut" from the previous year; every year thereafter allows spending to increase from one year to the next. Compare these numbers:

Projected Spending Levels (in dollars)

Fiscal Year	Balanced Budget*	CBO Baseline**
1994	1,474,000,000,000	1,474,000,000,000
1995	1,466,800,000,000	1,529,800,000,000
1996	1,475,000,000,000	1,613,900,000,000
1997	1,525,800,000,000	1,710,800,000,000

Projected Spending Levels (in dollars)

Fiscal Year	Balanced Budget*	CBO Baseline**
1998	1,607,900,000,000	1,800,100,000,000
1999	1,621,900,000,000	1,900,200,000,000

Figures based on Congressional Budget Office estimates.
*Actual spending levels from year to year (not baseline budgeting).
**Represents projected spending under the Congressional Budget Office's uncapped baseline. (Uncapped means that it does not take the spending cap on discretionary spending approved by Congress in OBRA 1993. This cap did not allow adjustments for inflation.)

According to the chart of projected spending levels, after "cutting" government spending by $800 billion over five years, the government still will be spending more money at the end of those five years than it did in the first year. Furthermore, with the budget balanced, the government still would be spending more money that it previously spent. Spending would increase by more than $327 billion over five years under our budget proposal.

The chart also illustrates how the projected baseline allows spending to increase at an extraordinary rate. If no new legislative changes are made in the baseline projections for any government programs, government spending will increase by more than $426 billion between 1994 and 1999. Many people find it amazing that the government designed a budget system that automatically increases spending from year to year.

As one member of our Task Force, Christopher Cox (R-California), has repeatedly pointed out, under current budget rules, Congress claimed in 1990 and in 1993 to be cutting a total of $1 trillion, when the actual spending will probably go up by more than twice that amount. If small-business owners and entrepreneurs attempted to plan and operate financially in a manner similar to the United States Congress, they would end up bankrupt, in jail for fraud, or both — and rightly so.

I believe Congress should be required to present budgets that clearly show how much the spending levels on each program change from year to year, rather than showing differences in projections. If that were the case, the starting point for presidential and congressional budgets would be a comparison of the actual numbers for the current year with the proposed numbers for the coming year. We would recognize increases in spending for what they are, and not talk about cutting spending when what we really mean is that we are not increasing spending as much as anticipated.

Passage of this budget process reform would be a victory for integrity, honesty, and common sense.

Such victory may come soon. On the opening day of the 104th Congress, the House of Representatives adopted substantial reforms to the budget process relating to baseline budgeting. I hope this important first step will be only the beginning of a long climb out of our fiscal troubles.

Prohibit Unfunded Federal Mandates

Two decades ago, the federal regulation of state and local governments operated as an incentive-based system of grants-in-aid designed to encourage state and local compliance with national policy objectives. Since that time federal regulation has become a command system that requires state and local compliance and often imposes penalties for failure to comply. For example, if the city of Albany, New York, does not comply with an Environmental Protection Agency mandate requiring a certain number of public trash incinerators per capita, it will be hit with a huge fine. However, if it does comply with the mandate, construction of a new facility for incineration may cost millions of dollars, thereby stripping out funding for emergency services or another important civic duty from an already-limited municipal budget. Compliance also may require levying new taxes to make up for the loss in revenue. It sets up a Catch-22 for local legislators when they must choose between compliance, fewer services, and higher taxes or large, annual environmental fines. Especially since the mid-1980s, the federal government has relied heavily on these "unfunded mandates" as a way of achieving national policy goals without paying the state and local costs for those achievements. Conveniently, the federal government has turned the principle of federalism on its head. Look at how it operates.

- First, it can establish federal standards that states are required to implement with their own limited financial resources.
- Second, it can claim credit for establishing important programs without having to subtract the costs associated with those programs as an expense on the government's balance sheets.

As a result, state and local governments are forced to devote a growing share of their budgets to complying with federal mandates, thereby shrinking the pie of available resources for other state and local priorities. Census Bureau data on sources of state and local government revenue show a decrease in federal funding to state and local governments. Direct federal aid to state and local governments dropped from $47 billion in 1980 to $19.8 billion in 1990. However, on the spending side, the cost of almost all categories of programs was increasing. In response, many states and municipalities have been forced to raise taxes and fees and to cut services. This situation has, in turn, caused increasing resentment by many state and local leaders to this federal practice. In anger, they call unfunded mandates "secret taxes." In frustration, they call the practice "coercive federalism."

An October 1993 Price Waterhouse study for the U.S. Conference of Mayors, *Impact of Unfunded Mandates on U.S. Cities*, contained a survey on the costs incurred by cities to implement these unfunded Federal mandates:

- Underground Storage Tanks
- Clean Water Act
- Clean Air Act
- Resource Conservation and Recovery Act
- Safe Drinking Water Act
- Asbestos Abatement
- Lead Paint Abatement
- Endangered Species Act
- Americans with Disabilities Act
- Fair Labor Standards Act

The study estimated that the total cost of those mandates for 1993 was $6.5 billion, and the estimated costs for the years 1994 through 1998 would total $54 billion.

The vice-president's *National Performance Review (NPR)* reported that, as of December 1992, at least 172 separate pieces of legislation were in force that imposed requirements on state and local governments. Many of those statutes are wholly or partially unfunded.

Most state and local officials recognize the potential value of mandates. We all want clean air and clean water. They benefit all of us. But the local costs of complying with lofty federal mandates often outweigh the benefits. Look at these examples.

- Michigan estimated that its spending would rise from $39.6 million to $136.9 million, a 245 percent increase over the six-year period from 1990 through 1995, due to federal Medicaid mandates.
- A 1991 Columbus, Ohio, study reported that the city would spend $1.1 billion on federal and state environmental mandates over the next ten years, consuming nearly 25 percent of the city's budget by 1996.
- The State of California will spend $7.7 billion to comply with unfunded and underfunded mandates in the fiscal year 1994-1995.[8]

I bring up this subject in our discussion of balancing the budget for two reasons. First, in its quest to be everything to everybody the federal government has overextended itself. As it attempts to withdraw back into its constitutionally created role, we must take care to ensure that responsibilities for certain programs are not just dropped on state and local governments. That was an important rule in our Task Force deliberations.

Unfortunately, we did not have as much time as I would have liked to assure that none of the proposed spending cuts we advocated would have resulted in unfunded mandates. Nevertheless, we did attempt to roll back the leviathan of government in a way that allowed for a clean and unburdensome transition for state and local municipalities. As we continue to develop this proposal, ongoing concerted efforts will ensure that such a transition results. The federal government should never take a burden off its own back only to place that same burden on the back of another government entity without its consent.

The second reason I believe it is important to review the record of federal unfunded mandates is because of the extreme importance of the role state and local governments will play in our attempt to downsize the federal government. There is little doubt that our efforts to balance the budget were derived from a belief that state and local governments, as well as the private sector, should be given more responsibility, while responsibility should be taken away from the federal government. The key to the success of our efforts to balance the budget is a successful transition from federal dominance to a true federal-state partnership.

The thirteen original states got together in 1787 in Philadelphia to create a federal government. Since that time, the federal government has become too expansive and intrusive. As power is extracted from the federal level, responsibilities must not be dropped on the states. If such an enormous amount of responsibility is transferred to the states in a quick, haphazard manner, the very engines of growth and prosperity at this level may be silenced. If our state and local governments serve as the foundation or feet of our nation and the federal government serves as the head, dropping current federal programs on the feet of the states will paralyze them, preventing those states and municipalities from meeting their new obligations.

Each level of government has an important role to play and each level, no matter if it is gaining or losing power, should recognize the importance of the other. This cooperative relationship is one of the beauties of federalism. Balancing the budget will require the United States to redefine the meaning of federalism. Prohibiting further unfunded mandates will assist in this period of redefinition. President Bill Clinton, along with 375 members of the House of Representatives and ninety members of the Senate, recognized the importance of this prohibition when in March 1995 he signed into law a bill to prohibit unfunded mandates.

Procedural restraints on the ability of government to exercise its power of the purse are consistent with the ideal of limited government. Government grows by collecting and spending money. Limited government necessitates restraints on the ability of government to collect and spend money at will. A teenager who goes to a shopping mall can spend only as much money as he or she has available. When the money is gone, the shopping trip is over. Government spending should be the same. The Treasury Department and the Internal Revenue Service must reach a point at which it is time to shut down for the day, time to let the private sector and the financial markets take over. Passing a balanced budget amendment, instituting the line item veto, eliminating baseline budgeting, and prohibiting unfunded federal mandates will curb such a spending environment and keep it from raising its ugly head again. The American people deserve such responsible reform.

---

1 See Glossary.

2 March 10, 1995.

3 *Congressional Quarterly*, Fax Report, 1994.

4 "The Line Item Veto Budgetary Implications of Selected GAO Work," *GAO Reports to Congress*. Washington, DC: U.S. Government Printing Office, January 22, 1992.

5 Ibid.

6 Congressional Budget Act of 1974.

7 Allen Schick. *The Capacity to Budget*. Washington, DC: The Urban Institute, 1990, page 96.

8 House Committee on Government Reform and Oversight. 104th Congress, First Session. "The Unfunded Mandate Reform Act of 1995." Page 9.

CHAPTER NINETEEN

Enjoying the Benefits of a Balanced Budget

> *Contemporary events differ from history in that we do not know the results they will produce. . . . [They lead] us into an unknown land, and but rarely can we get a glimpse of what lies ahead. It would be different if it were given to us to live a second time through the same events with all the knowledge of what we have seen before.*
> — Friedrich A. Hayek, *The Road to Serfdom*[1]

The United States has not operated under a balanced budget for more than twenty-five years. Not since 1969 has the economy been free from the monetary pressures of an increasing public debt. Consequently, it is difficult to determine accurately how our economy will respond to a smaller public debt burden and ultimately to smaller government. Nevertheless, we can reasonably project how the economy will react if we continue on our present course. Looking at that projection gives us little choice: We must alter our course.

Government spending is too high because government is too big. In 1969 America had a balanced budget. In that same year, the country was embroiled in the Vietnam conflict and the first stages of the "War on Poverty." The Great Society welfare programs of the Johnson Administration were encompassing an ever-growing share of the population, and the greatest expansion in the size of government since the New Deal was well under way. As the government ballooned, the private sector deteriorated.

As the late Nobel Prize-winning economist and social thinker F.A. Hayek stated, we have a glaring example of the effects of the fully grown welfare state and must learn from history. The complete failure of the Western European versions of socialism and welfare statism should serve as warnings to those seeking to "reform" our own welfare state. As we watch those European statist nations attempt to crawl out from under their failed centralized systems, we should realize that American renewal will not be achieved merely by replacing our current welfare state with a less expensive one. American reform must be a move in an entirely different direction.

For the purpose of determining the human impact of a balanced budget on the family, business, and the economy, we will equate higher spending with larger government and lower spending with smaller government. As stated earlier, balancing the budget is only one of the fundamental planks in our necessary transformation of the role of government in American society. To recap, the true benefits of a balanced budget can be realized only if our perception of government is accurate. As government grows, the private sector, where jobs are created and economic growth is fostered, shrinks.

The Federal Budget and the Economy: Strange Bedfellows

The Congressional Budget Office (CBO) offers four general rules of thumb — economic growth, unemployment rate, inflation, and interest rates — when attempting to project the relationship between the federal budget and the economy. Understanding this relationship is crucial to understanding how we will benefit from consistently balanced budgets. This relationship also demonstrates the volatility associated with economic forces in determining whether the budget stays balanced or not. The rules of thumb can serve as effective indicators of how a balanced budget and smaller debt burden will foster an environment better suited to create widespread economic opportunity.

First Rule of Thumb: Economic Growth. Strong economic growth narrows the federal budget deficit and weak economic growth expands it. From this rule, we can conclude that if the combination of a strong economy and effective spending restraints can produce a balanced budget and maintain it, real economic growth will continue to expand at a strong rate. Strong economic growth pushes down unemployment, thereby expanding the job market. With more people employed, consumption spending goes up, thereby further spurring the manufacturing sector to meet this increase in the demand for products. However, it must also be understood that if our nation experiences weak economic growth, the demands on government spending go up, which, in turn, may actually make it all that much harder to keep the budget balanced.

Stated another way, weak economic growth will increase government spending (growth), which could lead to a deficit and a higher unemployment rate. On the other hand, if economic growth is strong, pressures on government spending may be lower, while revenue growth may remain higher, granting the government a budget surplus.

Second Rule of Thumb: Unemployment Rate. Increases and decreases in the unemployment rate directly affect the budget deficit. The unemployment rate reflects the percentage of the national work force that is without a job. The more unemployed workers there are, the slower the growth in the gross domestic product (GDP), which measures the value of all goods that are produced domestically during a given period. Economist Arthur Okun has found that for every one percentage point increase in the unemployment rate, GDP is reduced by 2.5 percent.[2] From this rule we can conclude that higher unemployment also can result in higher government spending through increased activities for unemployment benefits and social welfare programs. Consequently, as the unemployment rate increases due to weak economic growth, GDP growth slows, resulting in government growth.

Third Rule of Thumb: Inflation. Those of us who remember the gas lines of the 1970s recognize the dangers of inflation. If other economic indicators remain unaffected, increases in inflation lead to increases in both tax revenues and spending. Consequently, inflation growth has no immediate impact on the deficit. However, over time, if other economic forces, such as interest rates, do not go up in tandem with the inflation rate, the deficit may begin to grow.

Fourth Rule of Thumb: Interest Rates. CBO's final rule of thumb demonstrates the sensitivity of the federal budget to interest rates. Currently, the Treasury Department carries the responsibility of financing the government's debt. This debt, financed at market interest rates, consists of short-, medium-, and long-term securities. As interest rates go up, so does the cost of servicing the debt.

In summary, economic growth, unemployment, inflation, and interest rates possess significant relationships to the ability of the federal government to stay in balance. Each of these economic indicators can dramatically affect the federal budget.

Many economists believe that the government's need to borrow money from the private sector can cause an increase in interest rates. If this is indeed true, then lower interest rates, in turn, as a result of lower deficits, would spur investment and diminish the cost of interest on the debt.

Budget deficits raise interest rates and cost everyone additional money. In statements before the House Budget Committee in March 1995, the Chairman of the Federal Reserve, Alan Greenspan, had this to say about the impact of a balanced budget for most Americans:

> *I think their real incomes and the purchasing power of their real incomes would significantly improve, and I think the concern, which I find very distressing, that most Americans believe that their children will live at a standard of living less than that they currently enjoy, that the probability would be eliminated and that they would look forward to their children doing better than they.*[3]

A balanced budget would lead to higher standards of living and a restoration of the American dream for my children and grandchildren. The Congressional Budget Office has concurred with Chairman Greenspan. According to CBO, the two largest impediments to increases in the standard of living are the federal deficit and low levels of private savings. The savings crisis in America is so well-documented by many private sector investment firms such as Merrill Lynch, Inc., who also have concluded that reducing the deficit would substantially improve the standard of living.

The Joint Economic Committee (JEC) of Congress recently formulated a number of scenarios to help us understand the impact of the presence of a deficit and a balanced budget on the family mortgage, the family farm, and the small business. According to their estimates, a balanced budget would produce a 2 percent lower interest rate for everyone — 2 percent lower on your car, your mortgage, your credit card, on building a new factory, and keeping a family farm in business. While 2 percent may not seem like much in the grand scheme of things, it adds up to a lot of money over a lifetime. Consider these scenarios.

What 2% Means for a 30-Year Mortgage		
Example: A $75,000 House at 8.75% Annual Interest Rate		
Annual mortgage payment	+ National deficit tax (2% + interest rate)	= What you pay every year
$5,832	$1,248	$7,080
Extra mortgage paid over 30 years due to the deficit = $37,440		

What 2% Means for a Car Payment		
Example: A $15,000 Car at 9.75% Annual Interest Rate		
Annual car payment	+ National deficit tax (2% + interest rate)	= What you pay every year
$3,624	$180	$3,804
Extra paid over 4 years due to the deficit = $900		

What 2% Means for a Family Farm		
Example: A $350,000 farm at 9.75% Annual Interest Rate for 6 Months		
6-month interest payment	+ National deficit tax (2% + interest rate)	= What a family farm pays
$13,936	$3,484	$17,420

Clearly, a 2 percent reduction in interest rates as a result of a balanced budget would substantially affect Americans — for the good.

This JEC study also found that 2 percent lower interest rates would make America more competitive in the world market. Specifically, experts learned that under such borrowing relief, the American economy will experience growth in the following ways:

- Create 6.1 million more jobs in ten years
- Increase per capita incomes 16.1 percent
- Generate $235 billion more revenue for the federal government, without a tax increase
- Generate $232 billion more revenue for state and local governments, without a tax increase

What does this mean for American citizens? More job creation means more employment opportunities for individuals and more business investment. Increases in the average per capita income lead to higher standards of living, just as more incoming government revenue provides the country with more fiscal resources to provide aid to those truly in need.

A Balanced Budget and Economic Growth

In a January 1994 report to Congress, the Congressional Budget Office predicted that balancing the budget though dramatic reductions in government spending would have an impact on the gross domestic product similar to that of the Omnibus Budget Reconciliation Act of 1993. Initially, balancing the budget will reduce short-term GDP growth by one-tenth of a percent in the first few fiscal years. Over the next two to three years, eliminating the deficit over a period of five to seven years will have a moderate effect on GDP growth. However, those short-term lulls will be more than offset by much higher-than-projected GDP growth over the long run. As with any major economic package, balancing the budget has the risk of reversing the economy's current trend toward continued growth. However, the economy is now strong, exerting healthy characteristics, and hence could handle any contractionary, or negative, effects resulting from slowing the growth in government spending.

The President's Council of Economic Advisors of the Clinton Administration also predicts positive gains associated with deficit reduction. In the *Economic Report of the President, February 1994*, the Clinton Administration stated:

> *Deficit reduction is generally associated with an improvement in the price competitiveness of U.S. goods and services abroad, and therefore an increase in net exports. This expansion in net exports provides a stimulus that partially offsets the contractionary impact of spending cuts and tax increases on domestic demand. While it is difficult to determine the magnitude of this offset precisely, studies suggest that net exports will rise by approximately 40 percent of the initial deficit reduction.[4]*

The economic advisors' statements were geared merely to reducing the deficit — not to balancing the budget — which means the positive impact on economic growth associated with balancing the budget would be even greater. They went on to state that "the key macroeconomic rationale for reducing the federal deficit is to increase investment and therefore productivity and real income in the future."[5] Balancing the budget will be consistent with this goal.

A Balanced Budget and the Dollar

Another important consideration will be the effect of a balanced budget on the value of the dollar. A hot topic in business centers around the world has been the continual decline of the American dollar in international markets. A lower dollar hinders the ability of American businesses to trade goods and services in the international market. Foreign investors continue to be skittish in their investments in U.S. securities and bonds.

A *Washington Times* editorial says the newspaper learned that the positions of a Japanese bondholder who invested $1,000 in a ten-year U.S. government bond in February 1985 took a 60 percent loss when that bond was redeemed early in 1995.[6] Such a dismal market greatly discourages foreign investment, which is desperately needed when the federal government's debt places such a burden on the private credit market.

That foreign hesitation is due to Washington's inability to control its spending habits was painfully obvious in February 1995 when the United States Senate failed to pass the balanced budget amendment by one vote after the House overwhelmingly passed it. The stock market reacted negatively to the defeat of the amendment, and foreign investors followed suit.

If the federal government can make a substantial effort toward controlling spending, the confidence of foreign investors will return and our own financial markets will rebound to new heights. Federal Reserve Chairman Greenspan furthered this idea again in testimony before the House Budget Committee. He said, ". . . all told, a credible program of fiscal restraint that moves the government's finances to a sounder footing almost surely will find a favorable reception in the financial markets." Balancing the federal budget and restructuring the federal government will surely place the nation's finances on a sounder footing. He went on to state that ". . . a key element in dealing with the dollar's weakness is to address our underlying fiscal imbalance convincingly." The editorial column of the *Washington Times* has interpreted this "Greenspanese" to mean "cut spending, cut spending, cut spending." If we balance the budget through spending reductions and program reform, the dollar will recover.

According to a study, *An Economic Analysis of the Jeffersonian Administration and the Louisiana Purchase*, conducted by the National Taxpayers Union, the projected 1994 federal budget deficit was, adjusted for the size of gross national product (GNP), about equal to the amount that President Thomas Jefferson borrowed for the Louisiana Purchase. But unlike that of 1804, 1994's borrowing was not buying us 306,573,740 acres of fertile prairies, navigable waterways, and abundant natural resources to resell at a profit and with which to enrich the lives and well-being of our children. Today's borrowing is for current consumption, simply allowing government programs to spend beyond their means. If those taxpayer dollars were used for investment or returned to taxpayers for private investment, our economy would experience unprecedented economic growth. Balancing our nation's accounts by downsizing government will provide a better economy for America's families, businesses, and financial markets.

The New Deal

As the Great Depression pressed down on the American people, President Franklin D. Roosevelt and Congress tried to reduce unemployment and restore prosperity to the country through a peacetime domestic program called the New Deal. Between 1933 and 1938 the federal government enacted innovative measures that endorsed a wide spectrum of new federal programs and agencies. Roosevelt won support for an unprecedented array of new services, regulations, and subsidies.

A flood of legislation during this period brought the American people many institutions that we know in our government today.

- The Emergency Banking Act provided for federal bank inspections and helped restore popular confidence in the wake of widespread bank failures.
- The Federal Reserve Act set stringent rules for banks and provided insurance for depositors through the Federal Deposit Insurance Corporation (FDIC).
- The Securities Exchange Act mandated detailed regulations for the securities market, enforced by a new Securities and Exchange Commission (SEC).
- The Federal Housing Authority offered loan guarantees for home purchasers.
- The Federal Relief Administration expanded existing relief grants to the states.
- The Civilian Conservation Corps (CCC) provided work relief for young men under a type of military discipline.
- The Tennessee Valley Authority (TVA) developed the Tennessee River in the interest of navigation and flood control. It also provided power to a wide area of the southeastern United States.
- The Agricultural Adjustment Act provided contractual reductions of surplus crops in return for government payments.
- The National Industrial Recovery Act (NIRA) provided for two major recovery programs — a public works effort and a program for regulating American business and ensuring fair competition.
- The Rural Electrification Administration provided subsidies for rural electrification.
- The National Labor Relations Act, best known for the role it plays in giving federal protection to the bargaining process, also established a set of fair employment standards.
- The Fair Labor Standards Act mandated maximum hours and minimum wages for most workers.

- The Works Progress Administration (WPA), a work relief program, provided jobs to the unemployed.
- The Social Security Act contained three major programs — a retirement fund, unemployment insurance, and welfare grants for local distribution that included aid for dependent children.

The passage of New Deal legislation and the creation of these numerous programs to help individuals, as well as the economy, is now sometimes referred to as a welfare state.

The Great Society

In 1965, President Lyndon B. Johnson outlined the Great Society, an extensive legislative program that he proposed to raise the quality of American life. The program spurred Congress into one of the most active legislative eras in our country's history. Among the acts enacted were the following:

- A new housing bill
- Medicare
- Numerous antipoverty measures
- Voting rights protection for African Americans, especially in the South
- The Department of Housing and Urban Development
- Abolition of the immigration quota system
- Several appropriation bills for secondary and higher education
- The National Teachers Corps
- The Model Cities urban redevelopment program
- An open-housing civil rights bill
- Gun control
- Conservation measures

By the expiration of Johnson's term in 1969, Congress had implemented 226 of Johnson's 252 legislative requests.

1 Friedrich A. Hayek. *The Road to Serfdom*. Chicago: University of Chicago Press, 1994 (reprint), page 3.

2 Congressional Budget Office. "The Economic and Budget Outlook, Fiscal Years 1996-2000, *Report to the Senate and House Committees on the Budget*. January 1995, page 79.

3 Paraphrased by the Budget Committee in testimony before the House Budget Committee, March 1995.

4 The President's Council of Economic Advisors, Economic Report of the President. Washington, DC: U.S. Government Printing Office, February 1994, page 83.

5 Ibid., page 85

6 "Deficits and the Declining Dollar." Editorial in *The Washington Times*. March 13,
   1995, page A-20.

CHAPTER TWENTY

Outlook

For far too many years, many politicians in Washington have been saying yes to everything and no to nothing. As a result, the federal government of 1995 hovers over the tax-paying family as a bloated bureaucracy — feasting on the toil of taxpayers and dashing all hopes of economic opportunity. With every passing minute, this bureaucratic leviathan swallows more slices of our limited financial pie. Left untamed this overreaching bureaucracy and its backpack of debt will bury our children and grandchildren and their futures. A new philosophy is needed. The time for America's renewal is here.

My personal hero, Ronald Reagan, called upon Americans in 1981 to dream heroic dreams, to believe in our own ability to overcome, and to persevere in times of crisis because we are Americans. It was in America that the greatest political experiment in history was undertaken and won. The American people must reach inside themselves once again to triumph and to find this same destiny. Once found, the nation must summon the courage to stand up and act decisively. It is our moral duty. It is our responsibility.

I believe the heart of this nation finally understands the seriousness of the crisis. It realizes that government expansion in the name of compassion has led us into a pit of amoral governing and that our actions, ironically, have become devastatingly incompassionate. The tide is beginning to turn.

The 1994 mid-term elections struck a nerve in the backbone of Congress, turning the House and Senate upside down. The American people sent a message and the new Republican majority must listen closely. After forty years of big government liberalism, a new governing philosophy in Washington is dedicated not to reinventing government but to shaking it up. For the first time in many years, politicians are beginning to look toward home for answers to society's problems. They are looking toward families and communities for answers, instead of looking toward Washington for more money and control.

The 104th Congress has a historic opportunity to enact fundamental change in the way we do business in Washington. However, many of the crucial decisions that this Congress will make will only place us on the road to recovery. The process of renewal will need to be followed through by future Congresses with the same courage and convictions of the citizen legislators sent to Washington in November 1994. Fundamental change takes time, but the American people need to keep legislators' feet to the fire so that the decisions made will be monitored closely and followed through to their completion.

Our Republican majority in the 104th Congress's House of Representatives, the first in forty years, is dedicated to fulfilling this process. House Republicans, united by the bonds of fiscal conservatism and moral conviction, have taken historic steps during the first 100 days of this Congress. Under the able leadership of House Speaker Newt Gingrich and Majority Leader Dick Armey, we have fulfilled our commitment to the American people in the Contract With America.

The Contract's list of party principles and campaign promises represents our determination to limit government, demand responsible fiscal policy, promote a renewal of values, and create a society of opportunity. Government was designed to be looked up to as an example of how society can collectively come together to solve problems responsibly. We want to emerge from this Congress as worthy exemplars of that intention.

The principles from the Contract With America permeate every piece of legislation that has passed the House this Congress with large bipartisan majorities. Remarkably for the American people, many conservative and moderate Democrats have crossed the aisle and supported many of these proposals.

Despite our success in the first 100 days and my own excitement in finally witnessing real change in Washington, there is much more to be done. Balancing the budget is perhaps the most important and demanding step, evidenced by the depth and width of the necessary reform outlined here. It may take years fully to implement such an ambitious undertaking. The people's business has just begun, and we have taken only the first steps. The electorate must continue to support leaders who truly possess the qualities necessary to steer us through the nation's sea of red ink and thereby restore fiscal sanity to government. Effective and principled leadership is crucial to averting the crisis that confronts us. Balancing the budget by restructuring the federal government, just as the world's largest corporations have done over the past decade, will foster an America that is capable of leading the world into the next century.

Part of the reason it took America so long — more than half a century — to reject big government liberalism is because much of the cost of this government was hidden from them as deficit spending. By requiring the federal government to balance its books, the 104th Congress will ensure that Americans continue to demand that their insatiably hungry federal government stay on a permanent diet.

Speaker Gingrich has called upon the 104th Congress to adopt a fiscal conservatism with optimism. Being fiscally conservative does not mean the government will be miserly with taxpayers' dollars. It simply means the government will have to spend taxpayers' dollars less often and more wisely. The call to fiscal conservatism requires the transformation of our welfare society into an opportunity society. The time for cheating our children has ended. The time for balancing our budget has arrived.

Postscript

The Balanced Budget Task Force continues an important role in the debate on restructuring the federal government and balancing the budget. With the new Republican majority in the 104th Congress, the purpose of the Task Force has changed from one of presenting a balanced budget resolution to one of devising a detailed menu of spending and programmatic reform ideas consistent with the ideal of balancing the budget.

Now with well over sixty Republican members and a working relationship with the Democratic Conservative Coalition, the Balanced Budget Task Force provides the House Republican leadership with solid support for the tough decisions needed to renew America. Most recently, the Task Force has drafted an actual legistlative bill — encyclopedia of legislative options — that outlines the specific laws that need to be amended or repealed in order to enact many of the spending reforms outlined in this proposal. As an introduced bill with a large number of cosponsors, the Task Force proposal will serve as a thorough and specific resource for anyone in Congress desiring to restructure the federal government. Those ideas can be taken up one by one as amendments to appropriations bills or as a complete unit. Our new proposal also includes many additional provisions such as merging some federal departments and transforming others into block grant programs to states. Not only is our new proposal specific and detailed but it outlines clearly, and begins to take, the first necessary steps down the road to balanced budget.

As this book goes to press, both the House and Senate have just approved seven-year balanced budget resolutions based in large part on many of the ideas outlined in this work. The American people are winning the war on the deficit, and the Balanced Budget Task Force has again been a major part of developing the strategy and advancing the cause.

Under the leadership of Speaker Newt Gingrich and with the efforts of Appropriations Committee Chairman Bob Livingston and Budget Committee Chairman John Kasich, the Balanced Budget Task Force will continue to hold Congress's and the president's feet to the fire on the tough decisions necessary to balance the budget for future generations.

APPENDIX A

The Balanced Budget Task Force

[Mr. Solomon gave the following speech before the House of Representatives, 103rd Congress, on March 9, 1994, one day before the Balanced Budget Task Force's proposal came to the floor of the House for a vote.]

Mr. Speaker, I appreciate the half-hour of the minority leader's time.

Mr. Speaker, let me just say that for a number of years now a number of us in the Congress have been so concerned about what is happening to the budget in this country and what has created these huge deficits that we, the American people, and the present generation and future generations to come are saddled with, and a number of months ago a few of us, about twenty-five of us, formed what we call the Balanced Budget Task Force. This has nothing to do with the balanced budget amendment. This is simply a task force put together to try to see if we could actually present to this Congress a balanced budget to vote on.

On Thursday, that is, tomorrow, the Balanced Budget Task Force will present to the U.S. Congress on this floor a balanced budget containing more than 500 specific cuts, and they are itemized right here, totaling more than $600 billion, and that is something that they said could not be done.

Our alternative budget contains the most comprehensive list of cuts ever put before this body or any other body. We included recommendations and suggestions from the credible Concord Coalition, the Grace Commission, the Congressional Budget Office, the Citizens Against Government Waste, a whole host of individual member initiatives, the National Taxpayers' Union, the Heritage Foundation, the Porkbusters Coalition, the reinventing government proposals, and many, many others, and this budget that we are presenting to this body tomorrow, if enacted into law, would result in a balanced budget by 1999, that is, the fifth year of this five-year budget, and even produce a surplus in the year 2000 and the year 2001.

During the recent Senate debate on the balanced budget amendment, President Clinton and our former colleague who is now the Office of Management and Budget Director, Leon Panetta, in twisting the arms of members of the other body to vote against the balanced budget amendment, which failed by a few votes over there, made the point time and time again that we do not need a balanced budget amendment; we do not need to change the constitution; what we need, they said, is a Congress willing to vote for a balanced budget.

Well, Congress is going to get this chance to do just that, and that is not easy, ladies and gentlemen. Other critics, including Senate Majority Leader George Mitchell, and I am ashamed to say even some Republicans over in that other body, and we have to place blame where blame is due, those Democrats and Republicans claimed that you could not balance the budget without dipping into the Social Security trust fund, without slashing earned benefits of veterans, and without raising taxes. They said you could not balance the budget without doing those things. Well, that kind of rhetorical scare tactic was wrong then, and it is wrong now, and we prove it with this balanced budget that we are presenting tomorrow.

I invite the public and the members of Congress and the press to look at it tomorrow morning in tomorrow morning's *Congressional Record*. This balanced budget does not touch the Social Security retirement trust fund. It does not cut a dime from earned veterans' benefits, and I used to be the ranking Republican on the Committee on Veterans Affairs, served on that committee for ten years before I went to the Committee on Rules, and was responsible for passing the legislation that created the Department of Veterans Affairs. I guess I have a fine reputation in fighting for the veterans of this nation, and I am one, as any member here.

But this bill does not cut a dime from veterans' benefits. And even more important it does not raise taxes in order to balance the budget.

Instead of decimating the defense budget, it actually restores about $50 billion proposed by President Clinton that is badly needed if we are going to be able to maintain a two-war strategy, that is going to maintain the young men and women in the best-equipped, the best army that we can produce.

In this budget, everyone will be asked to tighten their belts including Congress itself. Our budget is tough medicine. It is tough for all of us. It cuts Congressional spending by 25 percent over the five-year period. It cuts the White House spending by 25 percent over the five-year period. It consolidates departments like the Department of Energy and the Department of the Interior, which now, I think, they have given some other fancy name to, Natural Resources or something. It terminates many federal commissions. It eliminates programs like the space station, which is so controversial. It privatizes programs like the National Oceanic and Atmospheric Agency, which President Clinton has asked to do.

In this budget, everyone is treated fairly. We go on where we contract out items like the U.S. Printing Office, where the federal government has no business being in the printing business. It eliminates 90 percent of agricultural crop subsidies, which the American people just do not understand. It bars financial assistance to illegal aliens. It merges job training programs. It sells off the government direct loan portfolio to the private sector. All of these make good business sense.

And in all of this belt tightening, which touches every branch of government, we only cut spending by a mere 3.5 percent, a mere 3.5 percent; yet we managed to balance the federal budget. And this Task Force would ask this Congress, is a 3.5 percent over five years too much to ask of this body?

The American people do not think so and we do not think so. We will ask Congress to summon the courage to vote for this balanced budget tomorrow. That vote will take place around 7:00 or 8:00 tomorrow night, probably, and during that vote, ladies and gentlemen, the buck stops here on this floor. No longer can we, members of Congress, blame the past presidents or present presidents or future presidents for this deficit crisis: We can only blame ourselves if we fail to vote for a truly balanced budget.

Again, let me repeat: This budget before you balances the budget in five years. It cuts over $600 billion in federal spending with over 500 specific cuts. It does not raise taxes, it does not touch the Social Security trust funds, it does not touch earned veterans' benefits: It does restore defense spending to a level that is necessary to maintain a decent national defense.

In the year 1999 President Clinton's budget will have an annual deficit for that one year alone of $204 billion. That is $204 billion. A billion dollars is a thousand million dollars. This is 204 times a thousand million. That is the deficit that we will incur in just that one year of 1999.

Our budget that we present to you has a $5 million surplus. It is a very small amount of money, but it is a surplus as compared with a $204 billion deficit in that year.

And when you go to the next year, the year 2000, which is only six years from now, the President's budget has a $226 billion deficit, going up; and we show a $5 billion surplus. In other words, ladies and gentlemen, we have begun to make a dent in the federal deficit and we begin actually to pay it off. That is what the American people really want, and we do it by cutting, consolidating, terminating, eliminating, privatizing, contracting out, selling off portfolios, and by belt tightening in the branches of government.

Ladies and gentlemen, the point I want to make is that each member of our Task Force—and they come from all over this country, from New York, from Florida, from California, from every part of this country — and when you look through this budget, you will find things that hurt your district. But, ladies and gentlemen, if you are going to balance the budget, you have to tighten your belts. We have proved that it can be done. I would just say that this budget that we are offering is a credible document; it has been scored by the Congressional Budget Office as being a balanced budget. It is endorsed by such prestigious organizations as the Citizens Against Government Waste, by the National Taxpayers' Union, by Americans for Tax Reform, by Americans for a Balanced Budget, and dozens of other like organizations that have come out in support of this balanced budget.

That will begin to once and for all plug the dike that is hemorrhaging a sea of red ink that is slowly ruining this great country of ours and turning us into a debtor nation.

Mr. Speaker, I am happy to say that our efforts here in this House to adopt a balanced budget have now spread to the other body. Senate Republicans are preparing right now to offer a similar balanced budget just like ours. That is going to be the official Republican alternative over in the other body, without raising taxes, without cutting Social Security, without cutting veterans' benefits, and without decimating the defense budget.

I cannot tell you how pleased I was when I saw this come across the fax machine about an hour ago. It says, "fiscal year 1995 balanced budget resolution prepared by the Republican staff of the U.S. Senate Budget Committee." Ladies and gentlemen, that is a step forward toward a balanced budget.

I do not know if we are going to succeed tomorrow because I do not know if members of this body are going to have the guts to vote for something as tough as this because it is, again, tough medicine. But whether we win or lose, at least we have set the norm for future budget committees on both sides of the aisle in this House and in the other body, that the American people are going to get a balanced budget or they are going to know why.

I can tell you, with the elections only about seven or eight months from now, the thing on their minds is not health care but they are concerned about this budget deficit. They are concerned about jobs, about the economy. If we allow this deficit to continue to grow as the president's budget does, creating another $1.5 trillion in debt added to the already $4 trillion we have now, you are going to see inflation skyrocket, you are going to see unemployment skyrocket, and every time unemployment goes up 1 percent, it triggers in over $40 billion in social programs at the various levels of government.

We just cannot afford to let that happen. I would just implore members to take a look at the budget we present to you tomorrow. The Committee on Rules a few minutes ago made in order several alternatives, one of which is this balanced budget.

There is a Black Caucus substitute, which was also made in order, which does not balance the budget. There are several others.

I would just hope that members would give this consideration and get us on the road toward finally balancing the budget in this Congress.

Mr. Speaker, I appreciate the time of the Speaker and our staffs staying this evening to allow me this opportunity to at least tell you what is going to happen tomorrow.

APPENDIX B
Graphs and Charts

The Economic Outlook: January 1994

  For an accurate understanding of the total picture facing the nation at the time the Balanced Budget Task Force was formed, it is important to note the condition of the economy in January 1994 and the projections of its worsening condition over the next five years. The following charts vividly portray the dismal outlook.

Projected Federal Debt

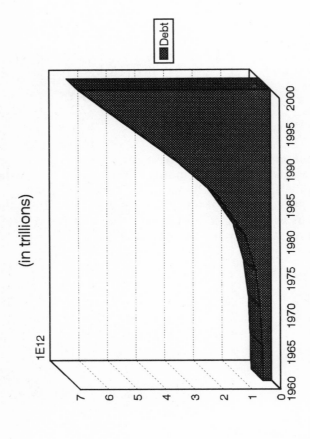

(in trillions)

Source: Office of Management and Budget, Fiscal Year 1995

CBO Deficit Projections

(in billions)

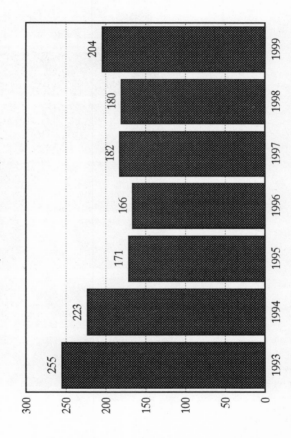

Based on Congressional Budget Office Projections - January 1994

CBO Real GDP Growth

(percentage change)

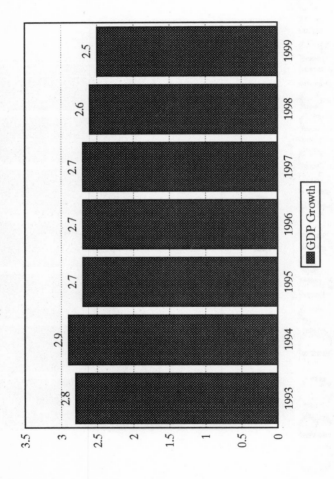

Based on Congressional Budget Office Projections - January 1994

Unemployment Rates
(national percent)

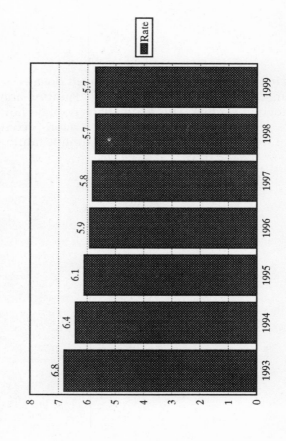

	1993	1994	1995	1996	1997	1998	1999
Rate	6.8	6.4	6.1	5.9	5.8	5.7	5.7

Based on Congressional Budget Office Projections - January 1994

Enhancing the Economic Outlook through Reform

Numbers, facts, and figures can be daunting and confusing if not understood in context. This set of charts portrays how the implementation of the spending and programmatic reforms contained within this proposal would greatly enhance our economic future.

Deficit Projections

With Enactment of Spending Reforms

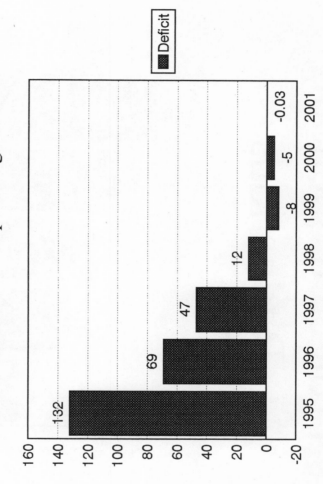

Source: Congressional Budget Office, 1994

Projected Spending Reductions

(in billions)

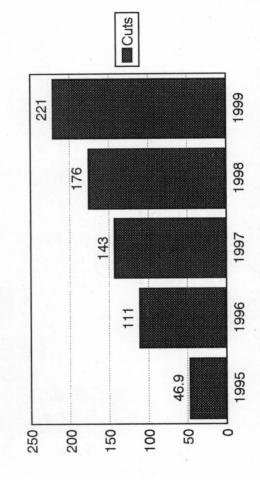

Year	Cuts
1995	46.9
1996	111
1997	143
1998	176
1999	221

Source: Congressional Budget Office; Reduction From CBO Baseline, 1994

Spending Level Comparisons

Current Law vs. Balanced Budget

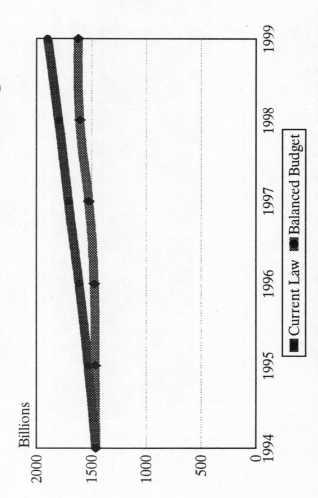

Source: Congressional Budget Office, 1994

Deficit Projections

(in billions)

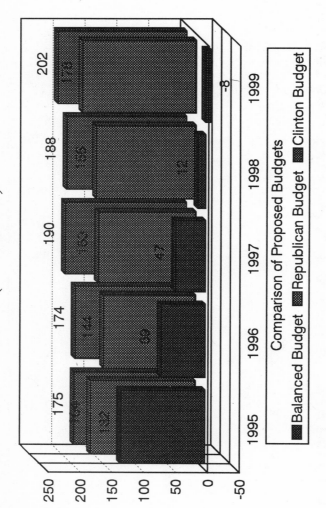

Source: Congressional Budget Office, 1994

The Economy: 1995

Since many of the proposed reforms have not been enacted, spending still skyrockets out of control and the budget still remains out of balance. Our economic future does not look very different now in 1995.

Current Deficit Projections

Under Clinton FY 1996 Budget

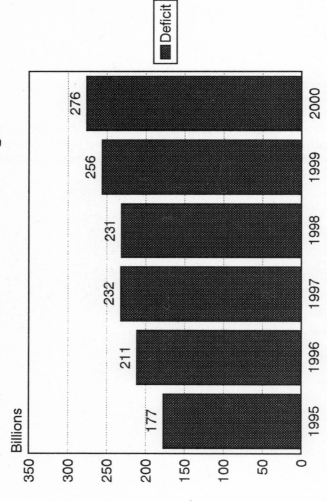

Billions

| | Deficit |

Source: Congressional Budget Office, 1995

FY 1995 Federal Spending

Total Spending $1,538 Billion

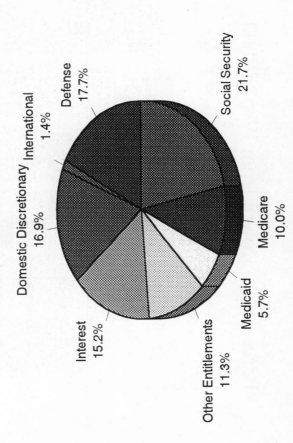

Defense
17.7%

Domestic Discretionary International
16.9%   1.4%

Social Security
21.7%

Interest
15.2%

Other Entitlements
11.3%

Medicaid
5.7%

Medicare
10.0%

Source: President's Fiscal Year 1996 Budget

Annual Spending Growth

Percentage Growth from 1995 to 2000

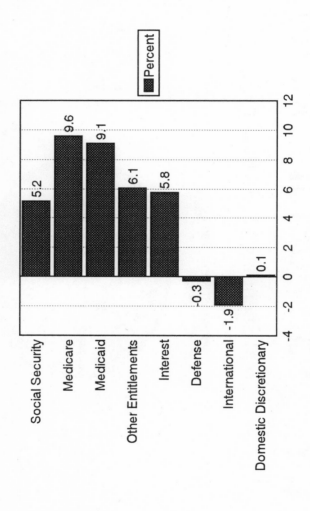

Source: President's Fiscal Year 1996 Budget

APPENDIX C
Glossary

The definitions cited for the terms in this glossary are specific to the usage in the context of this book.

A Vision of Change for America   A report describing President Bill Clinton's economic plan, which he submitted along with his State of the Union address on February 17, 1993, prior to submitting a budget for fiscal year 1994.

baseline   A benchmark for measuring the budgetary effects of proposed changes in federal revenues or spending.

Cato Institute   A nonpartisan public policy "think tank" in Washington, DC, dedicated to advancing a market-liberal policy agenda.

Citizens Against Government Waste   A grass roots nonpartisan organization that grew out of the dissolution of the Grace Commission to scrutinize legislation for porkbarrel and special-interest spending.

Committee for a Responsible Budget   A nonpartisan think tank based in Washington, DC, dedicated to responsible federal budgeting and the elimination of the deficit.

Concord Coalition   A not-for-profit, grass roots organization founded by former senators Paul Tsongas (D-Massachusetts) and Warren Rudman (R-New Hampshire). The coalition's mission is to educate Americans about the impact of the deficit on the economy and future generations.

Congressional Budget Office (CBO)   A nonpartisan part of the legislative branch established by Congress as a support organization whose

mandate is to provide objective and impartial analyses of the federal
budget and related issues. In Congress, it is widely regarded as the
authority on the federal budget.

Contract With America   A 1994 congressional campaign platform containing ten legislative planks, which Republicans in the House of
Representatives pledged in September 1994 to bring to the House floor
for a vote in a Republican-controlled House. Those campaign promises were fulfilled in April 1995.

deferral   To delay the expenditure of funds.

Grace Commission   A special panel formed during the Reagan Administration to study waste, fraud, and abuse in the ways that Congress
was spending the taxpayers' money. Chaired by industrialist J. Peter
Grace, the commission, in its "war on waste," delivered 2,478 recommendations for change. The report's reception, according to a Congressional Research Service study, was "cool and a disappointment to its
promoters."

Gramm-Rudman-Hollings   Also known as the Balanced Budget and
Emergency Deficit Control Act of 1985 or the Balanced Budget Act,
this law set forth specific deficit targets and a sequestration proce-
dure to reduce spending if the targets were exceeded. The Budget
Enforcement Act of 1990 established new budget procedures through
fiscal year 1995, as well as revised the targets, which exclude the
Social Security trust funds. The Omnibus Budget Reconciliation Act
of 1993 further extended various provisions of the Balanced Budget
Act, without including fixed deficit targets beyond fiscal year 1995.

gross domestic product (GDP)   The total market value of all goods and
services produced domestically during a given period. The components
of GDP are consumption, gross domestic investment, government
purchases of goods, and services and net exports.

gross national product (GNP)   The total market value of all goods and
services produced in a given period by labor and property supplied
by residents of a country, regardless of where the labor and property
are located.

Heritage Foundation   A nonpartisan, tax-exempt policy research institute established in 1973 and dedicated to the principles of free competitive enterprise, limited government, individual liberty, and a strong
national defense. Its research and study programs are designed to make

the voices of responsible conservatism heard in Washington, DC, throughout the United States, and in the capitals of the world.

leviathan   Figuratively, any great or powerful thing. In the Old Testament, some form of sea monster (Psalms 74:12-14; Isaiah 27:1). In Canaanite mythology, a huge sea monster who was defeated in combat with God.

mandate   An authoritative command, usually from a higher level to a lower level.

National Center for Policy Analysis (NCPA)   A nonprofit, nonpartisan research institute, funded exclusively by private contributions and headquartered in Dallas, Texas. NCPA's research specializes in tax policy and other economic topics.

National Performance Review (NPR)   An intensive, six-month study of the federal government commissioned by the Clinton Administration in 1993 and headed by Vice-President Albert Gore. The review was charged with devising recommendations on how the government could be more efficient at a lower cost.

National Taxpayers' Union (NTU)   A grass roots, nonprofit, nonpartisan organization dedicated to lower spending, lower taxes, and responsible governing. NTU, based in Washington, DC, has members throughout the country.

omnibus bill   A proposed law that covers many things at once. The term emerged from the Compromise Measures of 1850, a series of five legislative enactments passed by the U.S. Congress during August and September 1850. These measures, essentially the work of Senator Henry Clay of Kentucky, were designed to reconcile the political differences that were dividing the antislavery and proslavery factions of Congress and the nation. The measures, referred to collectively as the *Omnibus Bill,* dealt chiefly with the question of whether slavery was to be sanctioned or prohibited in the regions acquired from Mexico as a result of the Mexican War of 1846-1848.

Omnibus Budget Reconciliation Act (OBRA) of 1993   The official title of the Clinton Administration's 1993 tax and budget package, signed by the president on August 10, 1993. Also known as Public Law 103-66.

rescission   To terminate budget authority.

statism   The concentration of economic controls and planning in the hands of a highly centralized government.

statist   An advocate of statism.

statute   A law enacted by the legislative branch of a government.

statutory amendment   A congressional amendment that repeals or alters an existing law or statute, in contrast with a Constitutional amendment, which the Congress alone does not have the power to alter with a two-thirds vote of both Houses but must have the approval of three-fourths of the state legislatures or conventions.

unfunded mandate   A requirement by Congress that a state, municipality, or business perform a particular act or meet a specific demand without providing the financial resources necessary for compliance. Unfunded mandates can come in numerous forms and in various amounts.

Volcker Commission   A commission set up to study the functions of the United States government, under the chairmanship of Paul Volcker, former chairman of the Federal Reserve Board.

Index